Contemporary
Jewish Ethics

Recent Titles in
Bibliographies and Indexes in Religious Studies

Theological and Religious Reference Materials: General Resources
and Biblical Studies
G. E. Gorman and Lyn Gorman, with the assistance of Donald N. Matthews

Theological and Religious Reference Materials: Systematic Theology
and Church History
G. E. Gorman and Lyn Gorman, with the assistance of Donald N. Matthews

Healing Faith: An Annotated Bibliography of Christian Self-Help Books
Compiled by Elise Chase

New Religious Movements in the United States and Canada
Compiled by Diane Choquette

Bibliography of Published Articles on American Presbyterianism.
1901-1980
Compiled by Harold M. Parker, Jr.

Contemporary Jewish Ethics
A Bibliographical Survey

Compiled by
S. DANIEL BRESLAUER

G. E. Gorman, Advisory Editor

Bibliographies and Indexes in Religious Studies, Number 6

Greenwood Press
Westport, Connecticut • London, England

Library of Congress Cataloging in Publication Data

Breslauer, S. Daniel.
  Contemporary Jewish ethics.

  (Bibliographies and indexes in religious
studies, ISSN 0742-6836 ; no. 6)
    Includes indexes.
    1. Ethics, Jewish—Bibliography. I. Title.
II. Series.
Z5873.B74 1985   [BJ1280]   016.2963 '85   85-9895
ISBN 0-313-24594-0 (lib. bdg. : alk. paper)

Copyright © 1985 by S. Daniel Breslauer

All rights reserved. No portion of this book may be
reproduced, by any process or technique, without the
express written consent of the publisher.

Library of Congress Catalog Card Number: 85-9895
ISBN: 0-313-24594-0
ISSN: 0742-6836

First published in 1985

Greenwood Press
A division of Congressional Information Service, Inc.
88 Post Road West, Westport, Connecticut 06881

Printed in the United States of America

The paper used in this book complies with the
Permanent Paper Standard issued by the National
Information Standards Organization (Z39.48-1984).

10 9 8 7 6 5 4 3 2 1

Contents

Preface	vii

INTRODUCTORY SURVEY

The Problematics of Jewish Ethics	3
Distinguishing between Ethics and Morality	6
The Sources of Jewish Ethics	9
Ethics and Modern Judaism	15
Issues in Modern Jewish Ethics	25
The Essence of Jewish Ethics	34

BIBLIOGRAPHICAL SURVEY

1. General Works and Anthologies	37
Surveys of Jewish Ethics	37
Interpretations of Jewish Ethics	42
Anthologies of Jewish Ethics	63
2. The History of Jewish Ethics	70
Biblical and Talmudic Ethics	70
Philosophical Ethics	78
Pietistic Ethics	84
The Ethics of Jewish Mysticism	87
The Musar Movement	90
The Ethics of Hasidism	94
Modernity and Ethics: General Approaches	98
Modernity and Jewish Ethics: Liberal Options	111
Traditional Responses to Modernity	115
3. Issues in Jewish Ethics	120
Halakha, Aggadah, and Jewish Ethics	120
Theological Concepts and Jewish Ethics	136
Judaism and Social Ethics	147

4. Themes in Jewish Ethics   159

The Love Commandment and Self-Sacrifice   159
Human Dignity and the Divine Image in Humanity   163
Free Will, Evil, and Jewish Ethics   167

5. Jewish Ethics and Non-Jewish Ethical Theories   172

Kant, Kierkegaard, and Jewish Ethics   172
Psychology and Jewish Ethics   176
Jewish Ethics and Modernity   181

Author Index   187

Title Index   192

Subject Index   207

Preface

Numerous books, articles, and anthologies devoted to one or another aspect of Jewish ethics have been published between 1968 and 1983. In these fifteen years, Jewish thinking about medical ethics, social ethics, issues of war and peace, business ethics, and the basic philosophical foundations of Jewish ethics has flourished. Publishers, in particular Ktav Publishing House, Behrman House, and some of the university presses, have inaugurated a number of impressive series devoted to both the theory and practice of Jewish ethics and morality. Journals in widely diverse fields such as medicine, law, contemporary events, philosophy, religious studies, and ethics have published articles discussing specific issues in Jewish moral decision making. These works are frequently cited or indexed in widely scattered places intended for specialized readers whether a scientific audience in the case of articles concerned with medical ethics or a philosophical audience in the case of theoretical studies. They may thus be inaccessible to researchers seeking an overall or balanced view of Jewish ethical thinking. A bibliographical survey would solve these problems.

The two volumes now being prepared, of which this is the first, are meant to help scholars and students working in Judaic studies, religious studies, or ethics by documenting and annotating the various articles and books devoted to Jewish ethics in one reference work. The type of journals from which material is to be drawn, however, differs depending upon whether the subject matter is theoretical or practical in nature. This distinction suggested that two volumes should be prepared; further reflection confirmed that this separation of material is a useful procedure.

Two types of issues concern contemporary Jewish ethical thinkers. The first type focuses on the theoretical questions which Jewish thinkers have sought to understand and assess in relationship to moral life and ethical choosing.

Jews who take this process of confronting philosophical theories seriously are engaged in answering a number of problems which arise concerning the very nature of Jewish ethics. Among these are included questions of the relationship between ethics and morality, the presence or absence of an ethics independent of the traditional Jewish legal system, and whether Jewish ethics is essentially dialectical, monolithic, or organic.

Other theoretical issues concern interpreting the rich legacy of Jewish moral thinking. The variety of moral literature and its differing emphases in the Jewish heritage present a particular challenge. Still other issues arise from confronting general ethical categories--how Judaism stands in relationship to the questions of moral autonomy, imitation of the divine, love of neighbor, sacrifice of the self, and free will are important in the discussion of Jewish ethics. The modern Jewish movements--Orthodox, Conservative, Reform, Humanistic, and Reconstructionist--confront modernity in radically different ways and in so doing evolve different responses to the challenge of modern ethical thought. The writings in this present bibliography chronicle that evolution.

In addition to the attempt to understand Judaism through the perspective of non-Jewish theoretical systems, there is a second, more practical, focus in contemporary Jewish thinking. The issues associated with this focus are moral ones--questions on specific critical decisions. A second type of reference work is needed, one oriented to these practical issues of moral decisions. Jewish thinkers and leaders have found it necessary to confront the dilemmas of modernity. In the face of those dilemmas they have begun to rethink specific moral questions -- those concerning selfhood and sexuality, those focusing on the moral implications of war in the nuclear age, those raised by progress in science and technology, those associated with the pluralistic community in which most Jews live. What is needed is a comprehensive sketch of how different Jewish groups and specific Jewish thinkers have coped with the changing demands of moral decision making. Both institutional responses and trends among Jewish theologians need to be charted for the period from 1968 through 1983. Guidance is needed to put the mass of written response to these dilemmas in a general framework; an annotated bibliography alone is only a beginning; students will also need a theoretical structure as a means of putting the individual entries into perspectives. The projected volume will be a practical compendium of Jewish morality as it has evolved since the eighteenth century, its major concerns, the differences among various Jewish thinkers and the institutions they represent, reasons for those differences, and the spectrum of authentically Jewish interpretations of modern issues.

While the second volume looks at selected moral issues this present volume looks at philosophical questions and the way in which Jewish thinkers seek to resolve what often appears to be a conflict between traditional Judaism and contemporary ethical reflection. questions that can best be called ethical. This survey of ethical issues charts the differing concerns that have animated Jewish reflection on theoretical principles for solving moral dilemmas and the way in which traditional religion confronts the moral questions of modernity. In some instances non-Jews as well as Jews may be engaged in such reflection and in such cases they are included in this bibliographical survey.

In order to present an adequate survey of the material involved, the bibliographical entries are drawn from four major sources. The first are those sponsored by the major Jewish institutions in the United States-- the journals of the Reform Movement, Conservative Movement, and of Yeshiva University and the anthologies they have produced. While there are other forms of American Judaism and institutions associated with them (the Reconstructionists and the Society for Humanist Judaism) the thought of these groups is often represented in the publications of the major institutions. Other journals and publications which are more popular in nature, such as Sh'ma, Present Tense, and Moments, have been consulted and used where needed. Usually however either the same author or viewpoint represented in these journals has been expressed elsewhere at greater length and with more sophistication.

A second source is made up of scholarly articles and books published in the United States and Europe. These works analyze the history of Jewish ethics, the philosophical problems involved, and various solutions to both practical and theoretical dilemmas of Jewish ethics. Sometimes a major theologian chooses to write in a more popular journal and demonstrates in brief compass central ethical concerns; a few of these articles have also been included as easy introductions to the problem of Jewish ethics. Most books and articles included date from 1968 to 1983, but some earlier material was selected as crucial for understanding contemporary Jewish ethics.

A third source is difficult to assess and utilize: traditional collections of Hebrew ethical writings, both contemporary and classical. Sometimes older sources are reprinted; very frequently the classical moral literature appears in new editions and with useful notes. Often the works so reprinted or gathered anew are meant for devotional rather than scholarly purposes. Selected examples of this genre have been included in this bibliography as primary data for discovering the flavor and style of classical Jewish moral preaching and exhortation. The continuity of concerns throughout the history of Jewish ethical reflection which is evident even in the modern period is revealed in this literature.

The final source is material found in anthologies; while these anthologies focus on moral issues they also include articles that deal with ethical theory. Some material in these anthologies predate 1968 but taken as a whole these works represent the ideas and views that have shaped contemporary Jewish ethics. Perhaps the most important value in these anthologies lies in their testimony to continuity in Jewish ethical concerns.

All the categories noted above include writings in languages other than English. Entries in Western languages will be left untranslated. In the case of Hebrew books and articles, however, the case is different as often these texts include an English title page and when this is the case that is the title used; in other cases I have supplied my own translation indicating the original language in brackets thus:[Hebrew].

Where entries are relevant to more than one section of the topical bibliography, cross references are provided, utilizing the entry number of the citation and, sometimes, the author with the entry number in parenthesis.

The Bibliographical Survey annotates entries that analyze the basic structure, themes and debates characterizing contemporary Jewish ethics. It looks first at general interpretations of Jewish ethics. The purpose of this section is to prepare the reader for the more specialized sections that follow. A second section of this opening chapter focuses on interpretations of Jewish ethics, and a final section provides annotated entries of relevant anthologies of Jewish ethics. The following chapters will frequently refer back to this first chapter, especially in the annotations.

Chapters 2-5 are organized by subject matter. Chapter 2 presents studies of the history of Jewish ethics according to to the historical period investigated (general surveys of the history of Jewish ethics are included in the first part of Chapter 1). The third chapter brings together essays on internal issues of Jewish ethical reflection: ethics and Jewish law, theological issues, and concerns about social ethics. Chapter 4 looks at selected themes prominent in the theoretical studies of Jewish ethicists: the love commandment and self-sacrifice, human dignity and the task of imitating God, and the question of free will and the problem of evil. The final chapter, organized around the Jewish confrontation with modernity, open with articles grappling with the problems posed by Kantian ethics and Kierkegaard's rejection of that ethics, continues with the encounter between Jewish ethics and psychology, and concludes with essays coming to grips with Jewish ethics in a radically changed social and intellectual environment. The basic organizational structure of this work is thus topical rather than strictly chronological.

The rationale for the topical organization of the chapters and their parts in this Bibliographical Survey is explained in the Introductory Survey, which sketches the issues and concerns basic to the sources annotated in the bibliographical sections following and in which references to the bibliography are indicated by the entry number given in parenthesis. The importance of looking at the history of Jewish ethics, its sources, and its methods should be self-evident. The selection of particular issues in modern Jewish ethical thought is, perhaps, more subjective and therefore needs more defense.

In many ways the introduction should be seen as an interpretive essay that brings together and analyzes the various themes of contemporary Jewish ethics. It, together with the bibliography and its annotations, should provide readers with an explanation and a critical interpretation of contemporary Jewish ethics upon which future research and interpretation can build.

The three indexes provided are meant to guide readers in their use of the bibliography; access is to entry numbers, not page numbers. The index to authors refers to authors of the various entries rather than to authors mentioned in the annotations. Readers interested in the variety of writings by a single thinker will find this index useful. The index to titles also provides access to the enumerated citations. The actual title of the entry rather than, for example, the title of the anthology in which it appears, is cited. The

third index is more general and concerns the basic subject matter included in the bibliography. Subjects mentioned in the annotation as well as in the title of the entry are included.

**Contemporary
Jewish Ethics**

The Problematics of Jewish Ethics

Traditional Judaism challenges the modern world with an absolute standard, a religious philosophy a rooted system of values, and a legal system at odds with the current moral temperament. A look at the interaction between Jewish thinkers and the modern world can provide insight into the dynamic relationships between tradition and modernity, religion and secular society, and ethics and a changing world situation. This bibliography surveys the way in which Jewish thinkers have struggled to confront modernity, the ways in which ethical reflection has mirrored social crisis, and the importance that ethics has for the traditional Jew confronting modernity.

Jewish ethics presents a case history of a traditional religion that has lived with modernity for two centuries. Since the eighteenth century Jews have sought to evolve a religious ethics that is both consistent with traditional religion and relevant to modern life. The effort to produce such an ethical system has not been without its perils. The very endeavor is in many ways extraordinary. In expounding this view of Jewish ethics the Jewish medieval philosophers interpreted the meaning of normative Jewish ethics seeking to demonstrate how the precepts of Judaism illustrated the principles they had received from Greek philosophy. Kabbalists Jewish mystics advanced their moral and ethical system as self-evident and identical with the specific revelation given to the Jewish people as a whole. The task that classical Jewish moralists faced was that of motivating people to follow what, they considered to be the normal, traditional ethical obligations of Judaism. They had no need to justify their ethical system as such.

The modern Jewish ethicist faces a more difficult task, the task of justifying the attempt to articulate a Jewish ethics at all (see Kellner, 011). Modern women and men find their values in the secular world around them; society provides them with motivations and justifications for their actions.

These Jews perceive no need for Jewish morality or for a revealed system of ethical norms. The Jewish moralist must justify religious ethics in a way unparalleled in earlier Jewish thinking. Modernity, therefore, offers a unique challenge to the contemporary Jewish ethical thinker -- that of justifying the religious basis for ethics. Judaism must show itself of value in competition not with other religious systems but with a secular ethical tradition.

Ethical theorizing is suspect in Jewish tradition no less than in modern life. Traditional Jews have a system of behavioral norms that governs their lives. They need only follow these norms to live morally; they do not require an extensive ethical system to know how to choose the good and refrain from evil. Not only is an ethical system redundant in Jewish life, it is in many ways a difficult, almost impossible goal to attain. Judaism is as much a culture as a religious system, as much a way of living as a way of thinking. History and experience, no less than dogma and philosophy, shape the behavior patterns of Jewish life. This complexity makes Jewish ethics a particularly problematic subject area in Jewish philosophy.

Four controversies surround the attempt to develop a coherent Jewish ethics. The first concerns the question of whether there is any single value that is supreme, that is the touchstone of all particular moral decisions. The second argues over which strand within historical Judaism, the rabbinic, the philosophical, or the mystic, is most authoritative. The third seeks to define the place of ethics within the total structure of Jewish religion. The last arises from differing responses to the challenge of modernity. Each controversy represents a different problem within contemporary Jewish ethics.

The first debate reveals the problem that arises when a person seeks to organize the vast array of Jewish moral teachings in one coherent system. Jewish ethics begins by reflecting on the principles of Jewish life. One avenue of ethical investigation leads to the discovery of a single such principle in the name of which each of the variety of moral obligations can be affirmed. Traditional Jews seek an all-embracing norm to make sense out of the variety of minute details of Jewish law. Non-traditional Jews join in this search as well; for them such a virtue would provide a general principle in the name of which Jewish life and practice could be transformed.

The second debate reveals another problem, the diversity found in the rich moral legacy of Jewish ethical reflection. Medieval Philosophers have contended that intellectual virtues, knowledge, and self-perfection are the central moral goal. Rabbinic teachers have tended to emphasize piety, obedience and personal virtues. Kabbalists joined social and personal ethics as part of a unified moral task.

The third controversy grows out of the complexity of Judaism as a cultural and social as well as religious system This aspect of Judaism is problematic because ethics must be understood in relation to an entire pattern of existence extending beyond philosophy or religion to embrace ritual, history, literature, and nationalism. Some interpreters seek to show that humanistic ethics are the core of Jewish religion. They identify Judaism with its ethical ideals. Others argue that ethics is only a small part of Judaism; it is to be subsumed under the general category of fidelity to the divine. The on-going controversy between liberals and traditionalists often focuses on this question of priority. If Judaism as a whole system takes priority then humanistic ethics must play a secondary role in decision making; if Judaism is defined by its ethics, then ethical considerations are determinative in shaping Jewish life and practice. This issue becomes a pressing one in the modern world when universalistic ethics often conflicts with the particularism of Judaism.

The debate concerning modernity raises the problem of using an ancient tradition to confront new situations. This problem is not uniquely Jewish but should be understood as one of the major concerns in developing a contemporary Jewish ethics. Jews in the modern world must confront challenges from secular society. The ethical traditions of the general society must be taken seriously when Jews develop their own thought. How are Jews to respond to the ethics of the non-Jewish world in which they live?

Each of these four problems requires its own type of analysis. The question of whether there is a dominant ethical virtue by which all moral decisions are judged can be studied through concentrating on the relationship between morality and ethics as understood by Jewish thinkers. The way in which ethical principles are articulated, the role these principles play in making decisions, and the sources of these principles will be discovered by asking whether a thinker identifies a single ethical virtue with Jewish morality and, if so, what that virtue is.

The question of the variety of Jewish ethics can be addressed by considering each of the historical periods in which Jewish ethical writing developed. Such a historical survey focuses on the important sources and figures in Jewish ethical writing. A more methodologically oriented approach is that of identifying the major principles used in determining ethical and moral action. While the first approach looks at changing authors the second looks at constant methods in ethical investigation. These two approaches will be combined here in a historical review that considers both individuals who contributed to Jewish ethical reflection and the principles they used in establishing ethical standards. This survey will demonstrate the basis for variety within the tradition itself.

6 CONTEMPORARY JEWISH ETHICS

The last two questions can really be considered together: they are both responses to the modern predicament. The problematic nature of the place of ethics in Judaism is peculiarly modern and springs from the desire to find an "essence" of Judaism. The relationship of Judaism to the total human environment has become questionable only since the modern world has demanded that Jews see themselves as part of their general context. Considering these last two problems, then, is actually a consideration of modernity. A study of modern Judaism requires a double analysis. On the one hand the problems are historical and require a sketch of the modern movements in Judaism and their relationship to ethics. On the other hand, however, the theoretical issues raised by modernity need to be considered. The last three sections of this introduction, accordingly, are devoted to modern Jewish movements, some representative Jewish thinkers, and the problematic ethical issues facing the contemporary Jew.

DISTINGUISHING BETWEEN ETHICS AND MORALITY

The distinction between ethics and morality has proven useful to Jewish ethicists seeking to interpret their tradition (see 081, 094, 388). Ethics refers to a system of priorities, a set of criteria by which decisions are to be made. Moral norms, on the other hand, are specific decisions, legislated commands and prohibitions. An ethical system provides a framework by which a person can make moral choices. The relationship between morality and ethics has been compared to that between data and model. Moral commands are the data and ethical theories are the model that explains or tests that data. In Jewish religious life those moral commands are associated with the legal tradition, with <u>halakhah</u>; the theories or models, the ethical systems, are often associated with the nonlegal material of the tradition. Thus it could be said that the legal norms of Judaism provide examples of particular moral decisions that illustrate the way in which Jewish ethics actually works. The ideals and values of Judaism are said to generate specific moral rules. The ethics of Judaism, in this account, lie beneath the surface of the moral details spelled out in Jewish law. The principles by which morality is determined can be deduced by looking at specific moral choices. Judaism has, accordingly, both an ethics(a set of broad principles establishing moral priorities), and a morality (a set of specific rules of behavior to apply in concrete cases). Such an interpretation of Jewish ethics and morality, however, is not universally accepted.

The debate over the relative value of ethics, general principles and morality, represented by <u>halakhah</u>ty is controversial. While specific <u>halakhot</u> or legal decisions that govern daily life, are often assumed to have a vitality and legitimacy of its own, some interpreters argue that specific legal decisions are legitimated only by an all embracing ethical value (see 032, 042, 048, 082, 083).

This argument has led to the search for a single ethical standard by which to judge Jewish moral decisions, the enunciation of a set of ethical principles that explain the concrete laws of Jewish life, or a rejection of an independent ethics that can determine the validity of specific moral choices.

Some traditional thinkers eschew such a search. They suggest that morality is determined by the attitude of obedience that animates an act. Torah is the essence of ethics; to teach devotion to Torah is to teach ethics (see 024, 076, 088). The problem of determining the ethical value of Jewish law is solved by seeing in each moral act an ethical acceptance of the divine sovereign. No single virtue is, therefore, to be singled out as the ethical yardstick. Divine law rather than universal ethical principles supplies the justification for Jewish action.

Another approach, however, that may be equally traditional, does look for a central virtue that is the foundation for all Jewish ethics. What distinguishes liberal thinkers from traditionalists is often not the quest for an all-embracing virtue but the rationale for that quest. Liberals use the single virtue as a criteria in the name of which many details of Jewish law can be changed; traditionalists use the virtue as the basis for their contention that those very details are ethically justified. Some virtues which traditional and liberal Jews often see as the central Jewish ethical principle are humility (042, 085), love (048), humanism (049), or even politeness (083). In each case the author tries to condense the meaning of Judaism into a single principle. Included in the principle are all the details that govern Jewish life. The purpose of finding that principle is to discover the "essence" or central core of Judaism.

Some Orthodox Jews reject the quest for a "central core" on religious grounds--i.e., the Torah is either identical with ethics or beyond it as a moral law code. This theological approach is both consistent and simplistic. Other thinkers, both traditional and liberal, often reject such simplicity on philosophical grounds and contend that Jewish ethical thought is a complex system of dialectical interaction between a variety of moral values. Sometimes the dialectic is between two virtues like humility and human dignity (see 052, 093) and sometimes it is between universalism and parochialism (see 019, 097). In both cases the essential element in Jewish ethics is dialogue. No one virtue is permitted to gain total ascendancy. A balance of concerns prevents an ethical imperialism in which one virtue becomes supreme. The argument is made that this dialectic itself, rather than the specific virtues involved, is the ethical value in Judaism. Jewish ethics is identified with a moral caution that precludes any simplistic ethical yardstick.

There is a third approach taken to the quest for a central virtue in Jewish ethics. Some thinkers claim that Judaism is an organic system in which "value concepts" interact with specific situations, with "normal mysticism," and with cultural life in general. The life-situation itself and the value concepts that interact with it provide the dynamics of Jewish ethics. This idea is associated with Max Kadushin and is used by many Jewish ethicists influenced by him (see 057, 064, 142, 373). According to these thinkers it is inappropriate to seek to isolate a single virtue or even one or two virtues as the key to the meaning of Jewish ethics.

Three examples can show how a decision concerning the nature of Jewish ethics reflects a preconception about Jewish religion in general. The first is a traditionalist viewpoint in which an ethics independent of the moral code is rejected; the second considers ethics to be the result of an ethical dialectic rooted in Judaism itself; the last identifies Judaism with ethical thinking.

Zelig Plishkin (013) writes from a pietistic perspective and as a traditional Jew who happens to live in America but who has not imbibed American culture. His work centers on Jewish texts and Jewish values. He organizes his book around the weekly Sabbath readings, scatters references to the kabbalah, to the saints and heroes of Judaism in his work, and refuses to reduce Judaism to any single religious principle. His approach to Jewish ethics reflects an understanding of Judaism as an eternal, unchanging entity with no discontinuities of either content or style.

In many cases the view of Jewish ethics as dialectical is similar in its implications and consequences to the previous position. Many Orthodox Jews argue that the dialectics between individual and society, between humility and self-affirmation, and between human creativity and human destructiveness are inherent in traditional Judaism. They see no inconsistency in declaring that Judaism is both eternal and unchanging and also a religion of process and dynamic interplay of human moral forces. In general, however, this view of Judaism sees it as an evolving, changing entity. For these thinkers ideal dialogue entails compromise; encounter with diverging views leads to an acknowledgment that there are varieties of Jewish ethics. Conservative Jewish thinkers, representing the moderate camp in contemporary Jewish institutions, are among the most prominent proponents of this dialectical approach. The basic impetus to this view came from Max Kadushin (see 057, 142), who developed the position within the framework of "historical Judaism," the keynote of the Conservative Movement in American Judaism. This position argues that Judaism is an evolving culture in which ethics is the principle of growth and progress. The "value concepts" animating Jewish life take on concrete meaning in specific Jewish laws. These detailed and concrete laws, however, are only transient and imperfect representations of the ethical ideal. New situations call forth new actualizations of the same ideal. Proponents of this approach call for an evolving Jewish morality that responds to modern life on the basis of traditional ethics but with an openness to new ways of implementing those value concepts.

A peculiarly modern alternative rejects traditional Judaism's God-centered approach. Many modern thinkers calling themselves "humanistic" argue that humanity, not God or abstract principles, is central in Jewish teachings. Whether influenced by existentialist theologians like Martin Buber (see Bergman, 005, 006, 480) or by sociology or psychology (see Scult on Mordecai Kaplan, 321, or Bulka on Frankl, 323, 625, 626), or emphasizing the naturalistic context of modern thought (see Elkins, 035, and Cohen 431), these thinkers contend that whatever was best and is worth retaining in Judaism can be found in its ethics. Such a view has profound implications for a theory of Judaism and Jewish ethics. It suggests that the various religious forms and details of Jewish observance developed in the past were accidental accretions to an essentially ethical system. Whether this system is "prophetic ethics" as some American and European thinkers call it or "humanistic ethics" as other writers suggest is less important than the rejection of traditional Jewish forms which is entailed. This radical attempt to return Judaism to its ethical roots must be considered a vital force in contemporary Jewish thinking despite opposition to it (see Borowitz, 647).

Judaism may be peculiar in this multifold approach to ethics and to its own religious nature. In another way, however, the problem of determining what, if anything, is ethically distinctive about Judaism is symptomatic of a general challenge made to contemporary religion. The rapid changes in life occurring in modern times has demanded rapid responses from religious leaders. This necessity has required Jewish leaders, whether traditional, liberal, moderate, or radical in their approach to Judaism, to think critically about the nature of Jewish ethics. Such critical thought challenges ethical theory as well as particular moral positions. A not uncommon religious problem of modernity faces the Jew: justifying new answers to new questions on the basis of a traditional religion. Jews may not be unique in facing this dilemma; their answer, however, is distinctive because of the specialized language of Jewish ethics and the peculiar history of that ethics.

THE SOURCES OF JEWISH ETHICS

Another specifically Jewish characteristic stems from the way in which Jewish ethical investigation develops, from its peculiar process of religious study. The content of Jewish ethics is shaped by the canons of the process by which ethics is evolved, a process built into the very notion of

Judaic learning: that of interpreting traditional texts (see Fox, 008). The Jewish ethicist confronts theoretical questions of values and principles by studying the accumulated tradition. This procedure is organized and systematized through the use of a number of terms that can be divided into three general categories. The first of these is the category of normative, legal decision making. The technical term is halakhah--literally the way a Jew must walk, often interpreted as imitation of God (see 407). The details forming the basis of this imitation of the divine are the specific commandments of Jewish law , details often considered to be the building blocks of Jewish ethics. The ethical relevance of halakhah so understood is neither humanitarian nor utilitarian but theological: the moral details of Jewish law exemplify the ethics of obedience to the divine. This idea finds further confirmation in the Hebrew word that designates these moral norms, mitzvah, commandment indication that their authority lies in divine sanctions (see 343-346, 354, 257, 359, 380, 387, 420, 421).

In discussing the theology of Jewish ethics, however, the halakhah is only one element to be considered. An equally important element in Jewish tradition is that of the aggadah. This latter element is composed of various strands --folklore, anecdote, theological generalizations, fantasy, and philosophical speculation. While stimulating and influential, particularly in the shaping of Jewish liturgy, the aggadah is usually not considered "normative." It has no explicit behavioral implications (for the implicit normative power of aggadah see the writings by David Novak, 074, 075). The ethical significance of aggadah, however, should not be underestimated. It provides a perspective from which to regard the entire tradition. Its primary influence is on the individual's sense of self.

Musar, a technical term associated with aggadic rather than halakhic Judaism, refers to literature that disciplines through exhortation, inspiration, and advice. Musar strives to educate the soul so that it can fulfill its spiritual destiny. In addition to musar literature there is "reproof" literature. While musar literature concentrates on the path a person should take and provides explicit advice about that path, reproof literature admonishes, scolds, and provides lists of failings and shortcomings. Musar is a good example of ethics understood as a dimension of personal piety, of aggadic ethics. Halakhic ethics focuses on the the normative system of Jewish social behavior; aggadic ethics expands the range of ethical concerns to include personal responsiveness. The tension between these types of ethics is clearest in the controversies over the Musar Movement of the nineteenth century (see 215-234) although some scholars deny the existence of any such conflict. The debates occasioned by this movement, as well as those concerning Jewish mysticism suggest the multifaceted nature of Jewish ethics.

While both halakhic and aggadic ethics derive from rabbinic Judaism another approach is associated with the kabbalah. Usually translated as "Jewish mysticism" the term literally means tradition, basically the received esoteric tradition of Judaism, which seems rooted in social concern and ethical reflection. Members of Jewish mystical groups often call themselves hasidim, or pietists, a word with biblical associations that has been employed by various and unrelated movements in Judaism. The root of the word is a Hebrew term meaning devoted love, steadfast loyalty, covenantal devotion. The word hasid itself refers to one who practices that virtue of devotion. The name derives from the Bible where it is used in the Psalms and in the book of Daniel, apparently to refer to a sectarian-pietistic group of post-exilic Jews. Later it became a term by which mystical pietists referred to themselves in opposition to the rabbinic leaders of their times--as by the leaders of German Pietism in the twelfth century (see 188-200) and, beginning in the eighteenth century, by the popular mystical movement that is particularly noted for its ethical and homiletical teachings see 235-250).

A central ethical concern of Jewish mystics was that of tikkun, improvement of the world, the self, and the cosmos. On one level this concern motivated actions undertaken to improve the soul, to reach personal self-fulfillment. On another level it refers to social amelioration, to perfecting the world under the laws of God. These two values--personal self-improvement and social amelioration--are complemented by a third under which they are subsumed: perfection of the cosmos. In the most developed form of Jewish mysticism, that of Lurianic kabbalah in the sixteenth century, the cosmos is seen to be out of order, it has suffered a dramatic and catastrophic disaster. Holy sparks have been captured by evil forces and human deeds are needed to effect tikkun, to restore the cosmos to its original perfection. The purpose of ethical deeds is to free the sparks trapped in this material world.

To the three spheres of Jewish ethical concern--Law (halakhah), lore (aggadah), and mysticism (kabbalah)--should be added the variety of philosophical reflections on Jewish ethics that developed over the course of history. This development will be traced in the next section; before advancing to a historical sketch, however, the relevance of these three foci of ethical investigation should be noted. The halakhic stresses the relevance of social norms in ethical life; the aggadic centers concern on the inner life of the individual; the pietistic and kabbalistic cultivates a cosmic consciousness that embraces the individual and society in a wider universal context. While rabbis, philosophers, and mystics each developed their own unique responses to ethical challenges they shared a common vocabulary of discourse; rabbis, despite an emphasis on halakhah did not neglect the personal or the cosmic; mystics integrated the social and the personal into their wider perspective.

As important as a historical review is for understanding Jewish ethics, the unity that combines this diversity into a coherent whole should not be forgotten. A word of caution, then, is in order, before surveying the development of the Jewish ethical tradition.

Naturally the first period associated with Jewish ethics is represented by the Hebrew Bible. The Bible, however, can be read in different ways. Many scholars see the process of biblical interpretation evident even in the later books of the Hebrew canon. The technique of deriving new meanings from an old text is called midrash or searching. Jewish ethics looks at the Bible through the eyes of commentators and sages; the Bible becomes an ethical document in Judaism through the process of interpretation, of midrash (see 008). Biblical quotations are incorporated into various surveys of Jewish ethics, but they are integrated into a framework provided by later writers. Judaism shapes the Bible through categories derived from later authorities (see 013, 016).

The Bible is utilized in ways other than through midrash. It also provides a foundation, an organizational point of departure, for the study of Jewish ethics. An anthology of Jewish ethics may start each section with a series of biblical quotes before considering medieval philosophers (see 120). A biblical concept may provide the initial impetus for the study of a central Jewish ethical principle; the Bible thus becomes a stepping stone to later Jewish ethical thought (see 155, 160). Certain themes or stories from the Bible become of central religious concern--the binding of Isaac and the command that Saul slaughter the Amalekites are two such examples (See 026).

While the Bible often provides a pretext for Jewish ethical reflection, rabbinic Judaism actually begins the history of Jewish ethical reflection. Rabbinic Judaism, however, presents a more commanding example for the Jewish ethicist. There are three sources for an understanding of rabbinic literature: the Mishna, a compilation of Jewish law prepared by Rabbi Judah ha Nasi in about 210 C.E., the Talmud, an expansive discussion of the Mishna finally concluded about 500 C.E. , and finally later sources reflecting on these first two--the codes and the responsa. The rabbinic material is vast and often inconsistent so later authors compiled organized works to disseminate what they considered to be "authoritative" Jewish law. Two such works, the Mishneh Torah of Moses Maimonides (1135-1204 C.E.) and the Shulhan Arukh of Joseph Karo (1488-1575 C.E.), have become the standard reference works for Jewish law. In addition to these works another body of legal literature has been created to meet the changing needs of the growing Jewish community: responsa, collections of letters written by rabbis to in answer to specific problems. These letters often delineate ethical values and analyze moral issues and those who seek to study Jewish ethics look not only to works like the Talmud,

Mishna, and midrash, but also to the codes and the responsa which often provide both detail law and explicit reflection upon the ethical principles that undergird the process by which behavioral decisions are made (see the excellent summary of both these sources and their use in Jewish ethics in Feldman, 007).

Rabbinic Judaism provides the basis for contemporary Jewish ethical reflection in three major ways. It serves as a model of how ethical reflection should be carried out. The process of reaching moral decisions begun by rabbinic leaders is continued as an ethical ideal in contemporary Jewish life (see 134, 135, 138, 159). Rabbinic Judaism also sets the agenda for much of modern Jewish ethics. Moral issues raised in the Talmud, including questions of personal and social responsibility, are taken up by modern thinkers (see 129-162).

One fascinating example of this process is the discussion of the talmudic idea of "the law of the kingdom" (see 144, 478, 491, 509, 510, 520, 527). This idea suggests that the law of the non-Jewish king must be regarded as equal to that of Torah law. Contemporary thinkers examine the basis of this rule. Some conclude that it was meant to apply only to Jews in the diaspora and should not include a secular government like that in the state of Israel today. Other thinkers argue that the law remains in effect only when the law is a democratic reflection of the "kingdom" and not an autocratic whim of a tyrant. The relevance of these ideas to contemporary problems should be clear and the discussion of a halakhic principle often leads to a debate about contemporary ethics, a process with which some modern thinkers are uneasy, suggesting that illegitimate meanings are often read into classic texts (see 147 and 150).

While the biblical and talmudic sources can be used in a modern discussion of religious ethics they do not provide a philosophy of Jewish ethics. Medieval philosophers of Judaism--influenced by a variety of non-Jewish philosophical systems--did construct just such systems of ethical theory. It is in the works of these writers that the classical issues of freedom and determinism, the problem of evil, the virtues and vices of human behavior, and a philosophical anthropology of human motivations is presented. It is natural that modern Jewish philosophers should draw upon this medieval legacy.

While this philosophical ethics sets the agenda for a systematic approach to religious ethics, modern scholars often confine themselves to tracing how environmental and intellectual influences shaped medieval Jewish thinkers' ethics. Such academic studies, however, often provide important insights into Jewish ethical thinking. In one such study Alexander Altmann traces how the idea of free will was developed by three Jewish philosophers (see 163): Saadia Gaon who flourished in Babylonia, (882-942 C.E.);

Bachya Ibn Pakuda, a Spanish pietist in the eleventh century, and Moses Maimonides, perhaps the greatest medieval Jewish philosopher (see among other entries 164, 165, 171, 173, 177, 186). These three struggled with human rationality and its ability to verify religious doctrines. While Saadia mediated between doctrines and beliefs, Ibn Pakuda decided for doctrines in opposition to the philosopher's reliance upon rational belief alone; Maimonides identified the meaning of Jewish doctrine with the ideals of philosophy. This tension between reason and faith, the struggle to come to grips with the possible contradiction of the two, is at the heart of the ethical reflections in medieval Jewish thought and as Altmann presents it has modern relevance as well. This type of analysis makes the study of medieval Jewish philosophy relevant to modern ethical reflection (see 163-187).

It is, perhaps, surprising that Altmann analyzes Bachya Ibn Pakuda who, while a medieval Jewish philosopher, is actually best representative of Jewish pietism. The place of pietistic asceticism has been debated among modern Jewish thinkers (see 140, 148, 193). The roots of ascetic practice are controversial often being traced to non-Jewish sources whether Christian or Muslim.

It is clear, however, that Ashkenzic Hasidism in the twelfth and thirteenth centuries agonized over precisely this issue and studies of the movement emphasize its ambivalence towards pietistic self-discipline. Ivan Marcus has provided a number of studies on the movement (see 194-197) that illuminate the variety of pietism not only in Judaism but in religion in general. This strand of moralism and ethical rigor should not be ignored if the full range of Jewish ethical reflection is to be understood. Many of the elements of this rigorous piety were incorporated in later Judaism through the intermediary of kabbalah. Special pietistic moral practices were created to help repair a world that, it was felt had suffered an original catastrophe (see 201-214). Jewish mysticism answered the need of people who had suffered the vagaries of history, who knew first hand that the world was "out of joint." The themes of these mystics were often ethical despite a subject matter that often seemed remote from ethics (note the ethicalization of the idea of reincarnation discussed in 202). The social context if not the intellectual one of the kabbalah seemed to mandate an ethical concern. Jewish thinkers often interlink ethics and the kabbalah (see 101, 206, 208).

These five historical sources, the Bible, rabbinic Judaism, philosophy, pietism, and kabbalah, are pre-modern. The peculiar challenge of the modern period needs its own special treatment. Nevertheless when modern Jews, when faced with new problems, looks back to these five historical sources for inspiration. The Bible establishes broad themes and general concepts with which to confront modernity. The rabbinic literature provides the raw

INTRODUCTORY SURVEY   15

material from which to create a modern ethics. The philosophic literature offers a cogent model for self-conscious ethical reflection. Pietism justifies the personal the desire for self-perfection often necessary to reject the temptation of modernity. The kabbalah unites the various elements of behavioral norms, ascetic practice, and social concern through a comprehensive cosmology that supplies the modern Jew with a coherent worldview.

An example will show how the choice of which aspects of this tradition to emphasize shapes an individual's ethical approach. Contemporary Orthodox Jews are pressed to defend rabbinic Judaism as ethically persuasive. Since rabbinic Judaism seems to emphasize specific moral dicta rather than general principles it has been charged with ethical indifference. Many modern Jews accept the "ethics" of Judaism but reject the moral code of the rabbis. Philosophy, pietism, and kabbalah are often more convincing than rabbinic teachings just because they are expressed in discursive, abstract language rather than in the technical terms of the halakhah.

David Hartman, founder and director of the Shalom Hartman Institute of Judaic Studies in Jerusalem, is a modern Jewish philosopher (see 369) who as an Orthodox Jew, trained and educated in modern Orthodox schools, is aware of the need to look beyond a restricted traditionalist environment. He self-consciously takes Moses Maimonides, the medieval Jewish philosopher and philosopher, as his model. He sees Maimonides not only as a rabbinic scholar but also as a hasid who moved beyond halakhah into the spheres of aggadah (see 173). Hartman uses a modern philosophical approach and suggests that halakhah be understood not as rabbinic legalism but as a universal and symbolic language (368). Halakha, in this view, is not a set of answers but a set of principles upon which Jews can agree even if they disagree about the specific moral details generated by those principles. In this way Hartman follows Maimonides in transforming Jewish morality into a vital ethics. This move, however, precipitated considerable controversy (see 380, 388, 416). Those for whom rabbinic Judaism is the test of all ethics could not accept Hartman's philosophical bias. His reading of Jewish history which emphasizes the philosophical, places him at odds with others within his own Orthodox camp. Thus how Jews use the history of Jewish ethics will determine the shape their ideas will take and even the reception given to them.

ETHICS AND MODERN JUDAISM

What is modernity and how does it establish new problems in Jewish ethics? Jewish historians debate the exact point at which modernity began. Some place its origins in the Enlightenment, some in Napoleon's legislation, some with the rise of nationalism. For the purposes of this present

study modern Jewish ethics will be considered to begin with
Moses Mendelssohn (1729-1786 C. E.) and the enlightenment
tradition which he started (see 251, 257, 268, 293, 306).
Traditional Judaism faced a crisis in modernity: the Jew
was invited to join the non-Jewish world, but at the price
of giving up Jewish particularism. The Jew as an individual
with a peculiar religious set of beliefs could be accepted
within secular society. The Jew as loyal to a parochial
community with its own laws and social structure was totally
unacceptable. Modern Jewish ethics grew out of the need to
maintain continuity with the past tradition while meeting
the challenge raised by the invitation to become a citizen
of the world, a member of general society who, like all
individuals, was distinctive but who, like all citizens,
gave primary loyalty to the civil order. Moses Mendelssohn
demonstrated how a modern Jew could affirm the humanistic
values of the modern world and still retain a parochial
Jewish identity. He wrestled with the basic problem facing
modern Jews--how to reconcile a particularistic tradition
with a universalistic worldview that asserted the common
humanity of all rational beings.

Mendelssohn's response to modernity provided a model
followed by modern Jewish philosophers. He adapted Judaism
to meet the philosophical challenges of his time; he wrote
in a language derived from his environment, employing images
and symbols drawn from it, and he investigated problems of
interest to his contemporaries, not merely of interest to
Jews. In these three characteristics he was the prototype
of contemporary Jewish ethical thinkers. Jewish ethics has
been conducted with an awareness of modern philosophy (see
256, 266, 276, 281, 293, 297). The legacy of Mendelssohn
meant that Jews philosophized as part of universal humanity
and not merely as representatives of a parochial culture.
The struggle to balance parochial and universal elements is
evident as differing Jewish thinkers encounter the
philosophies of their times. This struggle can be witnessed
in liberals and traditionalists alike, in Orthodox and
Reform Jews, and in Israeli and diaspora-based theologians.
Some Jewish thinkers seek to derive a Jewish meaning from
Kantian ethics thus universalism Judaism. Hermann Cohen
(see 260, 261, 263, 265, 275, 279, 283, 291, 295, 299, 300,
305) is a classic example of a liberal Jewish thinker who
takes a Kantian approach to Judaism, but examples from
Orthodox Judaism can also be given (such as Isaac Breuer,
see 332). Not only Kant but other modern thinkers
influenced Jewish ethical reflection as can be discovered by
analyzing such thinkers as Martin Buber (see 258, 278, 282,
289, 301, 302, 304) Joseph B. Soloveitchik (see 0092-093,
325, 327, 337), and Emmanuel Levinas (285-288, 290, 303).

The significance of modernization lies in culture as well
as philosophy. The Jewish confrontation with secular
culture changed Jewish literature. Moses Mendelssohn
translated the Hebrew Bible into German as means of of
teaching Jews the vernacular; this aim went beyond a

pragmatic use of diaspora culture; it affirmed that culture. The marriage of Jewish ideas with diaspora form was carried out in the traditionalist and reformist camp alike, with neo-Orthodox Jews proclaiming the need to combine Torah (understood as all of Jewish learning) with derech eretz (understood as the way of the lands in which the Jews resided). This affirmation of the language and style of non-Jewish thinking has produced a distinctive quality about modern Jewish philosophy. Modern Jewish thinking by both traditionalists and liberals is done in the midst of a world culture and not only in the context of Judaism.

In an extraordinary extension of this characteristic many modern Jewish thinkers have chosen to utilize the language not of philosophy or tradition but of world literature. Thus the writings of contemporary Jewish novelists and poets serve as a new basis upon which to develop an understanding of the principles of Jewish morality. The works of American Jewish authors like Bernard Malamud and Saul Bellow or the challenging novels of Elie Wiesel have become the inspiration for new interpretations of Jewish ethics (see 254, 270, 274, 284, 294). Using metaphors and literary symbols borrowed from non-Jewish tradition Jewish authors explore the depths of the contemporary moral crisis. Interpreters suggest that there is a particular Jewish sensitivity that manifests itself in their work.

The new literature represents a new experience as well as a new language. Contemporary Jewish ethical thinkers have evolved a new style of writing and thinking not only as a reflection of their environment but also as a response to the catastrophes and threat of cosmic disaster that characterize the modern age. The work of these theologians resounds with new themes and concerns. One common theme in this work is that of persecution and suffering. Jewish ethicists since World War II have sought to extract meaning from the tragedy of of the Nazi Holocaust of six million Jews (see particularly 256, 259, 269, 281, 312, 313, 314, 317) The midrashic emphasis in the works of Emil Fackenheim (see 314) is an indication of the transformed literary style and the new themes arising from a consideration of the Holocaust. Thus, in philosophy, theology, and in literature Jewish ethical reflection confronts the moral dilemma posed by the radical evil disclosed in that event. Many modern thinkers emphasize that traditional thought patterns or modes of expression are inappropriate in the face of the Holocaust. The new form, that of modern midrash, using literary rather than discursive language, symbolizes the inability of older forms to capture the new reality.

Mendelssohn serves as a model for contemporary Jewish ethical thinkers, not only as an early example of how to combine Jewish and non-Jewish philosophy or how to integrate Jewish and non-Jewish styles of ethical reflection. His self-understanding is a model of modern Jewish identity. He was, self-consciously, a citizen of the world and responded

to the challenges of his times, not only to specifically
Jewish challenges like anti-Semitism but the broader
political and social issues of the general society.
Contemporary Jewish philosophy seeks to show the relevance
of Judaism to the wider concerns of contemporary society.
The final characteristic of modern Jewish ethics as a new
phenomenon is a willingness to confront problems perplexing
society as a whole. Such problems include ecology and the
environment, social life and civil responsibility,
nationalism and international peace, racism, poverty, and
other social ills, progress and technological challenges to
human life. Jewish ethicists view contemporary Western
civilization as both having benefited from Jewish ideas in
the past and as needing of the contributions of further
Jewish ethical reflection in the present (see 271, 276,
655). The theology of creation is an example of theology
that is socially responsibly because it creates an awareness
of the Jewish tradition as a resource needed by all
humanity. Thus modern Jewish philosophy extends its
concerns beyond the border of Judaism to embrace all of
modern life. Thus it is that a modern Jewish ethicist
cannot reflect only on parochial issues. Judaism becomes
relevant only when it offers solutions to the general
problems of humanity as a whole as well as to Jews as a
particular part of humanity.

   Mendelssohn contributed to German thought as a philosopher
of religion. His first major work was a defense of the idea
of immortality. His commitment to theology and religious
ideas as an important contribution that Jews can make to
modern life is continued by contemporary Jewish thinkers.
The theological categories of idolatry, creation, and
revelation are affirmed in a universal context by Jewish
ethicists. The relevance of contemporary events is not
merely "political" or historical; it is profoundly
theological. Jewish ethical thinkers emphasize the
religious basis of the moral problems confronting modern
women and men (see 049, 271, 652, 658, 661). A major theme
stressed by traditional and liberal Jewish thinkers alike is
the necessity to analyze, confront, and ultimately solve the
dilemmas of contemporary, secular society by means of
religious answers.

   While the term "the Enlightenment" refers to a specific
historical period (that of the eighteenth century in
particular), the model of the free Jewish thinker who
utilizes the philosophy, language, and current issues of the
day in evolving a Jewish ethics has a broader relevance. As
a whole it affirms the primacy of the non-Jewish environment ove
historical Jewish concerns and values, a tradition that
extends from the eighteenth century to the present and is a
symbol of the way in which Jews have accepted modernity.
This entire tradition, whether articulated by Mendelssohn or
evolved by more modern exponents of an "enlightened"
Judaism, presents precisely the challenge that Orthodox Jews
have faced since Mendelssohn and continue to face in

their affirmation of tradition: the challenge to reassert Jewish institutional constraints, to restore the traditional mode of Jewish ethical reflection, and to reestablish the historical agenda of Jewish ethics. These three challenges correspond to the three elements in enlightenment Judaism. When Orthodox Jews take up the enlightenment style and utilize contemporary philosophy they do so in order to ultimately reject that philosophy in the name of institutional commitment. When Orthodox Jews turn to contemporary literary forms it is in order to show how classical Jewish ethical reflection has merely been recast in modern terms (note in particular the way Reuven Bulka utilizes Logotherapy in 323, 624-626). When Orthodox Jewish moralists confront contemporary problems it is in order to show how traditional Jewish law solves current problems. Orthodoxy had already begun to respond to these challenges and evolve the shape of its new approach in the eighteenth century. Two movements during that period sought to respond to the challenge: the Musar Movement and hasidism (see 215-250). While these movements must be understood within the total framework of modernization and Judaism, they have a particular relevance for modern Jewish ethics.

The name of the Musar Movement is itself a clue to its ethical relevance. The term <u>musar</u>, or ethical discipline, is a sign that personal ethics, training in moral behavior and character education, was the foremost concern in the movement. Israel Salanter (1810-1883 C.E.), the founder of the movement, was convinced that the decay of traditional Judaism lay in the lack of moral training given to Lithuanian Jews in his time. He evolved a new educational system that upheld the ideal of traditional study and continued the rabbinic process, but added to it devotional studies for the sake of ethical self-improvement. Salanter was a respected rabbinic figure and his movement shared his prestige. During his lifetime few criticized the changed emphasis he gave to Jewish thinking. During that lifetime, however, his own system evolved. He came into contact with German Jewish enlightenment, began to address the crisis of modernity, and in his final stage he reaffirmed traditional study and religious practice. Following his example the Musar leaders who succeeded him were staunch traditionalists. They analyzed the crisis in modern Judaism as a moral one and suggested a program for revitalizing Judaism that in modern terms could be called sensitivity training as a means of motivating Jewish learning. This program was characterized by inspiring tales of ethical exemplars, enthusiastic support for Jewish scholarship, and astute mechanisms for reinforcing Jewish values.

Not only is <u>musar</u> ethical in content; its movement is central for contemporary Jewish ethics. Modern Jewish ethics draws as much on the psychology at the heart of the movement as at its orientation towards study and traditional Jewish values. (see 215, 223, 228, 229, 233). The movement reinforces traditional values of study and ethics. It also,

however, it addresses the problems of the modern Jewish
individual by using a sophisticated psychology of human
behavior that has enough similarity to behaviorism to be
respectable and enough traditionalism to be free from
suspicion of heresy. Young Jews are often attracted by the
Musar Movement because it fulfills their desire for a
personally compelling Jewish ethic (see 220-222).

While the Musar Movement manages to attract some Jewish
youth, the Hasidic Movement is by far more popular and has
generated considerable discussion (see 238, 239, 247, 248).
The movement is purported to have been begun by Israel Baal
Shem Tov (1700-1760 C.E.) in Russia and Poland; as it
developed it splintered into a variety of independent
groups, usually called by the names of the town where the
leader or Rebbe of the group resided (thus the following
names for current hasidic groups: Lubavitcher Hasidism,
Bratzlaver Hasidism, Karliner Hasidism). The movement
stimulated controversy and opposition during the early part
of its rise to prominence. Traditional Jewish leaders were
wary of this populist movement that threatened normative
Jewish values of study and practice. As it developed,
however, hasidism's traditionalism became clear, and it has
become a bastion of Jewish Orthodoxy in the modern world.

One way in which hasidism can be seen as a response to the
challenge of the modern world is in its ethics. Hasidic
ethics is often understood as a democratization of Judaism
as it emphasizes the contributions each individual makes to
the redemption of the world (see 235, 240). These
contributions include performing the normative Jewish
mitzvot, but also include personal, idiosyncratic
activities. Thus, hasidism is exalted as a model for the
modern Jew because it shows how to redeem the world through
ethical action. Some interpreters see hasidism as demanding
an ethical approach to religion by demanding a rigorous
morality, an uncompromising quest for truth and purity (see
241). Other interpreters stress community, the need for a
common ideal and purpose to hold a community together and
the interdependency of the leader and the members of the
community (see 246). Still others see in hasidism the
quintessence of Jewish ethics, an ethics balancing human
selfishness with human interdependency. This has been
called an "alter-centered" ethic in which one gains personal
salvation only through actions on behalf of others (see
246). Still another approach argues a peculiarly modern
relevance for hasidic ethics by maintaining that it provides
modern Jews with a sense of purpose, an argument buttressed
by sociological data (see 243, 244). Like many
psychological systems, it is argued, the teachings of
hasidic ethics give meaning and direction to life (see 236).

Thus far this survey has focused on personal, individual
concerns. While the search for meaning is a personal one,
much of contemporary Jewish ethics comes from institutional
sources. This survey of Jewish ethics would be incomplete

without including a look at the three major Jewish movements: Reform, Orthodox, and Conservative. In addition to these groups there have been "spin-off" sectarian institutions, often with their own ethical outlook. Traditionalists in Orthodoxy produced the Yeshiva movement (see 657); while the Reconstructionist movement is derived from Conservatism (see 310, 321, 322), and associated with Reform Judaism are Humanistic Judaism and Polydox. A look at the anthologies produced by the three major institutions, however, shows that they often include representative texts from the "spin-off" sects (see 102, 126, 411). A review of these three groups, then, will be useful in understanding the shape of contemporary Jewish ethics generally.

The Reform Movement in contemporary Judaism traces its roots back to Germany in the nineteenth century (see 305-309, 315, 320). Leading exponents of a liberalized and modernized Judaism like Abraham Geiger (1810-1874 C.E.) developed an institutional basis for transforming Jewish life and thought. German Reform Judaism stressed the "kernal" of Jewish religion which they saw as ethical monotheism. This ideology, close to the thought of Hermann Cohen, was refined by later theologians. Leo Baeck (1873-1956 C.E.), a liberal rabbi in Germany who suffered courageously in World War II, developed the idea of the "essence" of Judaism as a dialectic between ethical responsibility and religious sensitivity. In their search for an "essence" or "kernal" of Judaism that remained constant despite changes in form, outer appearance, and contextual, shape Reform leaders have stressed "prophetic ethics." This ethical stress is prominent in the American Reform Movement no less than in its European prototype. The Reform Movement in the United States had leaders who led the abolitionist cause against slavery (e.g., David Einhorn, 1809-1879 C.E.) and who were in the forefront of movements for social reform (e.g., Stephen S. Wise, 1874-1944 C.E.). Throughout its development the Reform Movement made ethical reflection and commitment primary. A central issue arising from this approach is the relationship of individual moral autonomy to group loyalty. While the Reform Movement is committed to moral independence--moral worth depends upon making a free ethical decision--it is also aware that there must be limits upon the individual's choices. The case of Felix Adler who broke with Reform Judaism in order to maintain intellectual honesty points up the Reform dilemma (1851-1933 C.E.; see 316). Reform Judaism clearly saw itself as within Jewish tradition and maintained its identification with the Jewish people. The commitment to ethical independence, however, created tension between group loyalty and personal decision making.

This tension provides the backdrop for modern ethical reflection among Reform theologians. They see themselves forced to balance both elements in Jewish moral thinking. Emil L. Fackenheim is one liberal theologian (see 311-314), who has confronted this issues, contending with the issues of autonomy within a tradition committed to God's revealed law and confronting the Nazi Holocaust, he has sought to find in its horrors justification for an ethically responsible particularism. He maintains that the world, and God, need the Jewish people and even a political State of Israel. For the sake of humanity as a whole the Jewish people must strive to survive. Survival has a religious implication, it is for the sake of God's ideals and not merely for chauvanistic pride. In order to maintain both universalism and the centricity of the Jewish people, Fackenheim has turned to midrash, aggadah, and Jewish mysticism as a means of using traditional sources to undergird a confrontation with modernity. Other Reform Jewish thinkers follow a similar pattern.

The Conservative Movement in Judaism traces its lineage back to the "Historical School" in Germany (see 081). Jewish leaders who dissented from Reform but who still sought some changes within Jewish religion looked to the Jewish past for examples and models they could use. Zechariah Frankel (1801-1875 C.E.) is associated with this approach. He advocated slow change that reflected the inner spirit of the Jewish people. This emphasis upon the spirit of the Jewish people was developed more systematically by Solomon Schechter (1847-1916 C.E.), who was the primary builder of Conservative Judaism in the United States. Schechter took as his central principle the idea of a "Catholic Israel," or the united collectivity of the Jewish people. This emphasis motivated Conservative Jewish ethicists to search for the dynamic principles driving the development of the Jewish people. Max Kadushin sees an organic system of value concepts as the source of those principles (see 057, 142); Mordecai Kaplan (see 058, 310, 319, 321, 322), whose Reconstructionist Movement in Judaism can be understood as an offshoot of Conservatism, stressed the idea of "civilization" as the key to Jewish development. What is important in both these systems is that Jewish ethics arises from the very existence of the Jewish people. Judaism is legitimized not by its ethics but by its existence; because there is a Jewish people and because there is a distinctive pattern of Jewish thought, the ethics of Judaism must be taken seriously. Jewish ethics is understood in the total context of Jewish survival and the meaning of being Jewish.

The general dilemma facing the conservative Jew is that of making a distinction between those aspects of Judaism that are vital and express the heart of the Jewish people and those that are no longer creative or persuasive. Differences among conservative leaders lead to the gulf between the radicalism of Mordecai Kaplan and the traditionalism of David Novak (see 410 and 411). The conservative Jew seeks to identify a moral tendency throughout the Jewish tradition that will provide a clear guide to what should remain unchanged within received practices and what is legitimately transformed.

Different systems of understanding Judaism within the Conservative Movement, however, point to different moral principles. No clear and unambiguous guide to show what Jewish practices should be changed or how change should proceed has been developed. The conservative Jewish moral thinker has two principle tasks--that of distinguishing the moral principles operating through Jewish tradition and that of demonstrating how a continuity of ethical principles can be maintained while changing concrete instances of those principles. While some conservative Jews have evolved complete systems of Jewish ethics (see, for example, that of Jacob Bernard Agus, 001-004), a more common approach has been to seek to define the meaning of halakhah, of mitzvah, and of morality. The relationship of Jewish law and Jewish moral ideals is explored. The process of defining new meanings for old terms is at the center of conservative Jewish ethical innovation.

The Orthodox Jewish community, on the defensive since the eighteenth century, takes a different approach to Jewish ethics. From its earliest exponents, Samson Raphael Hirsch (1808-1888 C.E., see 444) and his successor Isaac Breuer (see 332) in Germany, and Samuel David Luzzatto (1800-1865 C.E., see 324, 330, 331, 334) in Italy, neo-Orthodoxy has insisted upon the universal relevance of traditional Judaism. Judaism does not need to adapt to a Kantian world or to the modern scientific mode of thinking. It contains within itself the best the modern world has to offer. The world can learn its ethics from Judaism, and when rightly understood the most persuasive secular ethicists are merely restating established Jewish principles. The presentation of Jewish ethics by Orthodox Jewish thinkers takes one of two forms. It can either be persuasive and homiletical, utilizing traditional sources to cajole and inspire followers to adopt certain forms of behavior, or it can be polemical and apologetic. Jewish ethics is interpreted as the modern solution to the dilemmas human beings have created for themselves. In both cases Orthodox thinkers have a double thrust: towards universalism by their affirmation of the relevance of Jewish teachings for all humanity, and towards particularism because this ethics derives from the parochial duties of Jewish morality.

The reconciliation of these two strands in Orthodox Jewish ethics can be achieved in a variety of ways. The theology of Abraham Isaac Kook utilizes the mystical tradition to attain this goal; his ethical insight uses the language of the kabbalah to solve modern problems by reference to traditional law (see 060, 336). Yeshiyahu Leibowitz takes a different approach (see 063, 326, 335, 380). His traditionalism is integrated with a sensitivity to Kantian philosophy. He argues that ethics by itself must be universal and thus Judaism does not, cannot, have an independent ethics. Judaism is distinguished by its religiosity and its humility before God. Ethics by itself,

Leibowitz argues, is insufficient for a human life. Human beings need the religious humility of acknowledging their vulnerability before the divine, their weakness in the face of the infinite. Ethics correctly and naturally emphasizes what human beings as creative, responsible creatures can accomplish. Ethics points out the human task. Judaism augments this universal ethics with the realization of human limitations.

There are many contemporary Orthodox Jews who reject modernity completely (see representative material in 013, 032-034, 037-040, 050, 088, 105, 106, 113). Other traditional Jews, however, strive to be both modern and Orthodox; these Jews, however, often find themselves living in two worlds. They are both modern and Jewish, both traditional and contemporary. This tension is well represented by the work of Joseph Baer Soloveitchik (see 092-093, 325, 327, 337). Soloveitchik, born and trained in the intense Jewish scholarly atmosphere of Eastern European Jewry, teaches at Yeshiva University, an American seminary for Orthodox rabbis. By his disciples he is known as "The Rav," the teacher and model par excellence; he is respected by both traditionalists and liberals alike for his cogent talmudic thinking and philosophical rigor. His work reflects on the contradictions in being a modern Jew.

Soloveitchik posits two types of human impulses derived from the two portraits of Adam in the creation stories. Human beings are, on the one hand, creators, controllers, beings with a dignity that lifts them above the merely animal. They are also law abiders, halakhically inclined and submissive to the divine. Ethics, understood from a Kantian perspective as rational self-legislation, is certainly one of the poles of human existence. Human dignity depends upon taking responsibility for moral decisions. It reveals, however, but half of human nature. The other half demands submission, religious humility, and recognition of limitations. This dual approach, he claims, integrates ethics and humility, universalism and particularism, in a way superior that a secular ethics cannot. This view of Judaism is particularly appropriate for modern American Orthodox rabbis.

The differences between the different institutional forms of Judaism are matched by their similarities. Theologians from each of the three movements in Judaism are, thus, struggling with institutional justification as well as with theoretical issues. Reform thinkers not only seek to answer the question of autonomy but also to establish the legitimacy of autonomy as the foundation for a modern Judaism. Conservative theologians investigate the dynamics of Jewish moral teachings and seek to discover the organic system of Jewish ethical concepts from more than mere scholarly curiosity. As a movement based upon "Catholic Israel," Conservatism must discover the Jewish collective mind before making it into a governing principle. Orthodox spokesmen defend their traditionalism by showing that it is both compatible with and necessary for modernity. By investigating the dialectic between religion and ethics they do more than explore a theoretical issue. These leaders polemically support a particularistic set of practices as the needed balance to that universal ethics which is the hallmark of modern moral speculation. The thinking of liberals and Orthodox can legitimately be placed into denominational categories shaping the issues and manner in which thinkers look at modern Jewish ethics.

ISSUES IN MODERN JEWISH ETHICS

The issues faced by modern Jewish ethicists can be divided into four groups: issues raised by the internal dynamics of Jewish religion, issues raised by philosophical systems outside Judaism, issues raised by the social and behavioral sciences, and pragmatic considerations of living in the modern context. The internal categories of Jewish religion have been discussed earlier. The relationship between mitzvah and morality (acting beyond the limits of the law) and between aggadah and halakhah (the directives found within the Jewish tradition) serve as the basis for further ethical reflection in modern Judaism (see 352, 393, 404, 414). The basic aim of this reflection is to discover the way in which the legal prescriptions of Judaism interact with Jewish ethical principles. A traditional approach argues that Jewish law, the halakhah, is precisely the essence of Jewish ethics. Detailed legal prescriptions enable a community to live ethically according to this view. These thinkers reject the idea of an independent ethics that can judge whether any particular halakhic decision is valid (see 345, 346, 353, 367, 380, 385, 405). This view is defended by suggesting that halakhah itself is an ethics of love and concern for humanity which through its detailed rules provides ethical guidance. Thus obedience to Torah insures an ethical life without implying the existence of an external ethical standard.

A second approach, however, not only distinguishes between the halakhah and Jewish ethics but finds the latter to be the determinative value. Jewish ethics is understood as the dynamic set of values animating the halakhah. This view holds the halakhah to be not the ethical absolute of Judaism, but rather a changing and growing approximation of that absolute. Considerable debate goes on within the Conservative Movement in Judaism and between that movement and traditionalists on the one hand and liberals on the other over just this issue (see 339, 348, 360, 373, 374, 394, 395, 410, 411, 412). The shape of Jewish ethics follows the choices made on this question. Jews who separate ethics and halakhah claim that Jewish law does change in order to become more perfectly moral. Those who refuse to acknowledge such a separation resist all changes claiming that a divine revelation cannot be immoral.

Another implication of this debate is its understanding of the purpose of Jewish law. For many Jewish thinkers, both those today and those of the past as interpreted by thinkers of the present, the law is an instrument for the teaching of morality. This instrumentalism stands in contradiction to the traditionalist view that the commandments have moral value in themselves as intrinsically holy. This view is characteristic of non-traditional Jews. These Jews seek to reinterpret the injunctions of Judaism from the standpoint of contemporary ethical questions. Jewish law is presented as consistent with and often identical to American legal ideals. Thinkers employing this view argue that Judaism believes in the "moral law" as the only true halakhah and therefore expand the meaning of mitzvah to include many nontraditional moral obligations (see 344, 350, 354, 366, 387, 390, 399).

There are three central theological issues in addition to those of halakhah, aggadah, and the other terms associated with the Jewish legal system that are central in Jewish ethics. The three categories are monotheism, revelation, and creation. Associated with them are three general ethical , 8, 9 of the other, particularism and universalism, and freedom of the will. The discussion of the general ethical problem is pursued in Jewish ethics through the consideration of the specific theological issue.

The question of monotheism, for example, implies more than a consideration of the nature of divinity and the number of gods worshipped. Monotheism, as many modern exponents of Jewish ethics insist, is an ethical category (see, for example, 434, 441, 457, 461, 464, 467, 468, 472). Some thinkers argue that since God is perceived as a loving, caring person, human beings should strive to love and care for others. Others suggest that the unity of the divine is the example for the unification of the human self. While theology is, thus, often used in discussing Jewish ethics its problems are not ignored. There are difficulties in expounding the meaning of the divine nature for human ethics; Jews disagree on how much can be said about the correspondence between the human and the godly. Nevertheless the ethics of Judaism focus as much on the divine as upon the human, on a "theocentric" as much as on "anthropocentric" basis for moral actions.

One implication of this view is the imperative for imitatio dei, the imitation of God (see 579-593), an idea that roots human morality in the nature of divinity. This idea often become the basis for asserting the inherent dignity of being human, basing it on the radical claim that God needs the partnership of human beings in establishing a just and ethical world order. The divine concern for humanity is a central theological contention. Contemporary discussions of Jewish ethics focus lovingly on this concern for human value as a contrast to non-Jewish ethical systems.

This theological basis for ethics, far from elevating the divine above the human, it is contended, actually demonstrates the exalted position of being human and the cosmic responsibility involved in the human task.

The principle of imitating God enters into Jewish ethics as a consideration in the debate concerning self-sacrifice. Jewish thinkers are divided on this issue with some saying that just as God graciously limits divinity for the sake of human beings, individuals must also give up their personal welfare for the good of all. Others argue that because each person is an image of God self-sacrifice is in actuality a sacrifice of divinity, and therefore forbidden (see 539, 546, 549, 550, 553). An interesting solution proposed is to see self-sacrifice as a moral option but not a legal requirement. While such action cannot be commanded as part of the halakhah, the legislated walking in the way of God, it may be morally required as evidence of walking "beyond the line of the law."

The discussion concerning self-sacrifice shows the intimate connection in Jewish ethics between theology and revelation. To speak of imitating God implies a revealed pattern that can be imitated. The implications of imitatio Dei for human dignity and self-sacrifice are far-reaching, and Jewish ethics can be said to be constituted by the revealed command to imitate God. Jewish ethical principles are considered authoritative because they come from God; without a theological grounding in divine law Jews moral injunctions lose their force. Unlike a philosophical ethics which is authoritative because it is rooted in universal rational principles, the ethics of Judaism legitimates itself solely by reference to its divine origins (see 424, 425, 428, 435, 452, 456, 473), a particularistic claim.

There is a fascinating consensus among Jewish thinkers, whether liberal or traditional in orientation, that religious ethics alone can provide the absolute standard morality requires (see, for example, 340, 349, 380). Different thinkers disagree concerning the details of the revealed law; some identify revelation with each of the detailed moral requirements of the halakhah while others consider only the general moral principles essential. Naturally, there are opponents of supernaturalism; even they, however, agree that ethics must arise from religious soil and be reinforced by religious symbols, no matter how naturalistically they are interpreted.

The consensus that morality requires a religious ethics raises a problem in the pluralistic setting of modernity. How is the assumption of a universal ethics justified? The problem of secular ethics is answered through using the concept of the covenant with Noah, a Jewish form of "natural law" (see 149, 396, 469). The concept and its meaning is derived from the story of Noah in the Bible and the "Noahide Covenant" described there. After God destroyed creation through a great flood a covenant was made with all humanity through the one survivor Noah (Genesis 9). Jewish teaching insists that at that time a general revelation was given to all human beings. A sevenfold law was revealed, which (when all the ramifications extending beyond each of the basic seven commandments are taken into account) covers all human moral obligations. Jews can thus declare that all human morality, not merely Jewish morality, is basically religious and what is usually called "secular morality" is at its heart religious. The term "Noahides" refers to those for whom the covenant with Noah alone is the basis of their ethical and moral life. The root of this universalism is theologically derived from the idea that all humanity is created in the image of God. Much of the discussion in contemporary Jewish ethics seeks to elucidate the meaning of this Jewish universalism in contrast to Jewish particularism.

This universalism, however, is combined with the particularistic idea of the covenant made with the Jews alone. This idea is the basis of Jewish community and while some Jewish thinkers think community is possible on purely universalistic grounds, others deny it (see 089, 097, 096, 476, 494, 496, 513, 523, 526, 528, 529, 545, 555). This debate has more than merely theoretical interest. Jews usually live as part of a general, pluralistic society. That society has its own problems and concerns. How are Jews to interact with that society? Are the questions of economic, social, and political organization of an essentially non-Jewish community part of Jewish ethical responsibility? The shape this question takes is that of asking whether Jews have a general duty towards non-Jewish governments. There are two dimensions to this question. The first is the problem of deciding whether Judaism mandates any particular political program. Jewish ethicists have generally concluded that while Judaism is a realistic religion that takes politics seriously there is no one political program which can be identified with Jewish ideals (see 155, 482, 483, 485, 488, 492, 493, 501-505, 508, 512, 514, 517, 532).

The second dimension involves the choice between following the dictates of a government and the dictates of moral law (see 479, 487, 497, 498, 506, 511, 521). That choice was already an ethical issue in early rabbinic thought in the concept of <u>dina d'malchuta dina</u> (the law of the land is law) which became <u>a modus vivendi</u> for Jewish survival in the diaspora and was interpreted to mean that all laws not in direct conflict with Jewish law passed by an official government must be obeyed. This principle of obedience to political power, however, has been tested and challenged in recent times. It has been questioned particularly since the creation of the modern State of Israel. Does it imply support for an immoral war waged by a legal government? Does it apply to the secular government of Israel? What obligations can override that principle? Studies about the concept range from the homiletical to the scholarly and historical to the legal and exegetical (see 478, 484 490, 521, 520, 527). Politics cannot be separated from revelation if God's law is equated with the law of the land. Political ethics and social ethics are treated seriously in Jewish thought because they can be traced back to a divine legislation, a legislation seeking to create an ideal human community. Society is crucial for Jewish ethics since social value is rooted in the divine concern for humanity. Thus social ethics is understood in relationship to both revelation and the total divine design for creation.

Jewish ethics often sees this divine design as present in God's creative act and derives principles of ecology and of ethics from the mythology of divine creation. The third theological principle of major importance for Jewish ethics is that of creation. The world is not understood as the result of accident or chance. It is the product of a divine maker who has established order and meaning within existence. There are some immediate moral implications in such a view. One implication is that human beings are responsible for preserving and maintaining the creative order that God established. Ecology, scientific ethics, and the value and limitations of experimentation are all implied by the Jewish view of creation (see 426, 427, 429, 430, 436-440, 443-448, 450, 451, 453, 455, 459-460, 462, 465, 466, 470, 471, 474, 475). Human beings receive guidance, in this view, not only from divine imperatives given through covenant but also through the unwritten mandate of the created world.

The idea of a divine design certainly gives rise to an ethical expectation of how human beings are to interact with the created world. On the other hand, however, the idea of creation also raises questions about the nature of God's interaction with humanity. While Judaism conceives of human beings as "co-creators" with the divine--thus once again emphasizing the principle of imitating God--the conception of a divine blueprint for all of nature and reality seems to place limitations on human freedom. Modern behavioral science--particularly psychology--has also suggested the limits placed on human behavior.

Human free will has been challenged by the historical experiences of the Jew no less than by the advances of the social sciences. The grim realities with which an age of the Nazi Holocaust and the threat of self-destruction by nuclear power confront the Jewish thinker cannot be ignored. God's power and its relationship to human freedom and responsibility is a major concern of contemporary Jewish ethicists. During the Nazi slaughter of six-million Jews the shape of the divine plan was obscured. The meaning of divine covenant becomes problematic in its aftermath. In the wake of the Nazi Holocaust can Jews still affirm God's beneficent design? The experience of humanity in modernity suggests that both social pressures and catastrophe shape human life in tragic ways. This experience has caused modern Jewish authors to ponder the classic duality between freedom and determinism with particular urgency (see 581-601).

Reflections on both the problem of evil and the question of free will are found among liberal and traditional Jewish ethicists alike. In general the claim is raised that the possibility of evil is necessary for the possibility of free will. There are, however, some notable exceptions to this view. Steven Katz (see 281) suggests that moral teachings are needed; free will is asserted only when radical evil is a possibility. Moral freedom is not in itself a value; it becomes a value only when it is a necessity required by a less than perfect world. Richard Rubenstein (see 591, 592) takes a more radical approach and declares that in a world that God has abandoned people can only rely upon themselves. Jewish ethics, he claims, must abandon its claim of a grand divine design. The practical result of confronting the reality of evil in the world is both a reconsideration of the theology of creation and of human responsibility in which it is difficult to argue that humanity is truly in the image of God.

The passionate defense of freedom espoused by many thinkers combines a theological of humanity in the image of God with an awareness of modern philosophy. A challenge to Jewish ethics has been raised philosophically by both Kant and Kierkegaard. Kantian ethics claims that a theonomous ethics deprives the individual of that autonomy needed for a truly free moral choice; the Kierkegaardian response that religion demands a leap of faith seems to make light of the ethical choice that is an essential Jewish presupposition. Jewish ethical thinkers have been forced to come to grips with these two challenges.

Modern Jewish philosophy from Moses Mendelssohn onwards has been confronted with the Kantian view of ethics as a universal, *a priori* obligation placed on each individual as a rational being. Contemporary Jewish thinkers, no less than their predecessors in the nineteenth and twentieth centuries, have struggled with the Kantian demand for a "categorical imperative" that rational beings autonomously impose upon themselves (see 602-620).

Two foci in the argument can be discerned. The first is the relationship between revealed ethics and rational moral law. Does a revealed ethics undermine the autonomy of the moral agent? Some thinkers argue that revelation permits autonomy by liberating the individual from the constraints of the phenomenal world. Only by accepting the sovereignty of God is it possible to freely choose the moral good. Others suggest that Judaism makes adherence to a revelation more important than free will. There is in this view only one choice -- that of accepting or rejecting divine legislation. From this standpoint autonomy occurs not in each moral decision but when making the first and crucial ethical choice. The adherents of each position claim the strength of Jewish tradition behind them and accuse each other of manipulating texts or of misunderstanding the texts analyzed. Both groups, however, take the Kantian challenge seriously and legitimate Judaism despite the challenge from non-Jewish philosophy.

The second focus in this argument is on Kierkegaard's dichotomy between the "knight of faith" and the "knight of infinite resignation." The second represents the ethical hero who "rests in the universal." The former is the religious hero who accepts a "teleological suspension of the ethical" out of loyalty to a God who transcends the merely universal. As an illustration of the difference between the two Kierkegaard points to Agamemnon who sacrificed his daughter for the sake of his moral obligation and to Abraham who was called upon to sacrifice his child of the promise for the sake of the God who gave that promise. Jewish writers have wrestled with this midrash on the binding of Isaac, on the Akeda as it is called in Jewish tradition. They have sometimes argued that Kierkegaard misunderstood the tradition; Judaism sees God as the fountainhead of morality and so the Akeda cannot, by definition, contradict morality. Others suggest that Kierkegaard has seen an important element in Jewish ethics, the need to subsume rational thought under the rubric of service to the divine. Between the two comes a variety of interpretations: the story of Abraham and Isaac may be meant to teach that human beings must test God, that only by such a story can God's disapproval of child sacrifice be demonstrated, that Judaism, like Kierkegaard's Christianity, demands more than conventional religion. Whichever of these options is chosen the authors take Kierkegaard seriously as an ethical challenge to Jewish thought. Perhaps Abraham Heschel has gone the furthest in this acceptance when he draws the lines of similarity between Kierkegaard and a hasidic master, Rabbi Menahem Mendel of Kotsk (see 241). While hasidism and philosophy seem worlds apart, Heschel's thought shows how contemporary Jews use their tradition to respond to the challenge raised by the major trends in contemporary ethical theory as the confrontations with Kant and Kierkegaard demonstrate in great detail.

While the majority of Jewish thinkers are involved with the problems raised by Kant and Kierkegaard other ethical theories are not entirely neglected. Jewish writers explore the differences and similarities between modern theories of justice, progress, language, empiricism, and pragmatism on the one hand and Judaism on the other (see 646-666). These varied essays, some by traditional Jews and some by liberal Jews, show that Jewish thinkers are aware that Jewish ethics, to be compelling, must be attuned to the language and forms of expression of the modern world.

Another sign of this awareness of the challenges in the environment is the way in which Jewish ethics has confronted the behavioral sciences (see 621-645). Three areas of concern are central in this confrontation: the meaning of the human impulse to sin, the attribution of meaning to human existence, and the possibility of freedom in a science of behaviorism. The first question arises from the Freudian analysis of the human psyche. The impulses of the id are often identified with the "wayward impulse" that the rabbis attribute to each person; guilt is associated with the superego, the regulating principle that supplies the ought of human morality. For modern Jewish ethicists the questions this analysis raises are whether guilt and sin are appropriate ways of labeling human responses, whether the rabbinic view that the "evil impulse" is both necessary and useful to human life can be affirmed in Freudian as well as in Jewish terms, and whether anxiety might not be a positive rather than a negative element in personal development.

The problems raised by Freudian thought suggest that Jews must redefine the ethical sphere. The line between moral guilt and irrational disease has grown less and less clear. Questions of guilt, anxiety, and sin are ethical and moral: involve of evaluation of human activity; problems of mental health, however, evaluate a physical condition. Jewish ethical thinkers struggle with the meaning of disease, the positive implications of anxiety, and the possibility that "guilt" and "sin" are no longer viable categories. Most Jewish thinkers affirm that the terms are still useful, that anxiety can be productive, and that the "evil impulse" can be channeled through psychotherapy into creative alternatives. Some thinkers, like Richard Rubenstein (see 637, 638), contend that while the categories of Jewish ethics were useful and healthy in their own context they are no longer effective in the modern world. Freudian analysis has replaced the language of the rabbis.

Another set of problems raised by the behavioral sciences is the question of meaning and human purpose. Existentialist psychologists and sociologists stress the importance of meaning and purpose in human life, and many Jewish thinkers have integrated this emphasis into their ethical systems (see 624, 625, 626, 627, 629, 635, 645). They affirm that Jewish ethical and moral teachings provide just that meaning and purpose that social scientists define as essential in human existence. Others, however, suggest the quest for meaning, the desire for self-realization, and the centrality of individual development and experience spring from non-Jewish thought and that Judaism should reject such an identification of human human purpose with any mundane goal. The psychology of human purpose is perhaps useful if it points beyond ordinary goals to transcendent ones. Many Jewish thinkers, however, find that psychology ends just where it should begin--with aims that human beings take for themselves.

A final problem raised by psychology, particularly behaviorist psychololgy is that of human free will and responsibility (see 634, 642, 644). Behavioral science understands human actions as complex responses to both internal and external stimuli. The individual operates in an environment that conditions through experience; both prior training and present realities shape the way in which a person will act. Many Jewish thinkers accept this analysis of human behavior. Jewish law itself may be understood as a conditioning agent whereby the individual learns how to respond to the environment and to the self. Ethics can be taught by using behaviorist techniques; in fact the halakhic structure may be interpreted as a behaviorist conditioning device.

Many Jewish thinkers, on the other hand, are repelled by the implication inherent in behaviorism that human beings are not responsible agents for their own deeds. The contemporary Jewish ethicist wishes to preserve moral responsibility even while accepting the techniques of behavioral conditioning. After all, it can be argued, the individual self-consciously undergoes conditioning. Torah psychology moves beyond behaviorism by emphasizing, not radical freedom but the limited freedom of choosing the agents of conditioning. Jewish thinkers often accept the description of human nature given by psychiatry: people are both rational and irrational, both self-moved and motivated by subconscious impulses. A complete Jewish ethics must take both motivations seriously in order to affirm the value and meaning of Jewish law.

One theme seems underlies Jewish theological ethics whether when focused on responsibilities deriving from the nature of God, revelation, or creation or on the behavioral sciences. That theme is the distinctiveness of the Jew in the modern world. Jewish thinkers not only describe Judaism, they also compare it to the major trends in contemporary life (see 647, 649, 651, 653, 655, 656, 659, 660, 661) In this comparison they use the lessons of the social sciences to demonstrate the contribution Jews can make to society. Theologians claim that the Jew must stand apart from the main stream of society and must challenge that society by means of Torah ethics. Many analysts claim that the resemblance between Jewish views of freedom and those espoused in various "liberation movements" is merely illusory. They suggest that contemporary liberty is a license for abuse of both the self and others. Judaism, on the other hand, couples freedom with a sense of task. That task prepares the Jew for modesty, responsibility, and character. The theme of modesty in response to a society gone astray is constantly sounded by traditionalists. Even liberal Jews suggest that the values of modernity have become bankrupt and that Jews must now contribute moral teachings to a world bereft of ethical guidance. This sense of responsibility is an affirmation of a Jewish moral obligation towards an ethically wayward society. Since Jewish ethics takes the social sciences seriously it also contends that the divinely revealed principles it espouses are the best means to create a healthy, adjusted, and creative human being.

THE ESSENCE OF JEWISH ETHICS

This survey of themes and concerns in contemporary Jewish ethical discussion should set to rest any assumption that there is a monolithic Jewish ethics. The conception of a single value that unifies Jewish ethics into a coherent system must be abandoned in the face of the data. Various alternative views of Jewish ethics as based upon either a dialectical or pluralistic pattern of values must be rejected because of the vast differences each analyst discovers in the material. Whatever dialectical pattern emerges was already there in the mind of the scholar before it began to appear in the data. Even a division of Jewish ethics into categories corresponding to the major modern movements cannot be maintained since the representatives of those movements are often at odds with each other.

Certain common elements do reappear in various discussions. Any study of Jewish ethics must reckon with the meaning and interpretation of traditional texts. A comprehensive Jewish ethics must analyze the place of halakhah and aggadah in Jewish ethics, the theological concepts of monotheism, revelation, and creation, and the complex issues raised in regard to social responsibility, freedom, and determinism. A common element in all contemporary Jewish ethics has been the willingness on the part of every sector in contemporary Judaism to confront the intellectual and scientific theories of modernity. These common elements, however, lead in many different directions. Different themes, issues, and concerns arise in the pursuit of Jewish ethics; within the discussion of any one theme, issue, or concern a variety of equally valid options for Jewish belief is present. No one agenda can comprehend all issues discussed by Jewish ethicists.

Can an "essence" of Jewish ethics be discerned, a single characteristic by which the various theorists and their theories can be identified as Jewish? On the basis of the foregoing discussion some such characteristics can be isolated. It would be foolish to call them the essence of Jewish ethics as they are merely deduced from the data as external attributes that entitle the various works included here to be used as examples of Jewish ethical reflection. They do, however, show the principles at work in selecting items for this volume. They offer a sense of continuity linking Jewish ethicists from various traditions and transcending the differences in content between thinkers. It is therefore an appropriate addition to this introduction although not a definitive criteria of Jewish ethics.

The first principle is that of utilizing Jewish sources as both the basis of and illustration for the ethics being advanced. A work is included as an example of Jewish ethics if in addition to the Bible it draws upon one or more of the five basic resources of Jewish ethics: rabbinic Judaism, medieval Jewish philosophy, medieval Jewish pietism, or the ethics of the kabbalah. Two additional categories should be included by extension for in the minds of contemporary Jews they are considered traditional: the musar tradition and hasidism. The use of these sources provides evidence that the author is concerned with establishing credentials and with legitimizing the ethics advanced as rooted in Jewish tradition and Jewish precedent. While this legitimation may be aggadic rather than halakhic the choice of a Jewish source as the basis for ethical reflection indicates a willingness to stand within the Jewish tradition.

The second characteristic is a defense of Jewish ethics in confrontation with general theories of ethics. As Menahem Kellner (011) has pointed out, the modern Jewish ethicist is faced with a problem that earlier generations did not have: that of justifying the construction of a philosophy of Jewish ethics at all. Sometimes this justification may take the form of distinguishing between ethics and law, sometimes it may be an encounter with a particular non-Jewish system of ethics (e.g, the systems of Kant, Kierkegaard, or Empiricism), sometimes it may be an argument that the modern world needs Jewish ethics for its own salvation. Contemporary Jewish ethics has an apologetic strand within it, a defense of the relevance of exploring Jewish ethics. Traditional Jews may need to explain why ethics is necessary as well as the details of Jewish law; liberals may need to defend the particularity of a specifically Jewish ethics. Both seek to defend the relevance of a modern Jewish ethics.

The form in which these two characteristics appear may differ greatly from one writer to another. An article or book may investigate a historical figure in Jewish ethics and only indicate in passing the relevance of that thinker for modern Jews. An alternative approach would begin with the challenge of a specific modern idea or situation and then use traditional Jewish material to address that challenge. Throughout the works in this volume the reader will note that the authors perform the two functions indicated here: they look at the sources of Jewish ethics and they seek to explain the modern significance of those sources.

This introduction will, it is hoped, help readers find those issues or historical periods of most interest to them. Readers will find that a study of Judaism illuminates how women and men today confront both the contemporary situation and their own roots in the past. Not only Jews but all who are interested in bridging the gap between the past and present should find the entries in this volume of value comprehending the interplay between religion and ethics.

Bibliographical Survey

1
General Works and Anthologies

SURVEYS OF JEWISH ETHICS

001 Agus, Jacob Bernard. <u>The Jewish Quest: Essays on Basic Concepts of Jewish Theology</u>, New York: Ktav Publishing House, 1983.

The challenging and insightful essays included in this collection reveal Agus' on-going concern with Jewish ethics. They develop the idea that Jewish ethics is a dialogue between an ideal vision and a practical realism. The modern challenge of nationalism and survival is discussed in relationship to this dialectic of vision and reality. His openness to Jewish-Christian dialogue is particularly welcome and stimulating. See also 004, 340, 424, 425, 476, 477.

002 Agus, Jacob Bernard. <u>The Vision and the Way: An Interpretation of Jewish Ethics</u>. New York: Jacob Ungar Publishing Company, 1966.

This book-length survey of Jewish ethical thought from the biblical to the modern period, filled with lengthy quotations from original sources, is a basic introduction to Jewish morality. Agus interprets each period of Jewish thought as a dialectic between a "vision" and a practical "way". While not the definitive study this work should prove a valuable and encyclopedic road map to strands of Jewish ethical thought. The individual chapters are illuminating and enable the reader to glimpse the dynamics of Jewish history. See also 129, 130, 188, 251, 252, 341, 581.

003 Agus, Jacob Bernard. "Jewish Ethics," in <u>Dialogue and Tradition: The Challenges of Contemporary Judeo-Christian Thought</u>, 442-449. New York: Abelard-Schuman Publishing Company, 1971.

Agus claims that Jewish ethics is dialectical and characterizes Jewish theology as seeking the unity of God

38   BIBLIOGRAPHICAL SURVEY

and Jewish ethics as seeking the unity of the human person. He points to three models Jews have used to imagine the ethical ideal: the priest, the sage, and the prophet. The talmudic image of the "disciple of the wise" combines these into an ideal in which a balance between virtues is exalted. Jewish ethical systems from post-talmudic times through contemporary Zionism are used to illustrate these models. Compare this essay with 001, 002, 004.

004   Agus, Jacob Bernard. "Religious Ethics on the Contemporary Scene," in The Jewish Quest: Essays on Basic Concepts of Jewish Theology, 87-111. New York: Ktav Publishing House, 1983.

This essay surveys the basic principles used in Jewish ethics: reverence for law, development within the law, secularity and the modern problems facing Jewish ethics. Agus repeats his typology of priest, sage and prophet and offers a sketch of how Jewish thinkers in the past and in modern times (including Spinoza, Socialists, and Zionists) have utilized the principles of Jewish ethics. This mature presentation links the various themes that have characterized Agus' general thinking about Jewish ethics.

005   Bergman, Samuel Hugo. The Quality of Faith: Essays on Judaism and Morality. Trans. by Yehuda Hanegbi. Jerusalem: World Zionist Organization, 1970.

In this collection originally published in Hebrew as The Heavens and the Earth: Reflections on Human Responsibility (Tel Aviv: Tel Yosef, 1969), a major Jewish thinker studies ethical and moral theory from the biblical through the modern period. Bergman's ethical humanism pervades these essays making them valuable examples of one common modernist tradition that emphasizes religious values in a humanistic setting. See also, 026, 132, 479, 480, 603.

006   Djian, Jacques. Precis De Morale Juive et de Ses Rapports Doctrinaux avec les Morales Chretienne et Marxiste. Neuchatel: A. La Bacoonniere, 1962.

This important comparative survey based upon talmudic, medieval, and mystical Jewish writings, demonstrates one strand in the European tradition of comparative ethics that sets Jewish texts side by side with statements from the New Testament. The author concludes that both religions make significant contributions to contemporary secular society.

007   Feldman David M. "The Structure of Jewish Law," in Marital Relations, Birth Control, and Abortion in Jewish Law, 3-18. New York: Schocken Books, Inc., 1974.

This introduction to a study of sexual and biological morality is an exemplary survey of the principles and sources of Jewish ethics. It can be recommended as one of the best introductions to Jewish legal and ethical thought. Although an integral part of Feldman's book, the chapter can stand alone as an illuminating discussion of the process by which halakhah, Jewish law, develops and of the primary texts upon which it is based including mystical as well as halakhic materials. The article is reprinted in Kellner (111), 21-37.

008 Fox, Marvin, "Judaism, Secularism, and Textual Criticism," in Modern Jewish Ethics: Theory and Practice, edited by Marvin Fox, 3-26. Columbus: Ohio State University Press, 1975.

Fox, the editor of this excellent volume on Jewish ethics (see 107), explains one rationale for which a traditionalist can give seeking to renew Jewish ethical reflection. The argument of this essay is that Jewish ethics develops by responding to cultural challenges; texts are reinterpreted to meet new situations. Because it represents the method of traditional Judaism this essay is a helpful introduction to that tradition.

009 Goldman, Alex. Judaism Confronts Contemporary Issues. New York: Shengold Publishers, 1978.

This useful encyclopedic survey of contemporary Jewish moral thinking stresses the difference between Orthodox, Conservative and Reform Jewish moral teachings, not realizing that many analysts are discontent with this division. The bibliographical information, the introductory summaries, and the compilation of material makes this work helpful in sorting out the varieties of contemporary Jewish ethical positions. The issues examined are primarily those concerning bio-ethical moral decisions.

010 Greenberg, Simon. The Ethical in the Jewish and American Heritage. Moreshet 4. New York: Jewish Theological Seminary and Ktav Publishing House, 1977.

While focused on comparing Jewish and American ethics this book also surveys the development of Jewish ethics from biblical to modern times and provides a theoretical study of Jewish ethical concerns. The author considers religious and secular ethics, the love command, reward and punishment, and moral autonomy. The separate chapters are of independent interest but form a completed system of interpreting Jewish law as an ethical response to challenges of daily living. The work incorporates the two essays "Ethics, Religion and Judaism I," and "Ethics, Religion and Judaism II," appearing in Conservative Judaism 26 (1972): 85-126 and 27 (1972): 72-129, respectively. See also 365, 653.

011 Kellner, Menahem Marc. "The Structure of Jewish Ethics," in Contemporary Jewish Ethics, 3-18. Sanhedrin Jewish Studies. New York: Sanhedrin Press, 1978.

This introduction to a valuable and important anthology (see 111) surveys basic questions in Jewish ethics: the basis for deciding right from wrong, the source of moral obligation, the ethics of action in relationship to an ethics of belief. It analyzes contemporary alternatives in Jewish ethical thinking, emphasizing the divided voice of contemporary Judaism. Kellner presents a schema based upon differing views of revelation as a means of predicting differences in ethical thinking while this may be too limited to account for all variations among Jewish thinkers, it is a useful point of departure for further reflection.

012 Leiman, Sid Z. "Jewish Ethics 1970-1975: Retrospect and Prospect." Religious Studies Review 2 (1976): 16--22.

Leiman gives a brief analysis and critique of the developing field of contemporary Jewish ethics. He shows how titles may be misleading and notes the major controversies and laucunae in the field. He devotes offers a trenchant critique of the work of Louis Jacobs while commending the essay of Aaron Lichtenstein. The short bibliography needs updating but the critical analysis remains of interest in studying Jewish ethics. This essay was excerpted as part of Kellner (111), 58-60.

013 Plishkin, Zelig. Love Your Neighbor: You and Your Fellow Man in the Light of Torah. Brooklyn: Aish HaTorah. 1977.

This exploration of traditional Jewish ethics, expounded in connection with the weekly Torah readings, considers such ethical subjects as relationships between parents and children, business ethics, sexual morality, and personal virtues. The book has a devotional as well as educational purpose and is a useful introduction to traditional Jewish ethics. Many scholars may wish to pass by such devotional exercises as this and other pietistic works included in this bibliography for the sake of completeness (see 032-034, 037-040, 050, 088, 105, 106, 113.

014. Reines, Chaim Zeev. Essays and Investigations in Jewish Ethics and Law [Hebrew]. Jerusalem: Rubin Mass Company, 1972.

Reines combines essays on general moral issues -- women, marriage, treatment of animals, and the like -- with theoretical studies surveying Jewish ethics in the Bible, early postbiblical, and Talmudic writings. The book offers supportive evidence from primary textual material. The essays are to be recommended for their scholarly, if traditional, treatment of major ethical themes. See also 083, 157, 463.

015 Rittner, Steven. Jewish Ethics for the Twenty-First Century. Boston: n.p., 1977.

This privately published textbook on Jewish ethics and morality uses traditional material to look seriously at such issues as sexual ethics, ecology, war and peace, ecology, and medical ethics. While meant for young adults the book is helpful in capturing the variety of ways Jews have responded to moral dilemmas. The liberal ethics used as a basis for decision-making is often juxtaposed with very traditional statements from Jewish sources. Perhaps the text is most useful when seen as a contemporary introduction to Jewish ethics spiced with quotations from the Bible, rabbinic literature, and later Jewish writings.

016 Spero, Shubert. Morality, Halakha, and the Jewish Tradition. The Library of Jewish Law and Ethics 9. New York: Ktav Publishing House and Yeshiva University Press, 1975.

While the aim of this book is to provide a philosophical interpretation of Jewish ethics, it is also a useful survey of the tasks and history of Jewish ethics offering a compendium of biblical, post-biblical, medieval and modern quotation. Its review of the structure of Jewish ethics and major ethical questions make it an indispensable introduction to the basic elements of Jewish ethics. Spero uses a plethora of original source material and integrates traditional method with philosophical sophistication. See also 094, 414, 415, 560, 599, 619.

017 Unterman, Allan. "Ethical Standards in World Religions: I: Judaism." Expository Times 85 (1973): 36-40.

This brief article is an interpretive introduction to Jewish ethics that, in a popular, almost sermonic style, contends that unity of God is the central religious category of Judaism with the imitation of God as the central ethical ideal. Unterman offers evidence from a variety of Jewish sources to demonstrate his point that also illustrates the major forms of ethical writing -- halakhah, aggadah, pietistic morality, philosophical reflection, and mystical speculation. His presentation is often too facile (he concludes that the Musar Movement "won through" even though many modern Orthodox scholars would disagree). His balanced presentation of both social and personal ethics is valuable.

018 Weinfeld, Abraham C. Basic Jewish Ethics and Freedom of the Will. New York: Bloch Publishing Company, 1968.

Despite the impression given by the title this book surveys Jewish philosophical ethics from biblical through medieval and early modern times including early twentieth century Hebrew writers and American authors like Abraham Heschel and Mordecai Kaplan. These views are then contrasted with certain modern theories -- Marxism taking pride of place -- in order to demonstrate the superiority and value of Jewish ethics. While the thesis offered is interesting the book as a whole is far from persuasive and not to recommended as a serious contribution to Jewish thought.

INTERPRETATIONS OF JEWISH ETHICS

019 Agus, Jacob Bernard. "Polarity in Jewish Ethics." Sh'ma 7 (1977): 115-117.

Agus responds to a critical and provocative review by Steven S. Schwarzschild (089) of Marvin Fox's anthology on Jewish ethics (107). Agus presents a brief but well written precis of his model of dialectical development in Jewish ethics that draws on his other presentations of the themes, history, and literature of Jewish ethics (see 001-004). He responds to a variety of arguments made by other thinkers who also reacted strongly both to Fox's anthology and to the criticism of it by Schwarzschild.

020 Amiel, Moshe Avigdor. "Social Justice, Legal Justice, and Our Justice." In Between Man and His Fellow: Treatises on Human Relations in Judaism [Hebrew], 3-83. Translations and Collections From Israel's Wisdom. Jerusalem: Mossad Harav Kook, 1975.

Those interested in the way Jews have analyzed and defended their ethical views should look at this essay. This study contrasts the views of justice developed on the basis of social expediency, legal authority, and revealed religion. It contends, using an arsenal of rabbinic and musar quotations, that Jewish ethics is realistic in contrast to ascetic Christianity. The republication of this vigorous defense of Judaism shows the need that at least some traditionalists feel for demonstrating the viability and superiority of Jewish ethics.

021 Baruk, Henri. Tsedek. Edited and trans. by Michel Abehsera. Binghamton: Swan House Publishing Company, 1972.

This English language presentation of a French psychologist and ethicist utilizes both his later writings and an earlier work that covers much of the same ground. The book suggests Baruk's post-Freudian psychology and his use of Bible, Midrash, and medieval Jewish philosophy. Baruk is hardly a central figure in contemporary Jewish ethics but his combination of traditional orientation, psychological expertise, and clearly impassioned concern are fascinating examples of an alternative to the European tradition dominated by philosophers as represented above all by Emmanuel Levinas (see 72-75).

022 Baruk, Henri. Tsedek, Droit Hebraique Et Science de l'Homme. Collection: Civilisation Hebraique et Monde Modern. Paris: Edition Zikarone, 1970.

Baruk, an intriguing thinker, surveys the Bible, midrashic literature, some philosophers, as evidence for the "test of tsedek," that he revises into a clinical test whereby patients' responses to descriptions of situations are used to indicate whether they are affective, unfeeling, pragmatic, or synthetic in their ethical approach to the world to represent an ideal response to reality since it focuses on social and personal justice. This emphasis on justice, he claims, creates a sense of wholeness in Judaism that surpasses either Christianity or "neo-pagan" psychoanalysis.

023 Baruk, Henri. "La Science du Juste: Le 'Tsedek' et Le Monotheism Hebreu." Revue Metaphysique Morale 76 (1971): 257-282.

This short introduction to some of Baruk's major themes discusses the idea of justice or "zedek" as described in the Bible as an essential element in any ethical theory and intrinsically related to belief in one universal deity. For those who do not wish to work through Baruk's more extensive writings the ethical approach and psychological method he uses is made clear in this article.

024 Bekritsky, Morris. "Introduction to Jewish Ethics." In Building Jewish Ethical Character, edited by Joseph Kaminetsky and Murray Friedman, 203-212. New York: The Fryer Foundation, 1975.

This traditional interpretation of Judaism contends that Jewish ethics is not merely a human means of controlling social life. According to Bekritsky, Jewish ethics are based upon the eternal ideas of Torah rather than in the social world in which Jews live. This essay is a representative example of a traditional viewpoint.

025 Ben Horin, Schalom. "And God Formed Man in His Own Likeness": A Jewish View on the Corporeality of Man. Baarn: Unitgeverij Ten Have B.V., 1973.

Ben Horin contends in this monograph that Jewish realism is expressed in its view of human nature and in its ethical understanding of the human task. Corporeality is not seen as an evil but as a divine creation. For Judaism the human body, being created in the likeness of God, is natural and good. In this way Judaism advances beyond the dualism of Gnosticism and Christianity. This apologetic defense of Judaism is a valuable philosophical exercise.

026. Bergman, Samuel Hugo. "Expansion and Contraction in Jewish Ethics." In The Quality of Faith: Essays on Judaism and Morality, trans. by Yehuda Hanegbi, 32-40. Jerusalem: World Zionist Organization, 1970.

Any essay by Bergman demonstrates his grasp of philosophy and contemporary thought. This interpretive essay in Bergman's survey of Jewish moral concerns looks at the inner dynamics of Jewish morality. The most fascinating claim in the essay is devoted to "expansion and contraction" is that there is no Jewish ethics. The author says there is only human ethics derived from individuals struggling with their freedom. This struggle accounts for what Bergman finds to be the central tension in Jewish ethics -- that between universalism and particularism. This essay is found on pp. 29-38 of the Hebrew version (see 005)).

027 Blue, Lionel. <u>To Heaven with Scribes and Pharisees: The Lord of Hosts in Suburbia, The Jewish Path to God</u>. London: Darton, Longman and Todd Ltd., 1975.

Blue, a leading liberal rabbi in England, places a heavy emphasis upon Jewish moral behavior. Using the contention that Jews are to redeem the commonplace world of daily experience as his hermeneutic, Blue interprets the pattern of Jewish spirituality as an essentially moral activity. This book exemplifies the complaint of traditionalists (see Wyschogrod, 099) that liberals identify Judaism exclusively with ethics.

028 Borowitz, Eugene B. <u>Reform Judaism Today III: How We Live</u>. New York: Behrman House Publishing Company, 1978.

Borowitz has provided a three volume interpretation of a recent "platform" of Reform Judaism. This third volume describes Jewish actions and behavior focusing upon ethnicity, ritual practice, and moral obligation. Of particular importance is his contention that Reform Judaism no longer limits Jewish law to ethical and moral prescriptions. Borowitz reviews such issues as moral autonomy, the relationship between "oral law and moral law"(!), the tension between ethnicity and personal conscience, and the meaning of religious obligation. The historical perspective provided is also an interpretation of the development of Reform Judaism and its approach to Jewish thought in general and Jewish ethics specifically.

029 Breek, B. "La Probleme De La Philosophie Juive." <u>Tijdschrift Voor Filosophie</u> 34 (1972): 227-281.

This is an example of a common European Jewish tactic -- interpreting Jewish monotheism as exemplary ethics. Breek begins by concentrating on the neo-Kantian philosophy of Hermann Cohen but expands his article to include talmudic and medieval Judaism as well. His conclusion is that Judaism is not a metaphysical philosophy but a practical ethics that calls people to universalism and a concern for humanity as a whole. This article is an interesting example of a common style of contemporary Jewish ethical reflection.

030 Breslauer, S. Daniel. <u>A New Jewish Ethics</u>. Symposium 9. New York: Edwin Mellen Press, 1983.

This book is a useful example of modern Jewish ethical thinking that surveys some contemporary theories and adds its own perspective that suggests that Jewish ethics can be interpreted as a process of dialogue. Major moral dilemmas are studied together with the ethical principles

GENERAL WORKS AND ANTHOLOGIES   45

used to solve them. A confrontation with modernity leads to
a restatement of Jewish ethical thought. Concepts such as
covenant, halakhah, and Mitzvah, are given new meanings in
accordance with an open dialogue among Jews and between Jews
and non-Jews.

031   Damiel, Yitzhak. Faith in Man and What Is Above It
[Hebrew]. Tel Aviv: Mahberot LeSafrut, 1968.

This Israeli approach to Jewish ethics should be read as an
example of both a traditionalist viewpoint and of a modern
sense of philosophy and its demands. This collection of
essays shows humor, rigorous philosophical concern, and an
awareness of both theological and practical matters. Those
interested in modern Jewish interpretations of ethics can
learn much from this volume. Essays of particular interest
are "On Faith in Man and Its Meaning," 7-27 and "Religious
and Humanistic Ethics," 28-36. These focus on traditional
Jewish thought, the Talmud, and self-sacrifice but
demonstrate an awareness of and openness to modern thought.

032   Dove, Y. "Kindliness." In Building Jewish Ethical
Character, edited by Joseph Kaminetsky and Murray Friedman,
259-264. New York: The Fryer Foundation, 1975.

The chief value of this essay is that it shows how a
traditionalist can use a central ethical principle in
Judaism as a homiletical device to provide moral
encouragement for his audience. The virtue of "Chesed" or
kindliness is exalted as a central Jewish concern. It is
related to imitating the divine. As God in kindness allows
us life so we cultivate human life wherever it may be.

033   Dressler, Eliyahu. Strive for Truth: Michtavme Eliyahu,
the Selected Writings of Eliyahu Eliezer Dressler.
Trans. by Aryeh Carmell. New York: Feldheim Publishing
Company, 1978.

This collection and translation of musar lectures and
studies demonstrate the popularity and continued influence
of the pietistic tradition. Dressler gives brief and
homiletical interpretations of the virtues of
lovingkindness, mercy, and study and some philosophical
questions: evil, free will, love of neighbor. This
translation of a major musar teacher demonstrates the
continued importance of that ethical tradition and provides
a superb example of its style. See also 432, 541.

034   Efrati, Simhah. The Book of the Light of Joy [Hebrew]
Tel Aviv: Lipa Freidman Company, 1971/1972.

The scholar interested in an on-going musar tradition and
the traditionalist who desires an uplifting moral text will
find this work of value. It is a traditional collection of
Hebrew sermonic and homiletical reflections. The subject
matter includes ritual questions, moral issues, and general

ethical principles. This book immerses the reader in the classical Hebrew sources of rabbinic and medieval literature. For those who read Hebrew this is a fascinating introduction to the musar style of study and exhortation.

035 Elkins, Dov Peretz. Humanizing Jewish Life. New York: A.S.Barnes and Company, 1976.

This compilation of essays and pedagogical suggestions is not a rigorous interpretation of Jewish ethics. It offers some engaging reinterpretations of Jewish ethical terms, a useful primer in moral education, and interesting perspectives on various moral issues. It should be read as a fresh view of Jewish ethical thought but not as a profound investigation of the issues involved in that thought.

036 Etzion, Isaac Raphael HaLevi. "Ethics and Religion." In Studies in Questions of Faith [Hebrew], 71-83. Pardes Hanah: Midrashit Noam, 1969.

This sophisticated study of religion and ethics treats theoretical and practical issues in a serious and cogent way. Etzion maintains that it is easy to love humanity in general, but very difficult to love particular individuals. The difference between ethical obligation which is addressed to all in general and religious responsibility which falls upon the individual is, he suggests, that religion is realistic in coping with the greater difficulty and provides a specific obligation with detailed and concrete objectives for each individual.

037 Friedman, Murray I. "Introduction: The Sources of Jewish Ethics." In Building Jewish Ethical Character, edited by Joseph Kaminetsky and Murray Friedman, xi-xix. New York: The Fryer Foundation, 1975.

This essay is a valuable introduction to an intriguing anthology (see 110) and to traditional Jewish thought in general. It challenges a rational ethics from the perspective of revelation. Because the basis of Jewish morality is God's revealed word, Friedman rejects values rooted only in human culture. While some readers may be disconcerted by this view, it is an important alternative in contemporary Jewish moral thought.

038 Friedman, Murray I. "Solving Ethical Problems." In Building Jewish Ethical Character, edited by Joseph Kaminetsky and Murray Friedman, 61-70. New York: The Fryer Foundation, 1975.

Even non-traditional Jews can benefit by glimpsing the presuppositions involved in Orthodox Jewish ethics. In this essay Friedman describes the method of Jewish moral reflection. The Jew uses common sense even though basic moral commandments -- truth telling, responsibility, and the like are legislated by Torah. The response to unjust laws and to social crises is a reasoned one. The Jew combines the expertise of the Torah scholar (Talmid Chacham) and of the moral person (baal middot).

039 Gifter, Mordecai. "Ahavas Chesed." In Building Jewish Ethical Character, edited by Joseph Kaminetsky and Murray Friedman, 219-223. New York: The Fryer Foundation, 1975.

This essay is a rather naive celebration of a basic Jewish virtue that takes on significance in the context of this traditional volume as a whole. The virtue of "kindliness" is defined as a desire to help others and do the right. Talmudic stories are used to illustrate how training in kindliness brings about moral reform.

040 Glicksberg, Abraham Abba. "Fear and Love of God." In Building Jewish Ethical Character, edited by Joseph Kaminetsky and Murray Friedman, 225-229. New York: The Fryer Foundation, 1975.

While the naive approach utilized here may disconcert some this essay is a clear example of the devotional approach. It stresses the fear of God and obedience to the Torah based on love as the basis of Jewish ethics. This inspirational essay is an example of pietistic ethics at its most devotional and theoretic.

041 Green, Ronald Michael. "Abraham, Isaac, and the Jewish Tradition: An Ethical Appraisal." Journal of Religious Ethics 10 (1982): 1-21.

Green is a sophisticated scholar who brings broad knowledge and careful reasoning to his work. His essays are well argued and worth reading. Here he analyzes the well-known biblical story of Abraham's near-sacrifice of his son Isaac, using it as a focus for investigating a variety of Jewish moral issues. He contrasts what he considers to the rationality and morality of all Jewish interpretations with both Kantian ethics and the critique of Kierkegaard.

042 Green, Ronald Michael. "Jewish Ethics and the Virtue of Humility." Journal of Religious Ethics 1 (1973): 53-63.

While many Jewish thinkers stress the importance of humility this is an especially well constructed article. Green advances the argument that humility is the "constitutive virtue" in Jewish ethics. He notes its importance for the practice of imitatio Dei, for maintaining a moral sense of "election," for animating the Jewish sense of duty. He also provides a philosophical justification for maintaining that ethics in general presupposes humility.

043 Green, Ronald Michael. "Judaism: The Justice and Mercy of God," in Religious Reason: The Rational and Moral Basis of Religious Belief, 125-188. New York: Oxford University Press, 1978.

The first part of Green's book is a confrontation with Kantian and Analytic philosophies of ethics; it is a good summary and an illuminating discussion. He then gives his own rational, moral view and illustrates it in Judaism, Christianity, and Eastern religions. He argues that Judaism is a religion in which mercy is as powerful as justice.

044 Greenberg, Simon. *A Jewish Philosophy and Pattern of Life*. Moreshet 9. New York: Ktav Publishing House and the Jewish Theological Seminary of America, 1981.

Simon Greenberg, following Max Kadushin, (057), interprets Jewish ethics as the concretization of an organic system of values, including in his study the thought of modern thinkers such as Martin Buber, Will Herberg, and Abraham Joshua Heschel. Greenberg correlates the various activities making up a "Jewish pattern of life" and correlates them with certain values. The book is an interesting exercise in exegetical and hermeneutical thinking. Traditionalists would be uneasy with Greenberg's exaltation of values over their concrete representation; liberals would find his commitment to those representations limiting. The book is both valuable as an introduction to Jewish ethical thinking and as representative of one major strand in modern Jewish ethics. The ideas included in this study are similar to and should be compared with those in Greenberg's other writings as noted in Greenberg, (010).

045 Guibal, Francis. "Une Religion d'Adults." *Esprit* 9 (1980): 157-165.

This article is an extract from Guibal's book *Et Combien de Dieux Nouveaux* and looks at various ways in which Emmanuel Levinas has been influenced and has influenced thought about God. He emphasizes the effect of Kantian thought, an ethical rather than an eschatological focus, the importance of the "other" for the mature religious thinking Levinas advocates. This article is a good introduction to Levinas' ethical writings.

046 Harkavy, Solomon. *From the Words of Shlomo* [Hebrew], edited by Rabbi Epstein. Brooklyn: Art Scroll Publishing Company, 1975/1976.

This collection of ethical sayings, teachings, and interpretations of rabbinic literature, collected by students of a beloved master, shows the continued viability of the *musar* tradition. The text includes reflections on the weekly reading from the Torah and devotional material. It is a valuable example of traditional Jewish thought that emphasizes Jewish universalism.

047 Hartman, David. *Joy and Responsibility: Israel, Modernity, and The Renewal of Judaism*. Jerusalem: Ben Zvi-Posner, 1978.

David Hartman is a serious traditionalist whose essays on secularism, religious language, medicine, Israel, and contemporary Jewish thinkers, provide an ethical perspective that draws on tradition to confront modernity. Both traditional Jews and liberals should read clear and rational explication of major themes in Jewish ethics. For scholars of Jewish ethics it is essential reading. Compare 325, 368, 369.

048 Harvey, Warren Zev. "Love: the beginning and the end of Torah." Tradition 15 (1976): 5-22.

The focus of this essay, love or chesed, is a central virtue in Jewish ethics. The essay suggests that the command to love includes the three values of obedience to God , love of neighbor, and deeds of kindness and is, thus, both the foundation and most inclusive principle of Jewish ethics. The traditional orientation of the essay is blended with a sophisticated style and awareness of modern concerns.

049 Hel-Or, Yom Tov L. The Spiritual-Ethical Renaissance of the People of Israel. Trans. by Mendell Lewittes. Jerusalem: Or Yerushalayim, 1977.

Although packed with information and references to important modern figures this book may make many readers restless by its clearly partisan approach. This is an anthological, anecdotal argument that the State of Israel can be a spiritual center for Judaism only by returning to the basic ethics and values of Jewish religion. The author draws on classical sources and moderns who often disagree, but who, according to Hel Or, share certain common themes. The major influence on Hel-Or is Rav Kook whose philosophy can be found not only in the scope of the citations in the volume but also in the ethical compendium, a glossary of Jewish moral values, with which the book ends.

050 Herskovitz, S. A. The Rule of Ethics [Hebrew]. Bnai Brak: n.p., 1977.

As an example of devotional literature or traditional moral literature this essay is useful in defining the qualities found in musar teachings. It is neither a philosophical treatise nor a confrontation with modernity nor should it be used as such. This is a compilation of ethical teachings using the themes and discussions of the Musar Movement. It shows how ethical concerns are woven into homiletical musings on the weekly biblical readings of traditional Jewish life.

051 Herzog, Isaac. "Man's Smallness and Greatness," in Judaism: Law and Ethics, 29-33. New York: Soncino Press, 1974.

The theological reflections of contemporary rabbinical leaders and thinkers often suggest the general ethical approach of modern Jews. This essay, together with the others in this book, should be read in such a way. It is sermonic rather than theoretical and ponders the meaning of the Jewish High Holy Day season and the variety of views of human life enshrined in them.

052 Heschel, Abraham Joshua. The Insecurity of Freedom: Essays on Human Existence. New York: Schocken Books, Inc., 1972.

Heschel was a major figure in both American Jewish thought and American Jewish life; his works and his life should be studied as models of modern Jewish ethics. The series of essays in this book remain effective, even if they date from the 1960s. Heschel's interpretation of Jewish ethics is influential because it stresses the dialectic between humility and majesty that many find central to Judaism. He also shows how Jewish ethics may be applied to contemporary America. Two central essays in this volume are theoretical explorations of Jewish ethics: "Confusion of Good and Evil," (pp. 127-149), is both a tribute to Christian theologian Reinhold Niebuhr and an exploration of the rabbinic and hasidic view of human duality.

053 Heschel, Abraham Joshua. Who Is Man ?. Stanford: Stanford University Press, 1965.

Heschel's statement of his basic religious anthropology in general terms remains an important influence on Jewish ethics. This small volume has few Jewish quotations and speaks generally about "biblical man." It is, thus, accessible to non-Jews as well as Jews and has had an effect on religious moral thinking in general. The book can serve as an introduction to the major themes of any biblical ethics, whether Jewish or Christian.

054 Jacobs, Louis. "Jewish Ethics," in A Jewish Theology, 231-242. New York: Behrman House Publishing Company, 1973.

This is a useful introduction to Jewish ethics as a whole. Jacobs reviews the modern interest in ethics in both Reform Judaism and in the Musar movement; he provides interesting bibliographical notes on heroes of that movement, giving a detailed analysis of Maimonidean ethics in striking contrast to the ethics of compassion advocated by Samuel David Luzzatto. He acknowledges that Jewish ethics is motivated by religious fervor, not merely rational principles. The central ethical category turns out to be imitation of God. This is an excellent review of Jewish ethics -- its themes and some of its exponents.

055 Jacobs, Louis. "The Relationship Between Religion and Ethics In Jewish Thought." In Religion and Morality: A Collection of Essays, edited by Gene Outka and John P. Reeder, Anchor Books, 155-172. Garden City: Doubleday and Company, 1973.

This is a seminal study that analyzes various Jewish ethical and moral sources and themes. It looks at the binding of Isaac and the way the Jewish tradition has interpreted it. The issue of self-sacrifice forms a central concern in Jacobs' argument as is the question of autonomy and heteronomy in Jewish ethics. While criticized for using the tradition selectively it shows how contemporary problems can be studied from the perspective of Jewish sources. This article has provoked controversy and can be found reprinted in Kellner, (111), 41-57. Kellner also includes a response to Jacobs by Sid Z. Leiman (see 012).

056 Jung, Leo. Between Man and Man, 3rd enlarged edition. New York: Board of Jewish Education Press, 1976.

Leo Jung represented a sophisticated Orthodoxy that confronted modernity without compromising Jewish tradition. The works in this compilation illustrate his command of English and his ability to communicate the moral earnestness of Judaism. The book is worth reading for an understanding of the far ranging concerns of traditional Judaism and the traditionalist position on specific moral issues. An earlier version of this work was translated into Hebrew as "Human Relations in Jewish Law, " in Between Man and His Fellow: Treatises on Human Relations in Judaism [Hebrew], Trans. by Tzvi Bar-Meir. Translations and Collections From Israel's Wisdom (Jerusalem: Mossad Harav Kook, 1975), 113-215. See also 372, 503, 547.

057 Kadushin, Max. Worship and Ethics: A Study in Rabbinic Judaism. Chicago: Northwestern University Press, 1964.

This seminal work on Jewish ethics remains influential today. It is essential reading for both a sense of talmudic ethics and for the approach of many Conservative Jewish thinkers. Kadushin's analysis of ethics and the concretization of "value concepts" is used by contemporary Jewish ethicists. In this volume he traces how an organic system of values is expressed through such daily activities as eating, prayer, and interhuman behavior. The early chapters in the book provide theoretical reflection on the meaning and function of ethics, morality, and value systems in human culture generally and religion specifically.

058 Kaplan, Mordecai. The Religion of Ethical Nationhood: Judaism's Contribution to World Peace. New York: Macmillan Publishing Company, 1970.

Kaplan's thought was once the dominant one in American Judaism. While less pervasive now, it remains of interest. Kaplan argues that Judaism's unique ability to maintain a double loyalty -- to a diaspora nationality and to a universal spiritual nationhood -- is exemplary. Modern Zionism is a final flourishing of the ethical values of Judaism. When properly understood it transcends parochialism and offers a model of universalistic concern that all nations should emulate. His argument that the "Hebraic way" in opposition to the "Hellenic way" is the best path for contemporary humanity may seem both naive and self-serving. Kaplan's intellectual rigor, however, combined with his moral seriousness cannot help but impress the reader. Kaplan's work is indispensable for understanding the major themes in modern Jewish ethical reflection.

059 Klausner, Joseph. "Christian and Jewish Ethics." In *Faith and Reason: Essays in Judaism*, edited by Robert Gordis and Ruth B. Waxman, 100-114. New York: Ktav Publishing House, 1973.

Klausner's thought represents an earlier generation of Jewish ethical thinking and should be read for historical value rather than for its immediate relevance. Following the lead of Hebraist Ahad HaAm (Asher Ginzberg) Klausner defines Jewish ethics as more realistic than Christian perfectionism. He finds in Judaism demands that people can perform, a transcendent value system, and a humanism that is realizable in the modern world. This essay represents an older, fairly standard, presentation of Jewish ethics in contrast to the impossible idealism associated with Christianity. Its polemic quality can hardly be missed.

060 Kook, Abraham Isaac. "The Moral Principles." In *Abraham Isaac Kook: The Lights of Penitence, the Moral Principles, Letters of Holiness, Essays, Letters, and Poems*. Trans. by Ben Zion Bokser. Classics of Western Spirituality. New York: Paulist Press, 1978.

The mysticism and moral teachings of Rav Kook have influenced an entire generation of Jewish thinkers, primarily in Israel but in the diaspora as well. This essay is a translation of the second section of the following entry. It has historical worth but is also intrinsically suggestive as a creative approach to Jewish ethics. The work examines, in alphabetical order, the virtues of love, humility, giving of charity, faith, patience, and the mystical virtue of elevating fallen sparks of holiness to their divine source. The text also lists, as a warning, some of the undesirable qualities: anger, pride, timidity. The style is that of a traditional, mystic moral handbook. This translation was made from a Hebrew anthology that includes sections on the fear of heaven, fear of sin, and the self-discipline of study, *Musar Avicha* [Hebrew] (Jerusalem: Mossad Harav Kook, 1971). That original also includes essays on religious morality not included in the English translation.

061 Lamm, Norman. *Faith and Doubt: Studies in Traditional Jewish Thought*. New York: Ktav Publishing House, 1971.

These impressive essays range from theoretical and
theological discussions of revelation, creation, and human
freedom to the investigation of particular moral issues.
The traditional stand on Jewish ethics is well explained and
the relevance of revelation to contemporary life is given an
articulate exposition. The book should be read by liberals
and traditionalists alike. See also 225, 378, 450, 451, 656.

062 Lamm, Norman. "Introduction." In The Good Society:
Jewish Ethics in Action, edited by Norman Lamm. B'nai
B'rith Jewish Heritage Classics, 3-9. New York:Viking
Press, 1974.

Not only should this anthology provide a basic introduction
to Jewish ethics (see 116) but the editor's introductory
essay is illuminating and helpful. Lamm interprets Jewish
ethics as a polarity of individual and social concerns.
Because of the tension between self and society, public life
and privacy, individualism and social responsibility, Jewish
law must encompass a variety of elements. Halakhah, he
claims, is more than just legalism; it incorporates morality
and ethics within a framework of social legislation. This
view presents an attractive and persuasive argument for the
traditionalist claim that Jewish ethics must be interpreted
within the canons of tradition.

063 Leibowitz, Yeshiyahu. Judaism, The Jewish People, and
The State of Israel [Hebrew]. Tel Aviv: Schocken Books,
Inc., 1975.

The importance of Yeshiyahu Leibowitz for understanding
Israeli Jewish Orthodoxy cannot be overstated. His
influence is widespread, and his approach to religion and
ethics is controversial. This book collects his essays,
responses, and reviews that examine contemporary Jewish
thought from a traditional standpoint. Leibowitz is a
brilliant exponent of modern Orthodoxy and contends that
ethics and religion must be kept separate. His remarks on
Jewish education and the confrontation between humanistic
universalism and Judaism are controversial. Some of the
important essays will be described in more detail later in
the section on halakhah; see particularly 380-382.

064 Lelyveld, Arthur J. "A Distinctive Value Stance."
Journal of Reform Judaism (1978): 1-14

This essay is useful reading for those who associated
particular ethical stands with organizational affiliations.

It shows how ideas cross such boundaries. Lelyveld, a
Reform Rabbi, uses the views of Max Kadushin, associated
with the Conservative Movement, to argue for a distinctive
type of Jewish ethics. He notes that certain Hebrew terms
cannot be translated into English but represent a concrete
and complex structure of values that define the Jewish
stance. This stance is not to be confused with dogma or

doctrine but rather with a peculiarly Jewish response to certain situations and issues. He associates the stance with openness to others, abhorrence of bloodshed, valuing the sacredness of life, love, compassion, and the desire for equity, and a search for "whole and healthy relationships" among both groups and individuals. The article shows how a Jewish ethical perspective can be used to reinforce both the halakhic tradition and a more liberal approach.

065 Lelyveld, Arthur J. "Transient Isms and Abiding Values." In Tradition and Contemporary Experience: Essays on Jewish Thought and Life, edited by Alfred Jospe, 176-188. New York: Schocken Books, Inc., 1970.

Those interested in an "organic" interpretation of Jewish values should find this essay of value. While the "value terms" used in Judaism may differ, the important element is value judgment as evidenced in the "tone" used. Judaism emphasizes human dignity against all encroachments against it. The Jewish task is to make these value judgments our own through study of the past and applying them in new situations. This is a liberal interpretation of the idea of "value concepts" and uses that idea in order to emphasize contemporary Jewish ethics.

066 Levi, Zeev. "Judaism and Humanistic Values." In Sefer Yeshiyahu Leibowitz: A Collection of Essays on his Thought and in his Honor [Hebrew], edited by Asa Kasher and Jacob Levinger, 119-127. Tel Aviv: Tel Aviv University Student Association, 1977.

This essay explicates Leibowitz' view of Judaism; it goes beyond explication, however, and is also an independent statement on the relationship between ethics and religion that can be read profitably on its own. Levi reflects on Leibowitz's view that Judaism cannot have a distinctive ethics since ethics is universal. Jewish religion is particular; its halakhah is primary as a divine revelation. This view is clear in Leibowitz's criticism of Mendelssohn's interpretation of the Noahide laws. Levi, however, feels that Leibowitz is too close to Feuerbach. It should be possible to have a distinctively Jewish ethics that unites the ethical experience of human value with the religious experience of human dependency.

067 Levinas, Emmanuel. Difficile Liberte: Presences du Judaisme, 2nd edition. Paris: Albin Michel, 1976.

As the leading exponent of Phenomenology and as a luminary in European Judaism, Levinas commands respect and attention. His work is focused on the ethical and on human relationship no less than on metaphysics. Levinas' debt to both phenomenology and Franz Rosenzweig is apparent in the various essays in this volume. His wide range knowledge includes Zionism, Spinoza, feminism, and theoretical concerns for the meaning of monotheism, the teachings of

Torah, and human freedom. The ability to universalize even
particularistic elements in Judaism is impressive even to
those who may remain skeptical of the integration of Jewish
and nonJewish philosophical thought that underlies it.

068 Levinas, Emmanuel. "To Love the Torah More than God."
Trans. by Harriet A. Sugarman and Richard I. Sugarman,
with a commentary by Richard I. Sugarman. Judaism 28
(1979): 216-223.

This is an English translation of an important essay in
Difficile Liberte. It presents his argument that Jewish
teaching demands ethics, but that ethics is undergirded by
a sense of humility and unworthiness. The commentary by
Richard I. Sugarman is both illuminating and critical.
This article is a helpful introduction to the thought of
Levinas and its interpretation of Judaism.

069. Levinas, Emmanuel. "Exigeant Judaism." Debat 5
(1980): 11-19.

This popular article claims that Judaism creates, through
its orientation towards God, a different type of "existence"
from that of which philosophers speak. Its particular
characteristic is its moral seriousness and emphasis upon
deed. A student might well begin exploring Levinas' view of
ethics and Judaism through this article.

070 Levinas, Emmanuel. "Ideology and Idealism."
Translated by Arthur Lesley. In Modern Jewish Ethics:
Theory and Practice, edited by Marvin Fox, 121-138.
Columbus: Ohio State University Press, 1975.

This translation of an important paper by Levinas notes the
distance between modern thought and halakhah. Modernity
suspects all ideology as basically illusion. Judaism, he
contends, is not ideology but moral seriousness that finds
transcendence of self through concern for the other. The
essay is useful in combining Levinas' emphasis on Judaism as
ethics with his phenomenological analysis of both the modern
condition and the possibilities of transcendence of the
modern situation.

071 Levy, Bernard-Henri. The Testament of God. Trans. by
George Holoch. New York: Harper and Row Publishers, 1979.

Henri Levy is not an influential thinker on most of
contemporary Jewish thought but is an example of
"deconstruction" in philosophy, but interprets Judaism as an
ethical system much in the way of other Europeans (see
Levinas or Blue). He contrasts Jewish practicality with
the Christian love ethic that, he claims, undermines
ethical seriousness. A skeptical reader might question his
ability to transform parochial concerns -- Zionism, rabbinic
Judaism, legalism -- into universal ethical principles.

072 Lopian, Eliyahu. *Lev Eliyahu: A Collection of Talks*. Trans. by B.D. Klein. Jerusalem: Kalman Pinski, 1975.

This is an inspirational and devotional anthology of musar lectures that was first transcribed from tapes to a printed Hebrew text. It became popular in that form and then was translated into English. It includes lectures on faith, human nature, suffering, and the love of rebuke and provides a modern example of the devotional literature that mentions the holocaust, modern immorality, and secularism while using the traditional mode and language of classical Jewish moral writings. Of particular interest is the essay "The Right Way," pp. 249-257 that explains how the teachings of musar teachers and medieval Jewish thinkers can lead to repentance and the correction of sin. The psychology of ethical and moral life of the Musar Movement finds expression here as well as a psychological interpretation of Jewish literature. See also 575.

073 Marmur, Dov. *Beyond Survival: Reflections on the Future of Judaism*. London: Darton, Longman and Todd Ltd., 1982.

Marmur provides a popular, not scholarly, introduction to Judaism characteristic of liberal Jewish thought. This British explication of Judaism stresses "doing Torah" and claims that Judaism is a witness for hope in the future. Particular ethical principles -- love of neighbor, social politics, and moral choice -- are emphasized as characteristic of Jewish religiousness. See also 387, 514.

074 Novak, David. *Law and Theology in Judaism*. New York: Ktav Publishing House, 1974.

These essays on theological and practical issues illustrate the author's contention that Jewish ethics is a dialectical process in which the values of the aggadah enrich the concrete practice of the halakhah. Novak is a "traditionalist," a term that is more inclusive than his institutional affiliation to the Conservative Jewish Movement, and his interpretation of Jewish ethics should be studied in that context. See also 394.

075 Novak, David. *Law and Theology in Judaism*, 2nd Series. New York: Ktav Publishing House, 1975.

This companion volume to (074) examines ritual, theological and social questions from the perspective of Conservative Judaism. A particularly valuable essay is a study of revelation and its relationship to the halakhah as well as its aggadic dimension. The interweaving of the social and the ethical with a traditional approach to Jewish law makes this a fascinating experiment in devising a modern Jewish morality based in Judaism but responsive to contemporary needs.

076 Nulman, Louis. "A Personal Code of Ethics." In Building Jewish Ethical Character, edited by Joseph Kaminetsky and Murray I. Friedman, 105-112. New York: The Fryer Foundation, 1975.

This popular presentation of an Orthodox Jewish viewpoint argues that the worth of each individual despite differing abilities and talents is the central focus of Jewish ethics. It provides a traditional viewpoint on the way in which an individual develops personal ethical values through the study of Torah and how obedience to Judaism is the best guide to personal development.

077. Perez, David Jose. Judaismo E Universalismo. Rio di Janeiro: Sabedoria, 1968.

This Spanish language essay on Jewish ethics should be read with great interest. It defends Judaism as a universal faith drawing heavily on modern thinkers like Samuel Hugo Bergman (see 005, 026) and Norman Lamm (see 061, 062). He confronts Kant, Fichte, and other modern philosophers with biblical and talmudic ideas.

078 Petuchowski, Jakob J. Ever Since Sinai: A Modern View of Torah. New York: Scribe Publications, 1961.

This liberal Jewish interpretation of traditional rabbinic Judaism, its ethics, rituals, and laws, offers essential background for a study of Jewish ethics, while providing an imaginative and vivid evocation of moral teachings and ethical principles from talmudic sources.

079 Polish, David F. "Judaism and Human Rights." Journal of Ecumenical Studies 19 (1982): 40-50.

This careful study of the universalism implicit in Jewish ethics emphasizes the Jewish focus on this world and, following traditional sources, focuses on the two principles of the sovereignty of God and the sacredness of each human being. It claims that the Jewish doctrine of election does not impair Jewish universalism.

080 Rabinkov, Zalman Baruch. "The Individual and the Community in Judaism." In Between Man and His Fellow: Treatises on Human Relationships in Judaism [Hebrew], Trans. by Tzvi Bar-Meir, 85-110. Translations and Collections From Israel's Wisdom. Jerusalem: Mossad HaRav Kook, 1975.

This early classic of apologetic Jewish ethics is a good restatement of argument that various antithetical ideas -- universalism and particularism, law and ethics, optimism and pessimism -- unite in the idea of imitatio Dei.

081 Rabinovitch Nahum. "Halakha and Other Systems of Ethics: Attitudes and Interpretations." In Modern Jewish Ethics: Theory and Practice, edited by Marvin Fox, 89-102. Columbus: Ohio State University Press, 1975.

This complex and intriguing article is a basic statement of
contemporary Jewish ethics. Rabinovitch allows for
diversity within the specific details of Jewish law while
stressing unity of process in the halakhic method. He
suggests that Jewish ethics and morality are independent of
specific legal decisions. Traditionalists, however, are
uncomfortable with this pluralistic model, and liberals
reject the method itself.

082 Rackman, Emanuel. "The Centrality of the Concept of
Chesed". In The Jacob Dolnitsky Memorial Volume: Studies
in Jewish Law, Philosophy, Literature and Language, edited
by Morris Casriel Katz, 44-50 (Hebrew Section). Skokie:
Hebrew Theological College, 1982.

This exemplary study analyzes the value of chesed or
lovingkindness as the foundation of all Jewish ethics. It
offers a comprehensive survey of the use of the concept and
a clear exposition of its meaning. Unlike other studies
(compare 032, 033, 048, 105) this is a sophisticated
investigation of the theory and implications of an ethical
principle. It explores the ramifications of interpersonal
relationships for religious life and within religious
thought and is especially useful for its review of Jewish
literature from the Bible through the middle ages.

083 Reines, Chaim Zeev. "The Concept of 'Derech Eretz'."
In Essays and Investigations in Jewish Ethics and Law
[Hebrew], 130-131. Jerusalem: Rubin Mass Company, 1972.

This short Hebrew essay investigates the role of "good
manners" that is said to "preceed Torah." Jewish tradition
emphasizes that there are certain prescriptions that all
human beings must follow and that these "good manners" are a
prerequisite for any ethical activity. Reines agrees with
this analysis and therefore places "derech eretz" following
the correct way of human behavior as the cornerstone of all
Jewish morality. The essay is a valuable example of the
study of one moral concept as the basis of Jewish ethics.

084 Rosenberg, Shalom. "The Standpoint of Religious
Ethics." In Sefer Yeshiyahu Leibowitz: A Collection of
Essays on his thought and in his Honor [Hebrew], edited by
Asa Kasher and Jacob Levinger, 138-145. Tel Aviv: Tel Aviv
University Student Association, 1977.

This essay while illuminating Leibowitz also provides an
interpretation of Jewish ethics. Rosenberg notes that
Leibowitz rejects an independent Jewish ethics and
criticizes those like Moritz Lazarus who sought to establish
such an ethics. Ethics must be included within the
framework of Judaism and not identified with it. Autonomy,
however, is important since it reveals what it means to be
human. While ethics teaches the meaning of human choice,
Judaism gives a content to what should be chosen.

085 Roth, Sol. "Towards a Definition of Humility." *Tradition* 13/14 (1973): 15-22.

This is a traditionalist view of humility that marshalls various texts to show the centrality of this virtue in Judaism. It is actually a search for the central ethical value in Jewish religious teachings. Roth argues that Jewish ethics is based on the virtue of humility, an understanding of the limits of human achievement and the human being's need of divine guidance. The traditional approach here should be compared to the more philosophic approach of Green, (042).

086 Rubenstein, Richard L. *Morality and Eros.* New York: McGraw-Hill Publishing Company, 1970.

This is an example of radical theology using the insights of history, psychology, and sociology for an analysis of the shape of any future religious ethics. Rubenstein's revolutionary approach to contemporary Judaism is exemplified in this work. Many may reject his characterization of Jewish ethics as tribalism. His personal reflections on being in the State of Israel, on Jewish history, and on the psychology of God the Father are powerful reinterpretations of Jewish tradition in the light of contemporary thought and experience. The book should be read as a challenge for its perspective on Jewish ethical reflection as well as for its proposals for future action. Rubenstein offers more than a merely "Jewish" ethics. He sees his critique as applying to religious ethics generally in the American environment.

087 Samuelson, Norbert. "The Ethics of Preferring One's Own." *Sh'ma* 7 (1977): 41-42.

Samuelson, in response to an essay by Steven Schwarzschild (089), argues that Jewish ethics is an ethics of choice. The crucial question is how one can make difficult decisions. Where survival is at stake, he claims, life must always be a primary concern; where a life with morality, however, is pitted against a life without morality, the latter must be rejected. The entire controversy involved here warrants study and close attention.

088 Schwartz, Elkanah, "The Three Dimensions of Piety." In *Building Jewish Ethical Character*, edited by Joseph Kaminetsky and Murray I. Friedman, 251-258. New York: The Fryer Foundation, 1975.

This essay needs to be understood as an apologetic arguing that without religion morality is impossible. Ethics needs to be rooted in the divine, according to Schwartz ,and without such religious roots morality cannot flourish.

089 Schwarzschild, Steven S. "The Question of Jewish Ethics Today." *Sh'ma* 7 (1976): 29-36.

This essay is couched as a review of Fox's Anthology Modern Jewish Ethics (107), but goes beyond a critical analysis of the essays included in it. His organizing concept is that of the tension between particularism and universalism, or as he sees it between tribalism and universal moral standards. The essay is both provocative and useful as a confrontation with Fox's book. It is best read together with responses it evoked (see 019, 087, 096, 100, 545). Schwarzschild's response to the controversy can be found in entry 555.

090 Sole, Moshe Zeev. "The Ethical Values of Judaism." In On the Essence of Judaism [Hebrew], 61-66. Jerusalem: Keriyat Sefer, 1969.

Sole notes that ethics is an inherent part of Judaism that must be regarded as diverse and pluralistic rather than as monolithic. He points to the dialectic between law and morality, private and public ethics. Sole is a modern Israeli and merges traditional thought with an awareness of contemporary issues. His essay is a valuable restatement of basic Jewish ethical theory.

091 Soloveitchik, Aaron. "The Fire of Sinai." In Building Jewish Ethical Character, edited by Joseph Kaminetsky and Murray I. Friedman, 11-18. New York: The Fryer Foundation, 1975.

This essay argues that Jewish ethics and Jewish religion are identical. Soloveitchik rejects the search for an independent Jewish ethics and claims that by transmitting traditional Torah a Jew teaches ethics. The essay should be read as an example of traditionalist thinking.

092 Soloveitchik, Joseph B. Halakhic Man. Trans. by Lawrence Kaplan. Philadelphia: Jewish Publication Society of America, 1983.

Soloveitchik, a leading spokesman and scholar for Orthodox Judaism, should be studied as an articulate advocate for traditional Jewish ethics. His general philosophy is influenced by Existentialism, but it shows the mark of Kantian thought as well as traditional Jewish teachings. Judaism, in his view, provides both ethical realism and an ideal vision of perfection, combining Kant's moral universalism with Jewish ethical teachings. In this essay Soloveitchik develops his view of the duality of human nature, and the variety of religious types. Hebrew versions of this essay can be found in Halakhic Man: Revealed and Concealed [Hebrew]. Jerusalem: The World Zionist Organization, 1979 and in In Aloneness, In Togetherness: A Selection of Hebrew Writing [Hebrew]. Edited by Pinchas H. Peli (Jerusalem: Orot, 1976).

093 Soloveitchik, Joseph B. "Majesty and Humility." Tradition 17 (1978): 25-37.

This essay is a popular introduction to Soloveitchik's thought. He sees human nature as both exalted and as dependent upon the divine. This duality provides the basis for his dialectical view of Jewish ethics. He claims that it is neither based on humility alone nor on exalting human freedom. Like Heschel he emphasizes the double nature of Jewish ethics rather than reducible to one primary virtue.

094 Spero, Solomon. *Morality, Halakha, and the Jewish Tradition*. The Library of Jewish Law and Ethics 9. New York: Ktav Publishing House and Yeshiva University Press, 1975.

This book is an essential introduction to Jewish moral thought but is less impressive as a systematic interpretation of Judaism. It suggests that Jewish hermeneutics, logic, and method of categorization demonstrate philosophical rigor and attempts to derive the details of halakha from certain legal principles: explication, analogy, induction, generalization. These legal principles are said to be based on primary ethical principles such as love of neighbor and righteousness that themselves draw their power from the "ultimate" moral principle of imitation of God. While this systematic explication of Jewish ethics is intriguing the book as a whole fails to hold together. For the usefulness of the book as an introduction to Jewish ethics see 016. See also 414, 415, 599, 619.

095 Stitskin, Leon. *Jewish Philosophy: A Study in Personalism*. New York: Yeshiva University Press, 1976.

Although only one section of this book is called "The Ethics of Personalism" (pp. 181-205) the thesis is that Jewish philosophy is distinctive precisely because it focuses on the human potential to imitate the divine. In this sense the entire book is a reflection on ethics. The ethics of personalism is said to be the actualization of human value that Stitskin finds exemplified by moderns like Martin Buber no less than by medieval thinkers like Saadia, Maimonides, and Abraham Bar Hiyya. Stitskin is at home in both modern philosophy and Jewish medieval thought. The fruitful interplay of these three realms -- tradition, modern philosophy, and medieval writings -- makes a fascinating interpretation of Judaism. Nowhere is this interpretation more extraordinary than in the discussion of ethical values and the Jewish moral system. This book is worthy of intense study and review.

096 Weber, Stanley G. "Another Perspective on Jewish Ethics." *Sh'ma* 7 (1977): 48-49.

This is a response to the article by Schwarzschild (089) and should be read in connection with it. It argues that Jewish ethics is particularistic, but not thereby necessarily immoral. The question of Jewish self-preservation and its relationship to a universal ethics is central in contemporary Jewish reflection. Here Weber concedes that Jewish ethics places an emphasis on the survival of the Jew but concludes that this ethical parochialism is not a drawback but a necessary and important element in morality.

097 Weinstein, Deena and Weinstein, Michael A. "Jewish Ethics: The Tension Between Particularism and Universalism." Listening 14 (1979): 6-12.

This journal is neither a technical periodical nor one of the denominational presses. As a popular presentation of an enduring problem in Jewish ethics, however, the article merits attention. It shows how serious Jews grapple with the question of affirming parochial identity as part of a universal ethics. According to the authors Judaism is not best represented by the decalogue but by the exodus myth. Solidarity with slaves and recognition of the suffering of the oppressed is the central theme in Jewish ethics. This myth, however, has a double meaning. While it is universal in its concern for the oppressed, it is particularistic in being used as the basis for Jewish self-identification. The tension between these two elements in Jewish ethics gives it a characteristic creativity.

098 Weiss, Abner. "Ethics as Transcendence and the Contemporary World: A Response to Emmanuel Levinas. " In Modern Jewish Ethics: Theory and Practice, edited by Marvin Fox, 139-152. Columbus: Ohio State University Press, 1975.

The article explains Levinas' phenomenological categories and notes that for Levinas Jewish ethics is encounter. He explains difficult concepts and offers a criticism of the humanistic rationalism underlying much of European Jewish ethics. Weiss is not uncritical of Levinas but appreciates philosophic work and therefore provides a good introduction to Levinas.

099 Wyschogrod, Michael. The Body of Faith: Judaism as Corporeal Election. New York: Seabury Press, 1983.

This excellent book needs to be confronted by both liberals and traditionalists. Wyschogrod provides a sophisticated defense of Orthodox Judaism that he sees as the only modern version of Jewish religion that can claim to be "the" Jewish tradition. His review of Jewish ethics (primarily Chapter 5, but scattered through the book as well) notes that liberals have tended to interpret Judaism as an exclusively ethical system and have overlooked the particularistic elements within Judaism. Using his insight that Judaism is based on obligations flowing from divine commandment, Wyschogrod confronts Kant, the duality of law and ethics, the centrality of personhood, and questions of universalism and particularism. His is a cogent presentation of traditional Jewish ethics in the face of modernist philosophies of Jewish morality.

100 Wyschogrod, Michael. "The Particularism of Jewish Ethics." Sh'ma 7 (1977): 39-40.

As part of a continuing discussion of Marvin Fox's anthology on Jewish ethics (see 089 and the annotation there) Wyschogrod defends the particularism of Jewish ethics as a religious outgrowth of commitment to the divine plan.

101 Zacklad, Jean. Pour une Ethique de Dieu. Paris: Verdier, 1979.

This book should be read as a curiosity if at all. Despite its name this book is not really focused on ethics, but rather on a kabbalistic view of God. It begins with a "dialogue" in which the importance of mysticism, the name of God and the ethics of mysticism is stressed. It presents a subjective commentary on the text of the Tiqqunei HaZohar, a famous Jewish mystical work.

ANTHOLOGIES OF JEWISH ETHICS

102 Bulka, Reuven, ed. Dimensions of Orthodox Judaism New York: Ktav Publishing House, 1983.

This anthology traces the development of modern Orthodox Judaism, particularly in the United States but with references to other communities as well. Readers should use this accessible volume for its inclusion of a number of articles that illuminate the current ethical crisis in Orthodox Judaism. The editor provides a perceptive introduction that makes careful distinctions between observance, religiousness, and ethics. See 243, 329, 397, 423.

103 Bulka, Reuven, ed. Mystics and Medics: A Comparison of Mystical and Therapeutic Encounters. New York: Human Sciences Press, 1979.

This collection of essays focuses on the interrelationship of ethics, psychology, and mysticism. Most of the essays are nontechnical and partisan. The book is not recommended for those who stress academic or philosophical rigor. While focused on psychology many of the essays show the relationship between the value-system in Jewish ethics and that used in psychology. Bulka's own contributions to this discussion are ethical as well as psychological in nature as his interest in Logotherapy makes clear. See 236 and 242.

104 Carmell, Aryeh and Cyril Domb, eds. Challenge: Torah Views on Science and its Problems. New York: Feldheim Publishing Company, 1976.

Anyone concerned with the debate over evolution and creationism should look at this book. The quality of essays is uneven, but the book as a whole is important reading. It is a compendium of essays on traditional Judaism and science. A number of essays raise theoretical issues concerning creation, the ethics of experimentation, and the interaction between religious values and the scientific enterprise. Selected translations from classical and medieval Jewish sources are included in this collection. See also 430, 433, 453, 459, 460, 462, 466.

105 Eternal Life [Hebrew]. Bnai Brak: Bnai Brak-Katzberg, 1976.

This collection of devotional sayings culled from Jewish sources by an anonymous student of Jewish lore is meant for inspirational reading. Traditional Jews will be inspired by it and students of traditional ethical literature will find it a convenient summary of basic material. It includes rubrics relating to prayer, involvement in acts of lovingkindness, reproof and the need for discipline, honoring of sages, misuse of words, deeds, and various other moral concerns. References are made to medieval, modern, and classic Jewish sources.

106 Foundation for the Publication of Books of Musar and Hasidism. An Anthology of the Words of the Sages [Hebrew]. Jerusalem: Or HaSefer, 1974.

Readers seeking to become acquainted with or inspired by traditional Jewish moral literature should look at this book. This collection of hasidic passages is arranged alphabetically by moral themes including ethical concerns such as faith, trust, freewill, derech eretz, and such ritual concerns as the Sabbath, searching of leavening on Passover, the grace after meals, and such daily concerns as eating and drinking, family life, and commerce. It has the advantage of offering extended selections from pietistic works rather than mere aphorisms, and the reader will be rewarded by learning the major themes in hasidic morality and the way in which moral instruction is combined with the mystical cosmology of Hasidism.

107 Fox, Marvin, ed. Modern Jewish Ethics: Theory and Practice. Columbus: Ohio State University Press, 1975.

The central importance of this anthology that makes it indispensable reading can be glimpsed in the pages of Sh'ma (see 089); the various essays annotated there show the controversy that the orientation of this anthology produced. This is a peculiar anthology that focuses narrowly on love of neighbor within Judaism even while apparently dealing with such widely diverse concerns as the meaning of ethics in relationship to law and Israeli military procedures. This book is not a representative anthology but an in-depth review of selected issues. See also 008, 070, 081, 098, 170, 385, 409, 542, 549, 559.

108 Goldberg, Hillel, ed. Musar Anthology. Hyde Park, Massachusetts: Harwich Lithograph Company, 1972.

This labor of love by young men inspired by an encounter
with musar, provides vivid portraits in words and pictures
of the moral leaders of the Musar Movement. It should be
read for background on the Musar Movement and as an example
of the attractiveness of the musar for young Jews.

109 Gordis, Robert and Waxman, Ruth B., eds. Faith and
Reason: Essays in Judaism. New York: Ktav Publishing House,
1973.

This volume collects articles that appeared in Judaism
during the 1950s-1960s. The articles provide a good
introduction to the state of contemporary Jewish thought
including contemporary reflection on ethical and moral
issues and is a good introduction to the modern discussion
of Jewish ethics. See also 059, 431, 490, 548, 607, 610.

110 Kaminetsky, Joseph and Friedman, Murray I., editors.
Building Jewish Ethical Character. New York: The Fryer
Foundation, 1975.

This valuable assortment of essays on Jewish ethics by
traditional Jewish educators is divided into six parts:
general lectures, ethics in the classroom, the moral
curriculum, translations of Jewish classical moral
literature, essays on specific issues, and an exploration of
Jewish ethics and mental health. A common theme linking
these essays is that Judaism derives its ethics from
revelation; no distinction between the halakhah and an
independent ethical principle can be made. The essays
reaffirm the traditional argument that to divide Torah into
competing realms is illegitimate. The implications of this
theory for Jewish education is given detailed treatment.
Teaching revealed sources constitutes teaching Jewish
ethics. Moral training is also, thereby, training in
religious practice and belief. This ideology is translated
into practical terms when discussing classroom procedure or
issues of daily conduct. See also 024, 032, 037, 038, 039,
040, 076, 089, 091, 162, 226, 230, 233, 234, 352, 413, 420,
472, 488, 540 543, 621, 630, 634, 639, 644.

111 Kellner, Menahem Marc, ed. Contemporary Jewish Ethics.
Sanhedrin Jewish Studies. New York: Sanhedrin Press, 1978.

Together with the anthology by Marvin Fox (107) this
anthology is a standard work that should be read with care.
Its essays provide background on both theoretical and
practical concerns central in contemporary Jewish ethics and
consideration of selected moral issues. An introductory
essay provides historical background; a theoretical section
focuses on law, ethics, and halakhah. The book provides
a representation of the variety of approaches both within
and between organized Jewish groups in America as well as
a breadth of understanding of the types of moral concerns
that have animated contemporary Jewish ethical thought.
See also 007, 011, 012, 054, 385, 553, 564, 576.

112 Klagsbrun, Francine. *Voices of Wisdom: Jewish Ideals and Ethics For Everyday Living*. New York: Pantheon Books, Inc., 1981.

This anthology intermingles ethical reflection and consideration of particular moral positions in a wide-ranging selection of Jewish ethical material from classical, medieval, and modern sources. The editor has given a sensitive introduction to the book as a whole and to each section summarizing both recent debate and the older tradition. Taken as a whole the anthology is a welcome introduction to the variety of Jewish ethical thought.

113 Klein, Salamon J. *The Way of Torah and the Straight Path* [Hebrew]. Jerusalem: n.p., 1969/1970.

This devotional book is not of general interest but should be read by those specializing in contemporary expressions of traditional *musar*. It includes reflections on the holidays, the meaning of prayer, other matters of Jewish law and practice.

114 Kling, Simcha, ed. *A Sense of Duty*, Jewish Sources Speak Books. Washington, D.C.: Bnai Brith, 1968.

All readers should find this a useful anthology limited only by its brevity. The editor provides an introduction that argues that a distinctive feature of Judaism is its emphasis upon action. The anthology reinforces this claim by organizing under various ethical rubrics selections from classical, medieval, and modern Jewish literature.

115 Konvitz, Milton R., ed. *Judaism and Human Rights*. The Bnai Brith Jewish Heritage Classics. New York: W.W.Norton and Company, 1972.

This collection affirms Konvitz's belief that Jewish ideals and values constitute a reinforcement of the goals of democracy and freedom. The articles in this anthology focus generally on specific issues: equality, democracy, liberty, and peace being prominent. Certain essays are relevant to ethical theory: Samuel Belkin's article on creation and Konvitz on human dignity are particularly of interest. Not every essay is as useful as these but the anthology includes stimulating studies. See also 426, 437, 444, 572.

116 Lamm, Norman. *The Good Society: Jewish Ethics in Action*. Bnai Brith Jewish Heritage Classics. New York: Viking Press, 1974.

This is a valuable and well-conceived anthology that unites modern, medieval, and classical texts into a coherent whole. The book is divided into three sections "the individual" (love, compassion, the stranger, etc.), on the "family", and on "society," that the editor's introduction (see 062) seeks to integrate in one system. The book provides an integrated introduction to the themes of Jewish ethics.

117 "The Light of Ethics." In Shem U'Sheirit: An Anthology in Memory of Efraim Simhah Rozenfeld [Hebrew], 153-194. Bnai Brak: Yad Efraim, 1974/1975.

This anthology, put together in memory of Efraim Rozenfeld, includes some of his own writings and gathers essays from musar teachers like Isaac Blaser, J.D.Soloveitchik, and Eliyahu Dressler. The subject matter ranges from an interpretation of prayer to a discussion of the quality of absolute trust in God. This work is not for all readers but does offer the scholar a glimpse of the traditional expression of Jewish ethics.

118 Loewe, Raphael, ed. Studies in Rationalism: Judaism and Universalism. London: Routledge, Kagan Paul Ltd., 1966.

This work should be used selectively with certain outstanding essays being continual points of reference. This collection of articles, although slightly predating the majority of entries in this bibliography, is a brilliant assortment of ethical studies. See also 178, 386, 403, 569.

119 Mandelbaum, Bernard, ed. Choose Life. New York: Random House, Inc., 1968.

This is an anthology of source material arranged according to themes of the High Holy Days and is clearly meant to be of homiletical use to rabbis. Its appeal, however, is broader since it collects both Jewish and nonJewish statements on issues of general ethical concern. It can be used with judicious caution by those seeking to look at selective citations from Jewish ethical writing since the selections are short and impressionistic.

120 Moriel, Yehuda, ed. In the Good Way: Commandments Between Man and Man according to the Sources of the Bible and the Oral Law [Hebrew]. Jerusalem: The Histadruth of the World Zionist Organization, 1975.

This anthology collects material from a variety of ancient, medieval and modern sources to provide a good introduction to the variety of Jewish ethical thinking. The rubrics under which the material is gathered are both general ethical principles and moral directives.

121 Neusner, Jacob, ed. Understanding Rabbinic Judaism: From Talmudic to Modern Times. New York: Ktav Publishing House, 1974.

This collection of source material presents a variety of essays on Jewish thought, including many concerning Jewish ethics. The comments of the editor are always of interest and are helpful in understanding the rabbinic tradition generally. The companion volume Understanding Jewish Theology: Classical Issues and Modern Perspectives (New York: Ktav Publishing House, 1973) should also be consulted. See also 198, 199, 206, 219, 227, 392.

68   BIBLIOGRAPHICAL SURVEY

122   Porter, Jack Nusan and Dreier, Peter, eds. Jewish Radicalism: A Selected Anthology. New York: Grove Press, 1973.

Although not specifically devoted to "ethics" the type of reflection provided by various articles in this anthology demonstrate trends in contemporary Jewish ethics. Essays on Jewish self-defense, on the ideology of Jewish self-liberation, on Zionism, nationalism and internationalism, on women and youth, is useful for readers interested in modern Jewish morality and the ethics that generates it. Jack Nusan Porter's anthology The Sociology of American Jews:A Critical Anthology (Washington, D.C.: University Press of America, 1978) is also a valuable resource.

123   Reimer, Jack and Stampter, Nathanial, eds. Ethical Wills: A Modern Jewish Treasury. New York: Schocken Books, Inc., 1983.

Traditional Judaism has always included a genre in which the writer addressed his descendents with words of consolation, wisdom, and ethical advice. This tradition is continued even among secularized Jews in the modern world. This particular volume is remarkable for collecting a variety of examples of this genre from the contemporary period and can be used as a vital and human introduction to the ethical problems facing Jews in the modern world.

124   Rosner, Fred and Bleich, J. David, eds. Jewish Bioethics. New York: Sanhedrin Press, 1979.

   This volume on Jewish bioethics contains a number of essays on theoretical issues -- creation, evolution, the value of science -- and thus are useful for the study of Jewish ethics. While focused on specific issues they are valuable for a general view of Jewish ethical thought.

125   Shapiro, David S. Studies in Jewish Thought 1. Studies in Judaica. New York: Yeshiva University Press, 1975.

These valuable essays provide both theoretical consideration of the principles of Jewish ethics -- including three studies of the concept of imitation of God and its ethical implications -- and investigations of particular moral issues. Each essay is carefully argued and illuminates one aspect of an ethics of holiness. As a whole the book is a sophisticated presentation of traditional Jewish ethical thinking. See also 160, 407, 556, 576.

126   Silver, Daniel Jeremy, editor. Judaism and Ethics. New York: Ktav Publishing House, 1970.

This collection of essays originally appearing in the Journal of the Central Conference of American Rabbis, primarily resenting Reform Judaism, includes a breadth of subject matter and orientation. It may be helpful to read this anthology together with those associated with Orthodox Conservative Judaism. See also 147, 158, 266, 276, 318, 320, 393, 458, 487, 496, 500, 513, 525, 529.

127 Sobel, Ronald B. and Wallach, Sidney, eds., Justice, Justice Shalt Thou Pursue: Papers Assembled on the Occasion of the Seventy-Fifth Birthday of the Reverend Dr. Julius Mark. New York: Ktav Publishing House, 1975.

The papers presented in tribute to Dr. Mark's ethical concerns range in subject matter from theoretical questions about Jewish ethical principles to historical studies of ethics in rabbinic and medieval times and should interest all serious students of Jewish ethics. The contributors are drawn from varied backgrounds -- some academic, some Reform, some Conservative, and some Orthodox. See also 135.

128 Tishby, Isaiah. Hebrew Ethical Texts: Selected Texts With introductions, Notes and Commentaries [Hebrew]. In Collaboration With Joseph Dan. Tel Aviv: M. Newman Publishing House, 1970.

This collection of primary texts should be used by a beginning student. It offers a useful selection of Hebrew materials relating to ethics and morality. Many of the lesser known philosophers are included, pietists like Bachya Ibn Pakuda, philosopher-poets like Solomon Ibn Gabirol, and philosophical giants like Maimonides are all included. The latter has the entire last 100 pages of the books devoted to his work or to work attributed to him. This is a good textbook introduction to the style, themes, and mode of argumentation found in Jewish ethical treatises.

2
The History of Jewish Ethics

BIBLICAL AND TALMUDIC ETHICS

129 Agus, Jacob Bernard. "The Ideal Personality," in The Vision and The Way: An Interpretation of Jewish Ethics, 73-93. New York: Frederick Ungar Publishing Company, 1966.

In this chapter of his major interpretation of Jewish ethics (see 002)) Agus paints a picture of the "disciple of the wise" drawn from biblical prophecy, from rabbinic teachings, and from talmudic mystic saints. He focuses on atonement, charity, compassion, and other personal virtues quoting both halakhic and aggadic sources from rabbinic materials. Agus notes that the so-called "dry legalistic Torah-scholar" was also the mystic who made ascents to heaven and who sought the charisma that came from study.

130 Agus, Jacob Bernard. "The Ideal Society." in The Vision and The Way: An Interpretation of Jewish Ethics, 53-72. New York: Frederick Ungar Publishing Company, 1966.

This chapter of Agus' book (see 002) uses mainly rabbinic and biblical statements to show how Judaism conceived of the ideal society. While some later philosophers (Maimonides) and a few mystical authors are cited , the stress is on biblical and talmudic ethics. Mishnaic sources concerned with ethics, the messianic times, and war and peace are cited at length. The main argument is that rabbinic Judaism saw the Torah as a blueprint for an ideal society.

131 Altmann, Alexander. "Homo Imago Dei in Jewish and Christian Theology." Journal of Religion 48 (1968): 235-259.

This excellent philosophical study introduces the reader to a major idea of rabbinic ethics. Altmann surveys the development of the concept of the human being created in the image of God. He studies its development through biblical, rabbinic, medieval, and modern times. While the article is not confined to one historical period it shows how rabbinic ideas dominate Jewish ethical reflection.

132 Bergman, Samuel Hugo. "Can Transgression Have an Agent: The Law of the State and the Conscience of the Individual," in The Quality of Faith: Essays on Judaism and Morality 13-23. Trans. by Yehudah Hanegbi. Jerusalem: World Zionist Organization, 1970.

This useful examination of rabbinic ethics and its relevance in the modern world investigates the talmudic argument about agency to perform a transgression. It concludes that individual conscience and the responsibility for personal action supports civil disobedience. See Bergman (005); the essay can be found on pp. 9-20 of the Hebrew version.

133 Berman, Saul. "Lifnim Mishurat Hadin." Journal of Jewish Studies 26 (1975): 86-104; 28 (1977): 59-73.

The principle of acting "outside the lines of the law" is central in Jewish ethics, but has occasioned controversy: does it mean ignoring justice or does it refer to mercy that is in fact part of justice? This extended essay (separated because of length into two parts) is a major contribution that concludes that the principle suggests that the results of an application of the law are not always the expected pure justice but sometimes unexpected mercy. The principle suggests that within the law are untapped sources of mercy.

134 Faur, Jose. "Law and Justice in Rabbinic Jurisprudence." In Samuel K. Mirsky Memorial Volume: Studies in Jewish Law, Philosophy, and Literature, edited by Gersion Appel, Morris Epstein, and Hayim Leaf, 13-20. Jerusalem: Sura Institute for Research; New York: Yeshiva University Press, 1970.

This valuable exploration of the ethics involved in Jewish law and rabbinic teaching demonstrates the difference between a just law and a merely "legal law." The latter rules strictly; true justice may require mercy. The author claims that this difference lies at the heart of the principle of "lifnim mishurat hadin." See also 133.

135 Finkelstein, Louis. "The Ethics of Anonymity Among the Pharisees," in Pharisaism in the Making: Selected Essays, 181-198. New York: Ktav Publishing House, 1972.

This essay originally published in 1958 became the basis for an expanded investigation of Pharisaic ethics and has been reproduced in Sobel (127), 17-34. Finkelstein shows how rabbinic writing gives clues to rabbinic ethics. Authoritative statements are given anonymously, he claims, in order to subsume personality under the greater principle of searching for the truth. This essay is a useful exercise in the study of rabbinic literature and its ethics.

136 Finkelstein, Louis, "The Ethics of the Pharisees, " in Social Responsibility in an Age of Revolution, 39-94. Philadelphia: Jewish Publication Society, 1971.

This extended defense and explication of Pharisaic ethics makes use of material from previous work that Finkelstein has done. He surveys talmudic ethical principle --love of fellow human beings, imitation of God and the striving to be holy, and eschatological hopes -- as a means of correcting what he finds to be the misapprehension of the Pharisees as overly legalistic. He is clearly an expert on early rabbinic teachings, but at times, a polemical tone sounds too clearly in the writing.

137 Frankel, Yonah. "The Image of Rabbi Joshua ben Levi in the Stories of the Babylonian Talmud." In Proceedings of the World Congress of Jewish Studies 3, 403-416. Jerusalem: World Union of Jewish Studies, 1977.

Frankel analyzes stories in the Talmud about Joshua Ben Levi as ethical tales showing the development of concern for community. Joshua ben Levi develops from a private mystic into a social hero. The tale of him seeking the Messiah at the gates of Rome is interpreted as a moral test of his saintliness. This study is a good example of how aggadah can be used as the basis for moral reflection.

138 Goldenberg, Robert. "Commandment and Conscience in Talmudic Thought." Harvard Theological Review 68 (1975): 261-271.

This review of rabbinic method is a study in the ethical sensibilities of the Talmud. Goldenberg suggests that intention is as much a matter of ritual law as of criminal law in Judaism and that sometimes merely conscious awareness of a commandment is enough to consider it fulfilled. He finds the basis for this view in the centrality of learning in rabbinic Judaism. It is thus futile, he thinks, to contrast Judaism and Christianity as a religion of action and a religion of faith. This essay is a clear and needed antidote to religious polemics.

139 Greenberg, Moshe. "Rabbinic Reflections on Defying Illegal Orders: Amasa, Abner, and Joab." Judaism 19 (1970) :30-37.

This study of a rabbinic concept shows how talmudic thought can be applied to contemporary problems. Greenberg finds in the midrashic interpretation of biblical stories of "civil disobedience" a model for modern Jews   to follow. He argues that there is only minimal justification within the rabbinic tradition for civil disobedience. This essay is an example of how rabbinic literature serves as a model for current moral reflection. It is reproduced in Kellner (111), 211-220.

140 Halivni, David Weiss. "On the Supposed Anti-Asceticism or Anti-Naziritism of Simon the Just ." Jewish Quarterly Review, n.s., 58 (1968): 243-252.

Halivni reviews the controversy surrounding the anecdote of Simon the Just who approved of a nazirite vow in only one case which is often cited as an example of rabbinic anti-asceticism. The question of whether the Talmud has a realistic or ideal ethics is often raised regarding this example. After considerable study of alternative possibilities, Halivni concludes that the point of the tale is that only a nazirite who truly is dedicated to God should take the vow. For a differing view see entry 148.

141 Herzog, Isaac. "The Law of the Red Heifer," in Judaism: Law and Ethics, 37-40. New York: Soncino Press, 1974.

This essay analyzes a perplexing biblical and talmudic problem: why does the preparation of the ashes of the Red Heifer render the priest impure while the use of them purifies? Herzog suggests that even the rabbis of the Talmudic period had forgotten the meaning of this law. He provides a new interpretation that makes the law a relevant commentary on the meaning of human life.

142 Herzog, Isaac. "Philosophy in the Talmud and the Midrash," in Judaism: Law and Ethics, 95-103. New York: Soncino Press, 1974.

Herzog uses this essay to review the wealth of evidence showing rabbinic concern for philosophical and moral issues. He emphasizes the intellectual humility that the rabbis exhibited. Not philosophic ethics but "the spirituality of the God-idea" was, according to him, the major moral contribution of rabbinic Judaism.

143 Kadushin, Max. The Rabbinic Mind, 3rd edition, New York: Bloch Publishing Company, 1972.

This influential study in talmudic Judaism emphasizes value-concepts, the meaning of halakhah, aggadah, philosophy, and "normal mysticism." Kadushin suggests that rabbinic thought is an ethical system in which the various elements of morality, ritual, and law interact creatively. His work has shaped the way many Jews, especially in the Conservative Movement in Judaism, have understood rabbinic tradition. See also 057.

144 Kimmelman, Reuven. "Nonviolence in the Talmud." Judaism 17 (1968): 316-334.

This essay reviews the talmudic tradition on nonviolence and concludes that while rabbinic Judaism is not pacifist it emphasizes the values of peace and justice. Kimmelman's exploration demonstrates how a study of traditional Jewish teachings can be applied to modern ethical issues.

145 Kimmelman, Reuven. "The Rabbinic Ethics of Protest." Judaism 19 (1970): 38-58.

This essay demonstrates the relevance of rabbinic ethics for contemporary Judaism. Kimmelman surveys the rabbinic teachings about political dissent and concludes that while rabbinic teachings did not deny the value of political protest they did circumscribe it. Such protest was to begin in self-criticism and was to be directed against offending actions, not against persons. Kimmelman uses his findings to suggest that Jews moderate their protest against the American war in Southeast Asia.

146 Kirschenbaum, Aaron. "The Bystander's Duty to Rescue in Jewish Law." Journal of Religious Ethics 8 (1980): 204-226.

The command not to stand idly by while people suffer becomes the focal point around which this essay examines the principles of love, self-sacrifice, and concern for neighbor in rabbinic ethics. This is a well crafted article but not an original contribution to contemporary Jewish ethics.

147 Kravetz, Julius. "Some Cautionary Remarks." Journal of the Central Conference of American Rabbis (1968): 75-81.

Kravetz suggests that many liberal rabbis have been less than cautious in their interpretation of talmudic teachings on abortion, conscientious objection to war, and penal reform. His conclusion is that texts must be used with care and respect for their original context. This article is reprinted in Silver (126), 273-281.

148 Landman, Leo. "The Guilt Offering of the Defiled Nazirite." Jewish Quarterly Review, n.s., 59 (1968): 9-23.

Landman enters the controversy over whether the anecdote about Simon the Just is anti-ascetic or not (see 140). He suggests that the tale concerns only those nazirites who become polluted before the original time of their self-imposed vow has not elapsed. Are they required to renew their vow after this forced abandonment of it? He suggests that such renewal of vows should be allowed only in extraordinary circumstances.

149 Lichtenstein, Aaron. The Seven Laws of Noah. New York: Rabbi Jacob Joseph School Press, 1981.

Lichtenstein investigates the talmudic contention that God gave to Noah seven laws that govern the social and ethical life of all humanity. He reviews the literature and discovers many ramifications of each of the laws finding that the Noahide code and its implications cover the entire range of human justice, overlapping in important areas with the commandments applied to the Jews. He concludes that a considerable number of laws thought to be exclusively Jewish are in fact integrated into the Noahide system. His important and useful point is that the Noahide covenant is an inclusive rather than exclusive theory.

150 Lightstone, Jack N. "Problems and New Perspectives in the Study of Early Rabbinic Ethics." *Journal of Religious Ethics* 8 (1980): 199-209.

Lightstone's careful scholarship merits attention by those seeking a comprehensive system of Jewish ethics no less than those desiring an understanding of rabbinic ethics. This study urges caution in using the basic texts of rabbinic Judaism as a basis for discovering a "normative" Jewish ethics. The texts need to be decoded historically as well as intellectually. When this is done the perils of trying to discern a single normative Jewish ethics are revealed. There is no uniform and unambiguous "rabbinic ethics" that can be established with absolute certainty according to Lightstone. Any attempt to create a normative system of values based upon the rabbinic material is, thus, inevitably arbitrary, selective, and reveals the prejudices of the person creating it.

151 Mandelbaum, Bernard. "Two principles of Character Education in the Aggada." *Judaism* 21 (1972): 84-92.

Mandelbaum uses the *aggadah* as a model for modern Jewish ethical reflection. He claims that Judaism provides an inner world of its own that uses the activity of Torah study to provide moral education. He notes two central principles that are inculcated in this way: the values of study and sensitivity to ethical concerns. The author, a Conservative Jewish leader, takes these two principles as indications of the dynamic moral thrust of the tradition.

152 Petuchowski, Jakob J. "The concept of 'Teshuva' in the Bible and Talmud." *Judaism* 17 (1968): 175-185.

Petuchowski investigates classical Jewish sources to find the meaning of the moral idea of repentance, *teshuvah*. Moral responsibility, he argues, is possible only on the basis of two presuppositions: that human beings have the capacity to do either good or evil and that they can right the wrongs they have committed. Judaism, according to this fascinating study of rabbinic teachings, emphasizes the power and value of repentance for just this ethical purpose, that of making morality truly possible.

153 Pines, Shelomo. "Two Who Walk in the Desert," in *Studies in the History of Jewish Philosophy: The Transmission of Texts and Ideas* [Hebrew], 9-11. Jerusalem: Bialik Institute, 1977.

A famous talmudic dispute concerns two who walk in the desert only one of whom has a flask of water. The moral question is both one of self-sacrifice and of concern for others. Pines contributes to the discussion of the relationship between this passage and stoic parables and puzzles and so provides useful findings for the history of Jewish ethics.

154 Pines, Shelomo Zalman. *Biblical and Talmudic Ethics* [Hebrew]. Jerusalem: Akiva Joseph Press, 1976.

This fascinating study and useful introduction to Jewish ethics analyzes the fundamental sources of Judaism. It surveys biblical literature, the so-called "Ethics of the Fathers" from the Mishna, the *aggadah*, and the legal material. The book concludes by suggesting the meaning of "a sense of ethics," with particular reference to modern concerns and philosophies.

155 Priest, James E. *Governmental and Judicial Ethics in the Bible and Rabbinic Literature*. New York: Ktav Publishing House; Malibu: Pepperdine University Press, 1980.

This survey of the biblical and rabbinic principles of governmental ethics provides useful facts about talmudic and biblical judicial procedure. It also investigates the relationship between law and ethics. Particular examples of Jewish judicial ethics are discussed: laws concerning war and peace, capital punishment, and civil legislation.

156 Reines, Chaim W. "Beauty in the Bible and the Talmud." *Judaism* 24 (1975): 100-107.

In considering the biblical and rabbinic sources concerning beauty, Reines notes an appreciation of nature and natural beauty as divine creations. The natural impetus to value beauty, however, was checked in favor of moral value. *Aggadah* from rabbinic literature is used to show how the ugly can still be of moral worth.

157 Reines, Chaim Zeev. "Morality and Wisdom in Bible, Ben Sirah and the Rabbis," in *Essays and Investigations in Jewish Ethics and Law* [Hebrew], 18-30. Jerusalem: Rubin Mass Company, 1972.

This examination of the principles, examples, and major concerns found in biblical and postbiblical Judaism suggests that wisdom in Judaism refers to moral knowledge. It is sought after as an aid to fulfilling the divine precepts. This thesis is challenging and presented with insight, passion, and scholarship.

158 Sandmel, Samuel. "Confrontation of Greek and Jewish Ethics: Philo's *De Decalogo*." *Journal of the Central Conference of American Rabbis* (1968): 54-63.

Sandmel shows that Philo's interpretation of Jewish law in his discussion of the decalogue is influenced by stoic thought. While Philo does argue that Torah is revealed law, this revealed law is found on examination to be identical with the stoic conception of natural law. Philo is an example of how Jewish thinkers have wrestled with their tradition to show that its ethics are as exalted as, if not superior to, that of the culture around them. This is a useful historical study reproduced in Silver (126), 161-176.

159 Schweid, Eliezer. "The Authority Principle in Biblical Ethics." *Journal of Religious Ethics* 8 (1980): 180-203.

Schweid combines good scholarship and an advocate position for traditional Jewish thought in analysis of authority in biblical ethics. Ethics or discipline (musar) is a non-coercive principle, he suggests, emphasizing free choice. The human being can will to obey or to be disobedient, but needs training in order to will obedience. Discipline or ethics is a means of training the will for obedience, it is self-imposed authority put into practice.

160 Shapiro, David S. "Wisdom and Knowledge of God in Biblical and Talmudic Thought." *Tradition* 12 (1971): 70-89.

This seminal study contrasts Jewish views of the knowledge of God with Greek views. Whereas the Jew seeks a wisdom that allows imitation of the divine through following moral principles the Greek seeks mastery through the attainment of skill. Shapiro argues that this difference is relevant not only in rabbinic times but through medieval Judaism and into contemporary Jewish life. The modern Jew should seek moral rather than technical knowledge as did the traditional one. The essay is reproduced in Shapiro (125), 44-62.

161 Worob, Avraham. "Stoic and Talmudic Ethics: The Acceptable and the Adequate," in *Duties of the Mind: Essays on Jewish Philosophy*, edited by Nova Worob, 40-43. Spring Valley: Shaare Emet, 1975.

Worob's popularized version of debates on basic questions of philosophy is less rigorous and more general than most readers would wish, but is valuable as an expression of a rather common traditional viewpoint. He looks at philosophy defensively from a Jewish standpoint. This essay argues that despite similarities Jewish ethics is distinctive from Stoic ethics and must be considered a unique moral advance. This view should be contrasted with Pines, 153.

162 Yaged, Moshe. " 'Kibbud Ov': An Analysis." In *Building Jewish Ethical Character*, edited by Joseph Kaminetsky and Murray I. Friedman, 236-245. New York: The Fryer Foundation, 1975.

This study of the biblical command of honoring parents interprets its place in the ten commandments as a transition from God-directed to human-directed actions. An interesting contrast between this clearly rabbinic and biblical approach and that of Philo's stoic influenced approach can be found by looking at Philo's view of this commandment as summarized by Sandmel in 158. Yaged's traditionalism stands in marked contrast to Sandmel's academic method; Reines provides a more sophisticated contrast of Jewish and Hellenistic thought. This essay is best read as an example of a devotional approach to the Jewish ethical tradition.

PHILOSOPHICAL ETHICS

163 Altmann, Alexander. "The Religion of the Thinkers: Free Will and Predestination in Saadia, Bahya, and Maimonides." In Religion in a Religious Age, edited by S.D.Goitein, 25-52. Cambridge: Association for Jewish Studies, 1974.

Altmann demonstrates how the intellectual contexts of Jewish thinkers shapes their understanding of certain ethical conceptions. Saadia prefers the "beliefs" of the philosophers, rationally defensible arguments for ethical ideals and shows that "doctrines" -- accepted religious claims -- can be demonstrated to be actually well founded beliefs. Bahya, a pietist, emphasizes the primacy of reliance upon the divine. Maimonides, working out of just that Islamic rationalist tradition against which Bahya, rebelled has a "deterministic free will" that is identical to that of the philosophers. Each thinker argues for the value of Jewish ethical categories in radically different contexts and so transform the meaning of those categories. This is not only an article of high academic excellence but one that is highly recommended even for nonspecialists in medieval Jewish thought. It is reprinted as "Free Will and Predestination in Saadiah, Bahya, and Maimonides," in Essays in Jewish Intellectual History (Hanover, New Hampshire: University Press of New England, 1981), 35-64.

164 Atlas, Samuel. "The Contemporary Relevance of the Philosophy of Maimonides." In Reform Judaism: A Historical Perspective, Essays From the Yearbook of the Central Conference of American Rabbis, edited by Joseph L. Blau, 481-519. New York: Ktav Publishing House, 1973.

This essay is interesting both for Maimonidean scholarship and as an example of how Maimonides is made to fit differing molds, in this case a Kantian one. Atlas presents Maimonides as an exemplar of a modern Jewish ethics. The categories of imitation of God, ethical monotheism, and a categorical ethical ideal make Maimonides a better guide than Moses Mendelssohn for the modern Jew. Atlas contends that Maimonides' ethics fits the Kantian model and as such is useful in the modern context.

165 Berman, Lawrence V. "Maimonides on the Fall of Man." Association for Jewish Studies Review 5 (1980): 1-15.

This scholarly article written for historians of Jewish thought is also important for a study of the Jewish view of the human condition. While primarily philosophical in its emphasis this study looks at an ethical problem in terms of its biblical roots and later explication. Berman explores Maimonides view of humanity, particularly in relationship to the Adam story in Genesis. He concludes that Maimonides' position can be falsified only by showing it at variance with the original intention of the biblical text.

166 Blomberg, Zeev. "The Ethical Systems of Abraham Bar Hiyya, Joseph Ibn Zaddik, and Abraham Ibn Daud." [Hebrew] Tarbiz 46 (1977): 231-244.

This well argued investigation of the ethical perspective of three Jewish thinkers analyzes their interpretation of the ten commandments and of other halakhic practices, of reward and punishment, and of free will. It suggests that the ethical systems of these thinkers was shaped by their historical and philosophical contexts.

167 Blumberg, Harry. "Theories of Evil in Medieval Jewish Philosophy." Hebrew Union College Annual 43 (1972): 149-168.

This scholarly analysis of various ethical treatments of the problem of evil is of interest mainly to philosophers and historians of philosophy. It studies how some medieval thinkers interpreted the book of Job and wrestled with the problems of free will and theodicy.

168 Davidson, Herbert. "Maimonides' Shemonah Perakim and Al Farabi's Fusul al-Madani." In Essays in Medieval Jewish and Islamic Philosophy, edited by Arthur Hyman, 116-133. Studies from the Publications of the American Academy for Jewish Research. New York: Ktav Publishing House, 1977.

This technical study investigates the relationship between Maimonidean ethics and that of a major Muslim thinker. Davidson shows how Maimonides borrows Al Farabi's moral and psychological teachings but not his theology. Maimonides accepts ethical truth from whatever source it comes; he does not, however, according to Davidson, compromise his religious beliefs by citing sources from an alien tradition. This historical study is also useful for its perspective on the relationship between Jewish and non-Jewish ethics.

169 Etzion, Isaac Raphael Halevi. "Maimonides' system of Ethics: Its Sources and Its Source," in Investigations in Questions of Faith [Hebrew], 84-103. Pardes Hanah: Midreshit Noam, 1969.

This popular essay investigates the relationship between Maimonides and and non-Jewish ethical systems. Etzion contrasts the "median way" as understood by Maimonides to its use in Aristotle. Whereas Maimonides seeks the rational way in order to learn to know God, he claims, Aristotle sought extrinsic success and happiness. According to Etzion this difference shows that despite apparent similarities Maimonides and Aristotle hold a radically different ethics.

170 Fox, Marvin. "On the Rational Commandments in Saadia's Philosophy: A Reexamination." In Proceedings of the Sixth World Congress of Jewish Studies 3, edited by Avigdor Shinan, 33-43. Jerusalem: World Union of Jewish Studies, 1977.

This essay combines the best of technical expertise with an awareness of current philosophical issues to suggest that Saadia defends rational commandments as an effective means to a religious end. The ethical relevance of Saadia's distinction between revelation and reason is explored as part of an entire religious system. It is reproduced in Fox (107), 174-187.

171 Galston, Miriam. "The Purpose of the Law According to Maimonides." Jewish Quarterly Review, n.s., 69 (1978): 27-51.

Galston points to a contradiction in Maimonides' defense of religious diversity. While diverse moral traditions enable individuals to find their way to self-perfection, social stability requires uniformity. Maimonides, according to Galston, shows that Jewish laws serve both purposes -- not only are they a means to self-perfection but they also bind the individual in loyalty to the group. In this way his view of ethics shows the superiority of Judaism to a purely political morality that lacks the means for self-perfection, and to a purely philosophical one that may lead to a destabilizing diversity.

172 Goodman, Lenn E. "Saadiah's Ethical Pluralism." Journal of the American Oriental Society 100 (1980): 407-419.

This challenging study demonstrates the variety within the Jewish ethical tradition. Its close reading of Moses Maimonides discloses that at almost every turn he is rejecting views previously supported by Saadiah Gaon. Maimonidean ethics may be considered the reversal of that of Saadiah. Goodman notes that while Saadiah's technique works well as a critique of material values it fails as a defense of religious ethics and suggests that Maimonides presents a positive approach to spiritual values.

173 Hartman, David. Maimonides: Torah and Philosophic Quest. Philadelphia: Jewish Publication Society of America, 1976.

This excellent study of Maimonides also lays the foundation for Hartman's own treatment of Jewish ethics. Hartman, an articulate defender of a common Jewish ethics that is independent of halakhic detail, finds the prototype for a pluralistic community of Jewish thought in the work of Maimonides. This study of the entire corpus of Maimonides -- including legal codes, philosophy, and ethics -- culminates in the chapter "Morality and the Passionate Love for God." This chapter suggests that Maimonides' philosophical quest for God was part of an ethical struggle for imitatio Dei that combined the universal (philosophy) and the particular (Jewish law) in a way that Hartman finds persuasive even for the modern Jew.

174 Herzog, Isaac. "Order and Sequence in Maimonides Code," in *Judaism: Law and Ethics*, 43-51. New York: Soncino Press, 1974.

The importance of Maimonides, according to Herzog, lies less in his biography than in his thinking. The two essays reproduced in this volume suggest the moral rationale for his organization of Jewish law. He finds such ethical principles as the sanctity of human life, the spiritualizing of the body and the purification of the mind, and the messianic vision. From this perspective the great legal work of Maimonides was also a great ethical work. Judaism, then, becomes a way of ethical striving rather than merely a philosophical approach to eternal human questions.

175 Lazaroff, Allan. *The Theology of Abraham Bibago: A Defense of the Divine Will, Knowledge, and Providence, in Fifteenth Century Spanish-Jewish Philosophy*. University: University of Alabama Press, 1981.

This academic work is connected with Lazaroff's commitment to the Jewish pietistic tradition and interest in Jewish ethics. The subject matter is clearly one central to any academic study of ethics. This is a scholarly and well researched analysis of a medieval text and is of primary interest to scholars.

176 Niewohner, Frederich W. "Das Verhaltnis von Naturphilosopie und Ethik im More Nebuchim." *Neue Zeitschrift fur Systematische Theologie und Religionsphilosophie* 14 (1972): 336-358.

This study looks at Maimonides from the perspective of later Jewish thinkers and investigates whether their interpretation of his ethical universalism is actually found in the data of his work. It focuses attention on the controversy over whether Maimonides' thought was universalist or not. This study traces history of Jewish universalism from the story of creation through the Babylonian Talmud and medieval thought until Maimonides and then concludes that Maimonides uses the mystical speculation on creation as the basis for a universalist and natural philosophy. This essay is a valuable study of German Jewish thinking as well as an exploration of Maimonides.

177 Rawidowicz, Simon. "Philosophy as Duty," in *Studies in Jewish Thought*, edited by Nahum N. Glatzer, 305-315. Philadelphia: Jewish Publication Society of America, 1974.

Rawidowicz comments on Maimonides' contention that through philosophy one learns to love God. Since love of God is an ethical and religious duty, philosophy itself becomes an ethical obligation. The conclusion Rawidowicz draws, one shared with others including Agus and Abraham Joshua Heschel, is that led by his ethical sensitivity Maimonides the philosopher develops into Maimonides the pietist.

178 Rosenthal, Erwin, J. "Torah and Nomos in Medieval Jewish Philosophy." In *Studies in Rationalism: Judaism and Universalism*, edited by Raphael Loewe, 215-230. London: Routledge, Kagan Paul Ltd., 1966.

Rosenthal's excellent scholarship is utilized here to uncover the meaning of "Torah" as an ethical category. He notes that for Jewish philosophers Torah denotes faith and not merely reason. The following of Torah is said to create spiritual well-being. As such it has an ethical as well as merely legal significance. The often cited dichotomy between law and love is overcome by seeing Torah in a wider philosophical and religious context.

179 Samuelson, Norbert. "Causation and Choice in the Philosophy of Ibn Daud." In *The Divine Helmsman: Studies on God's Control of Human Events*, edited by James L. Crenshaw and Samuel Sandmel, 223-233. New York: Ktav Publishing House, 1980.

Samuelson suggests that the issues of free will and determinism on the one hand and of causation and choice on the other are intrinsically different. The first of the two sets of contradictory terms refers to God's activities in the world. The second refers to the moral question of human responsibility and human decision making. Samuelson finds that for Ibn Daud the two can be taken together: nature determines how we choose; choice determines who we are as people.

180 Schwarzschild, Steven S. "Moral Radicalism and 'Middlingness' in the Ethic of Maimonides." *Studies in Medieval Culture* 11 (1977): 65-94.

This study combines academic precision with contemporary sensitivity to investigate Maimonides use of Aristotle's "median way." Such a compromise ethics is indeed part of the political vision that Maimonides presents. His religious view, however, is more radical. His moral imperative is the imitation of God; such imitation cannot be "middling" but must be extreme. While extremism is not a model for the social order, it is a goal of the individual.

181 Schweid, Eliezer. *Studies in the Shemoneh Perakim* [Hebrew]. Jerusalem: Offset Ha'amanim, 1969.

Schweid offers a traditional commentary on Maimonides' ethical explanation of the Mishnah. This type of supercommentary is in the traditional style and shows how interpretation of classical texts becomes the basis for moral inspiration for contemporary Jews. This work is rich in exegetical insight but is best read by scholars.

182 Stitskin, Leon D. *Eight Jewish Philosophers: In the Tradition of Personalism*. New York: Feldheim Publishing Company, 1979.

The title of this work is misleading since Stitskin goes beyond the eight "minor" philosophers indicated to survey medieval Jewish thought in general. He contends in a stimulating, controversial, and illuminating investigation, that personalism, the ethics of imitation of God, and the understanding of the commandments as means of actualizing human potential, are the central themes of that thought.

183 Tishby, Isaiah. <u>Hebrew Ethical Texts: Selected with an Introduction, Notes and Commentaries by Joseph Dan</u>, [Hebrew]. Tel Aviv: M. Newman Publishing House, 1970.

The general introduction, pp.xi-xxiv, to this anthology (see 128) is a good discussion of the relationship of Jewish moral literature to the <u>aggadah</u>, to philosophy, and to folklore. The influence of the moral writings of the middle ages upon later authors is discussed. The anthology itself is an excellent introduction to the major Jewish ethical thinkers in the Middle Ages.

184 Twersky, Isadore. "Some Non-Halakhic Aspects of the Mishneh Torah," in <u>Studies in Jewish Law and Philosophy</u>, 52-75. New York: Ktav Publishing House, 1982.

This instructive and scholarly article shows that Maimonides' <u>halakhic</u> compendium includes more than merely legal matters. The entire system of Jewish <u>halakha</u> is presented as an ethics, a means of perfecting the human being as a moral, intellectual, and spiritual creature. <u>Halakhah</u> for Maimonides, according to Twersky, is an instrument of ethical instruction.

185 Vajda, Georges. "Sagesse Humaine et Morale Revele d'Apres Quelques Theologiens Juifs." In <u>Sagesse et Religion</u>, 127-134. Paris: Presses Universitaires de France, 1971.

Vajda surveys the conflict between revealed morality and rational ethics as in developed in Jewish and Muslim thought. He looks particularly at the way in which Saadia, Ibn Gabirol, and Ibn Pakuda sought to solve the dilemma. Compare Altmann, (163), who focuses on the same issues.

186 Weiss, Raymond L. with Charles E. Butterworth. "Introduction," in <u>Ethical Writings of Maimonides</u>, 1-26. New York: New York University Press, 1975.

In a useful introduction to a valuable anthology Weiss suggests that Maimonides discovered that the way of piety led to greater serenity than the way of Aristotle. He charts Maimonides' growth from prudential ethics to piety.

187 Wigoder, Geoffrey. "Introduction." In <u>Meditation of the Sad Soul by Abraham Bar Hiyya.</u> Trans. by Geoffrey Wigoder. The Littman Library of Jewish Civilization. London: Routledge and Kegan Paul Ltd., 1969.

This introduction seeks to, but does not quite succeed in, justifying the value of Bar Hiyya's work as a model of Jewish ethics worthy of emulation today. The ascetic tradition within Judaism is acknowledged although the scheme as outlined by Bar Hiyya is considered exceptional. Wigoder considers this approach to moral self-discipline necessary and relevant in the modern world.

PIETISTIC ETHICS

188 Agus, Jacob Bernard. "The Infinite Dimension of Piety," in The Vision and The Way: An Interpretation of Jewish Ethics, 128-166. New York: Frederick Ungar Publishing Company, 1966.

While including later pietists, "mystics" like Moses Chaim Luzzatto, and philosophers like Maimonides this chapter (see 002) presents a good introduction to the pietistic movement in Judaism. Agus suggests that piety has an ethical component as it seeks to balance the two poles of law and nearness of God. He emphasizes the ideal of imitation of God and the ethical implications of Jewish mysticism. This is an important investigation of the ethical thrust in Jewish mystical thought.

189 Appel, Gersion. A Philosophy of Mizvot: The Religious-Ethical Concepts of Judaism, Their Roots in Biblical Law and the Oral Tradition. New York: Ktav Publishing House, 1975.

A thirteenth century work, Sefer HaHinnuk, serves as the framework for this analysis of faith and reason, the meaning of the commandments, and the ethics of revelation. This is a useful paraphrase and interpretation of the relevance of the moral literature of the early middle ages. An earlier statement of Appel's interpretation can be found in his "A Rational Conception of Mitzvot," in Samuel K. Mirsky Memorial Volume: Studies in Jewish Law, Philosophy, and Literature, edited by Gersion Appel, Morris Epstein, and Hayim Leaf (Jerusalem: Sura Institute for Research; New York: Yeshiva University Press, 1970), 21-33.

190 Dan, Joseph. Hebrew Ethical and Homiletical Literature: The Middle Ages and Early Modern Period [Hebrew]. Jerusalem: Keter Publishing House, 1975.

This learned and well written introduction to Jewish ethical writings provides an encyclopedic view of moral and sermonic literature from the early middle ages to the early modern period. Dan investigates the evolving aesthetic forms used to convey moral teachings, the relationship between Jewish and Christian homiletics, and the differences between philosophical, mystical, and rabbinic approaches to ethics. The book is clearly, if popularly, written and provides a good introduction to the moral tradition in Judaism.

191 Dan, Joseph. "Samael, Lilith, and the Concept of Evil." Association for Jewish Studies Review 5 (1980): 17-40.

This study of German Hasidism which has relevance to such issues as feminism, the idea of evil, and the demonic, shows how belief in demons and their work can influence ethical reflection. The struggle between good and evil can mirror a duality in the human soul. Dan traces how certain Jewish thinkers advanced a monistic understanding of the world and how others, influenced by their view of human nature, were led to a dualistic system.

192   Hagi, Ben-Artzi. "Asceticism in Sefer Hasidim." [Hebrew]. Daat 10 (1983): 39-46.

This essay suggests, in the context of an analysis of asceticism in Judaism (compare 140, 148, 193) that despite its denigration of the material world as a temptation the Sefer Hasidim actually requires that world as a test for moral virtue. From this Hagi argues that the ascetic model is not the highest value in Sefer Hasidim. This argument should be compared to the work of Ivan Marcus that shows a development in German Hasidism that moves from asceticism at one stage to its denial at another (see 194, 195, 196, 197) that may explain the seeming tension in Sefer Hasidim.

193   Lazaroff, Allan. "Bachya's Asceticism Against its Rabbinic Background." Journal of Jewish Studies 21 (1970): 1-38.

Lazaroff is to be commended for drawing attention to the ascetic teachings of Bachya. He does, however, have an apologetic purpose. By contrasting Bachya with his sources he suggests that rabbinic teachings softened Jewish pietism and made it less extreme than the non-Jewish models that served as its inspiration. A comparison of this work with the study of Altmann (163) is instructive as Altmann's aim is the academic one of tracing Bachya's sources while Lazaroff has a more polemical goal.

194   Marcus, Ivan G.   Piety and Society: The Jewish Pietists of Medieval Germany.   Etudes Sur Le Judaism Medieval. Leiden: E. J. Brill, 1981.

Marcus uses keen scholarship and imaginative insight to analyze the rise and decline of German Pietism (Ashkenazic Hasidism) in the eleventh and twelfth centuries. The investigation begins with the father of Judah the Hasid, then moves to Judah and the Sefer Hasidim, and concludes with Eleazar Rokeah. The main argument is that pietism grew into social reform and that social reform was later abandoned for the sake of personal self-perfection.

195   Marcus, Ivan G. "Religious Virtuosi and the Religious Community: The Pietistic Mode in Judaism." In Take Judaism For Example, edited by Jacob Neusner, 93-115. Chicago Studies in the History of Judaism. Chicago: Chicago University Press, 1983.

86 BIBLIOGRAPHICAL SURVEY

While repeating familiar themes from Marcus' work, this essay (194, 196, 197) focuses on leadership and its relationship to social settings. Marcus suggests that the pattern of pietist leadership shown by German pietism can be applied generally to religious communities and religious leadership as social groups.

196 Marcus, Ivan G. "The Politics and Ethics of Pietism in Judaism: The Hasidism of Medieval Germany." Journal of Religious Ethics 8 (1980): 227-258.

Marcus restates his major theme (see 194, 195, 197): there were two strands in German pietism, one that focused on inner spirituality and self-perfection through ascetic practice and one that sought social change. This dichotomy is generalized as a principle operating in the history of religions. The story of how these strands developed and were synthesized into one piece by Ashkenazic Hasidism is used to illustrate this thesis.

197 Marcus, Ivan G. "The Recensions and Structure of Sefer Hasidim." In Proceedings of the American Academy for Jewish Research 45 (1978): 131-153.

Marcus compares the Bologna and Parma editions of the Sefer Hasidim and discovers that considerable extraneous material has been added to the received text. He suggests that this material was inserted by French Jews who rejected ascetic practice in favor of Maimonidean piety. What is unfortunate is that this inserted material has changed the tenor of the book and is, in fact, the basis for the very selective English translation (see 199). This biased view of the text obscures its very radical asceticism, a point of importance when considering the controversy concerning asceticism (see also 140, 148, 163, 192).

198 Neusner, Jacob. "Mysticism and Ethics." In Understanding Rabbinic Judaism: From Talmudic to Modern Times, 301-302. New York: Ktav Publishing House, 1974.

This introduction to the selection from The Book of the Pious in Neusner's anthology (see 121) discusses the close ties between mysticism and ethics in Judaism. Neusner notes that Judaism is a religion of action and dwells on behavior rather than on faith. When pietism develops in Judaism it does so as an ethical expression rather than in an speculative or introspective form.

199 Singer, Sholom Alchanon. Medieval Jewish Mysticism: The Book of the Pious. Northbrook, Illinois: Whitehall Company, 1971.

Both the title and subtitle of this work have been criticized as being misleading (see 012). Nonetheless this translation is a valuable addition to the study of Jewish ethics. The introduction suggests that pietistic ethics is a morality "beyond the law", a piety that surpasses normative Jewish tradition. The section translated is only a small portion of the entire Book of the Pious and, some claim, (see 197) an unrepresentative portion. The ascetic, prayer-oriented, and sexually focused text, however, is a fascinating example of the pietistic ethics. Selections from both the introduction and the translation are presented in Neusner (121), 303-313.

200 Soloveitchik, Hayim. " Three Themes in the Sefer Hasidim." Association for Jewish Studies Review 1 (1976): 311-357.

This scholarly article evaluates the categories of the "righteous" and the "wicked" given in The Book of the Pious concluding that they are a response to the new talmudic dialectic that had developed in the Franco-German Jewish academies. The author shows how pietistic ethics is a contrast and alternative to rabbinic ethics and that modern Jewish historians have been so sympathetic to the latter and antagonistic to the former that they have distorted both the evidence when interpreting The Book of the Pious.

THE ETHICS OF JEWISH MYSTICISM

201 Bokser, Ben Zion. The Jewish Mystical Tradition. New York: Pilgrim Press. 1981.

This anthology of representtative mystical texts provides evidence for the moral nature of the kabbalah. It includes selections from Bachya Ibn Pakuda, Maimonides, and then literature from German pietism, later mystics and Polish Hasidism reflecting their ethical orientation. Bokser's provides useful introduction to the basic Lurianic myth.

202 Breslauer, S. Daniel "The Ethics of Gilgul." Judaism 32 (1983): 230-235.

This article begins by reflecting on the claim by Gershom Scholem that Hasidism transformed mystical concepts into ethics. The particular concept of reincarnation, gilgul, is analyzed from Lurianic Kabbalah through its use in early modern Hebrew and Yiddish literature. Its development is said to demonstrate how a mystical concept became an expression of Jewish ethics.

203 Cohen, Seymour. "Introduction." In The Ways of the Righteous, xv-xxii. Trans. by Seymour J. Cohen, augmented edition. Bernard Feinberg Library of Jewish Ethics. New York: Ktav Publishing House, 1979.

In an introduction to this anonymous work Cohen shows how it is a synthesis of ideas found in earlier writings, noting its emphasis on study rather than asceticism. The ethical importance of the book is stressed with particular reference to the opposition to study as an abstract art.

204 Jacobs, Louis. "The Kabbalistic Worldview." <u>Ultimate Reality and Meaning</u> 2 (1975): 321-329.

Louis Jacobs, a foremost exponent of both Jewish mysticism and Jewish ethics, emphasizes that the values of Jewish mysticism are those of traditional Judaism but with a slightly different meaning. The central ethical category, he suggests, <u>imitatio Dei</u>, would seem to eliminate ethical autonomy. Jacobs denies this and claims that the <u>kabbalah</u> restores that autonomy through its stress on the cosmic importance of human deeds.

205 Martinez-Miller, Orlando. <u>La Etica Judia Y 'La Celestina' Como Alegoria</u>. Miami: Ediciones Universal, 1978.

This analysis of an important document in Spanish letters shows how the writings of Jewish mystics were integrated, through the efforts of "conversos" or new Christians, into general Spanish thought. The author seeks to relate the ethical ideas of Fernando de Rojas, author of <u>La Celestina</u> not only to the medieval Spanish mystic Isaac Aboab but also to Jewish ethics generally. This effort, while fascinating, seems a bit forced as statements from such varied sources as modern biblical critics and Hermann Cohen are marshalled to evince a "Jewish ethics" that is reflected in a medieval work.

206 Neusner, Jacob. "Beyond the Law: Ethics," in <u>Understanding Jewish Theology: Classical Issues and Modern Perspectives</u>, 121-122. New York: Ktav Publishing House, 1973.

Neusner's brief introduction to Moses Hayyim Luzzatto in his useful anthology (see 121) notes that Jewish thinkers do not give a philosophy of ethics; they provide advice and maxims to be practical and He comments on the importance of purity and impurity in Jewish ethics and suggests that it falls between legalism on the one hand and philosophical speculation on the other. Neusner, unlike Tishby (212) does not mention the mystical elements in Luzzatto's views.

207 Newman, Eugene. <u>The Life and Teachings of Isaiah Horowitz</u>. London: G.J. George and Company, 1972.

This summary of the life and works of Isaiah Horowitz (1570-1626 C.E.) shows how intertwined Jewish <u>kabbalah</u> and moral reflection are. The ethical treatise in Horowitz's major work, <u>Shnei Luhot HaBrit</u>, is based on mystical views of creation and the human task. Newman offers an outline and summary of this major work in a superficial but useful sketch of the ethical elements in a major Jewish mystic and scholar.

208 Pachter, Mordecai. <u>Homiletical and Ethical Literature of the Sages of Safed</u> [Hebrew]. Jerusalem: Keter Publishing House, 1976.

This study of sixteenth century Safed and the ethical literature associated with it shows the relationship between ethics and mystical speculation. The work reviews the guidebooks that were developed during that period and examines the ideology behind them. It offers a wealth of quotations from and examples of early Jewish ethical thought and shows the beginnings of Jewish moral style.

209 Piekarz, Mendel. The Beginning of Hassidism: Trends in Drush and Musar Literature [Hebrew]. Jerusalem: Bialik Institute, 1978.

This important work traces the emphasis on personal repentance and moral self-discipline that later surfaced in Polish Hasidism to earlier Jewish mystics. He investigates the pietism of Isaiah Horowitz (see Newman, 207) and of Jonah of Gerona as prototypical of moral thinking based upon mystical categories. This book is expert scholarship and analysis as well as an investigation of early texts.

210 Schimmel, Solomon. "Education of the Emotions in Jewish Devotional Literature." Journal of Religious Ethics 8 (1980): 259-276.

Schimmel discusses how Elijah De Vitas integrated piety, mysticism, and ethics. It is argued that his program of controlling anger and training the emotions is worthwhile today by providing an example of that self-control needed in contemporary life.

211 Sherwin, Byron. Mystical Theology and Social Dissent: Judah Loewe of Prague. Littman Library of Jewish Civilization. East Brunswick: Associated Universities Press, 1982.

In this significant study Sherwin characterizes the work of Judah Loewe of Prague united kabbalah and social dissent in a radical social, moral, and ethical program. Judah Loewe is conceived of as an ethical dissenter from normative Jewish tradition. His ethical works and moral writings are surveyed as responses to controversies during his lifetime. Mysticism is shown to be morally relevant since it can be argued that moral abuses continue the exile and disturb the cosmic order.

212 Tishby, Isaiah. "The Influence of Moses Hayyim Luzzatto on Hassidism." [Hebrew]. Zion 43 (1978/1979): 201-234.

Tishby suggests that Luzzatto's importance as a precursor of Polish Hasidism lies in his emphasis on serving God through material action as well as spiritual dedication. Luzzatto gave importance to concrete activities, to ethics within the daily world. This emphasis of piety in the midst of experience shows that Gershom Scholem's view that Luzzatto did not influence Polish Hasidism must be rejected.

90 BIBLIOGRAPHICAL SURVEY

213 Wigder, Shabsie and Brog, Shmuel Elchonen. The Challenge of Eternity: Reflections on Our Times in the Light of the 'M'silas Yeshorim.' New York: Bashon Printing Company, 1968.

This devotional tract, in the style of the latter musar writers and quoting many of the masters cited in the next section, including Israel Salanter, founder of the Musar Movement, exemplifies ethical exhortation in modern Judaism. The form of the work is that of a commentary on the classic The Upright Path by Moses Hayyim Luzzatto into which is interspersed pithy sayings and anecdotal illustrations of ethical imperatives. A traditional moral outlook is here integrated with concerns arising from the atomic age.

214 Zacklad, Jean. Pour Une Ethique de Dieu. Paris: Verdier, 1979.

See the annotation at 101.

THE MUSAR MOVEMENT

215 Amsel, Avrohom. Irrational Rational Man: Torah Psychology. New York: Feldheim Publishing Company, 1976.

The author draws on musar teachings as an alternative to Freudian psychoanalysis. He finds in musar insights into character and character formation important for contemporary psychology. The sixth chapter of this book makes clear the debt Amsel has to the Musar Movement. His view of the unconscious and of training rational self draws on the teachings of Israel Salanter, Eliyahu Dressler, and others from that movement. The book deserves study as both a modern version of musar and for its application of musar to contemporary psychology.

216 Eckman, Lester Samuel. The History of the Musar Movement: 1840-1945. New York: Shengold Publishers, 1975.

The Musar Movement is presented as the third alternative in Jewish life created as a response to modernity. Hasidism sought to avoid the crisis by a retreat to mysticism; the Haskalah or Enlightenment assimilated into the modern world; musar stressed the charisma of learning and reeducation of the emotions. Eckman traces the relationship of the Musar Movement to other modern events -- the history of the Jews in Russia, Zionism, educational institutions in Europe and in the Land of Israel. He stresses the primacy of both morality and religious observance. The various schools of the musar are described and their differences and characteristics are given. The survey is as much a defense of musar as a modern form of Judaism as a historical study. It should be read as an interesting study of one period in the development of Jewish ethical thought and also as an expression of one type of modern Jewish ethical approach.

217 Eckman, Lester Samuel. Revered by All: The Life and Works of Rabbi Israel Meir Kagan. New York: Shengold Publishers, 1974.

This devotional biography of the "Hafetz Hayyim" (1838-1933 C.E.) shows the continuity and appeal of the musar teachings in modern times among traditional Jews. His teachings are a call for traditional morality in the face of such modern secular realities as Zionism and assimilation. The book reviews his theology and ethical injunctions as valid possibilities for the modern Jew.

218 Etkes, Emannuel. "The Systems and Works of Rabbi Hayyim of Voloshin As a Response to the "Mitnagdim" of Hasidism." Proceedings of the American Academy for Jewish Research 38/39 (1970/1971), Hebrew Section: 1-45.

This work which has historical and scholarly merit studies the opponents of Hasidism on their own terms. It interprets the characteristics of the Musar Movement -- a stress on Torah scholarship and a contention that devekut (that cleaving to God which is central in Hasidism) can be attained only by Torah study -- as responses to Hasidism. The musar method, he claims, maintains the structure of traditional Judaism but infuses it with the moral fervor found in Hasidism.

219 Ginzberg, Louis. "Israel Salanter." In Understanding Rabbinic Judaism: From Talmudic to Modern Times, edited by Jacob Neusner, 355-382. New York: Ktav Publishing House, 1974.

This glowing tribute by a modern scholar to the Yeshiva training of his youth demonstrates the power of the Musar Movement to inspire its disciples. It evokes the feeling and devotion associated with the Musar Movement.

220 Goldberg, Hillel. Israel Salanter, Text, Structure, Idea: The Ethics and Theology of an Early Psychologist of the Unconscious. New York: Ktav Publishing House, 1982.

This scholarly and impassioned in-depth study reviews all previous theories about Salanter's teaching, its relationship to modern psychology, and its historical context and importance. Goldberg provides a chronological schema by which to understand how Salanter's ethical system evolved in relationship to his changing contexts: the orthodoxy of his time first faced an internal crisis of moral and spiritual sterility; it then face the challenge of modernism and the assimilationist Enlightenment leaders.

221 Goldberg, Hillel, ed. Musar Anthology. Hyde Park: Harwich Lithograph Company, 1972.

See the annotation at 108.

222 Goldberg, Hillel. "Toward an Understanding of Israel Salanter." Tradition 16 (1976): 83-119.

A general reader may want to look at this brief article rather than at the lengthy study of 220. Here Goldberg suggests that Salanter's contribution to Jewish ethics is his program for training the moral soul. A bibliographical survey reveals that scholars have overlooked his most important insights on training human behavior.

223 Gottlieb, Mel. "Israel Salanter and Therapeutic Values." Tradition 14 (1974): 112-129.

This popular and nonscholarly article argues that Salanter's psychological insights can help modern Jews cope with contemporary problems. Human conflict and irrationality are part of daily experience, and Gottlieb illustrates how musar ideas can cope with them by using anecdotes about Salanter.

224 Katz, Dov. The Musar Movement: History, Personalities, and Method [Hebrew]. 2nd Edition, five volumes. Jerusalem: n.p., 1982.

While uncritical in approach this work is a magisterial survey of leading musar personalities, their lives and thought from Israel Salanter into the mid-twentieth century. Primary sources from the movement itself are used uncritically to produce an enjoyable and fascinating, but intellectually unsatisfying narrative.

225 Lamm, Norman. "Scholarship and Piety," in Faith and Doubt, 212-246. New York: Ktav Publishing House, 1971.

Lamm offers a valuable critical study of the relationship of study and piety and reviews the example of moral heroes who were also heroes of Torah and suggests that the pursuit of morality does not conflict with or contradict the commandment to devote oneself entirely to the study of Torah. The essay is not entirely favorable to the Musar Movement as such. He demonstrates the primacy of scholarship even among its leaders to show that more than just piety is needed for a full Jewish life.

226 Leibowitz, A.H. "Chochmas HaMusar." In Building Jewish Ethical Character, edited by Joseph Kaminetsky and Murray I. Friedman, 55-60. New York: The Fryer Foundation, 1975.

This traditionalist explanation of musar which should be used with caution as an "insider" presentation, emphasizes that its purpose is self-perfection. It considers ethical training a complement to the learning of Torah law and as motivation for halakhic living.

227 Neusner, Jacob. "Reform Through Tradition," in Understanding Rabbinic Judaism: From Talmudic to Modern Times, 353-354. New York: Ktav Publishing House, 1974.

In a useful introduction to Ginzberg's article on Israel Salanter (see 219) Neusner points out that two movements as different as the traditional Musar Movement and the radically oriented German Reform Movement were both responding to the challenges of modernity by stressing ethics. The movements differed since while Salanter considered ethics as rooted in traditional religion; the Reformers used ethics to make religion less traditional.

228 Pachter, Mordecai. *Israel Salanter: Selected Writings* [Hebrew]. Jerusalem: Bialik Institute, 1972.

This scholarly presentation of primary material by Israel Salanter and the useful introduction accompanying it is a valuable introduction to musar teachings and to Salanter in particular. Pachter selects texts that indicate Salanter's view of the moral value of study, of ethical training, and of human nature. The relationship between ethics and traditional Judaism becomes clear in these selections.

229 Rachlis, Arnold. "The Musar Movement and Psychotherapy." *Judaism* 23 (1974): 337-345.

In this popular and uncritical presentation of the Musar Movement, Rachlis advocates its modernity and importance. He interprets the Musar Movement as one response to modernity that in contrast to Hasidic emotionalism stresses self-understanding. This approach, he argues, is peculiarly modern and is parallel to Adlerian psychotherapy.

230 Schwartz, Elkanah. "The Pursuit of Perfection." In *Building Jewish Ethical Character*, edited by Joseph Kaminetsky and Murray I. Friedman, 246-251. New York: The Fryer Foundation, 1975.

This advocate position should be read as part of an "insider's" argument. While not essential reading it shows how contemporary Jews utilize musar teachings. The article demonstrates the continuity of a peculiar moralistic style that blends traditional scholarship and piety.

231 Sher, Isaac Aisik. *Collection of Ethical Discourses* [Hebrew]. Bnai Brak: Slovadka Yeshiva of Bnai Brak, 1968.

This collection of Hebrew writings encapsulates the musar tradition from Lithuania to contemporary Jerusalem and offers fruitful material for scholarly study. The varied discourses included center on themes of fear and love of God, ritual observances and the virtuous life. Remarkably the themes and ideas show no change in a period that includes life before and during the Nazi Holocaust in Europe and afterwards in Israel.

232 Ury, Zalman F. *The Musar Movement*. New York: Yeshiva University Press, 1970.

This study of the Musar Movement is meant to awaken an imitation of its qualities in American Jews and is not an academic study but a call for committed emulation of an ideal model. Ury surveys the history of the movement and gives anecdotes about its great leaders. He sees the movement as relevant today in teaching the necessity for self-discipline, the study of Torah and training of the emotions and personal character. The last section is devoted to theological and philosophical issues that concern the modern Jew -- freedom of the will, the problems of contemporary morality and social life.

233 Ury, Zalman F. "Bridging the Gap Between Ethical Theory and Practice." In Building Jewish Ethical Character, edited by Joseph Kaminetsky and Murray I. Friedman, 38-46. New York: The Fryer Foundation, 1975.

Taking Israel Salanter as a model Ury develops the idea that musar is the striving to go beyond Jewish law. Salanter contributed to the development of Jewish ethics by developing his ideas in action and thereby, according to Ury, provided a needed model for modern Jews struggling to give meaning and significance to their lives. Ury suggests that contemporary Jewish day school movement should be understood in terms derived from the nineteenth century Jewish ethical movement.

234 Ury, Zalman F. "The Legacy of Rabbi Israel Salanter." In Building Jewish Ethical Character, edited by Joseph Kaminetsky and Murray I. Friedman, 159-167. New York: The Fryer Foundation, 1975.

Once again the nineteenth century model of the Musar Movement is used, through a study of its founder, in order to demonstrate the new roles and responsibilities of contemporary Jews. Jewish ethics today draw strength from that earlier period. Ury is clearly a disciple of the Musar Movement who sees in the work of Rabbi Israel Salanter and his followers a model that contemporary Jews can use to cope with modernity. In this work he argues that this resource of Torah study should not be overlooked and must play a leadership role in shaping the future of traditional Judaism in the modern world.

THE ETHICS OF HASIDISM

235 Bratzlaver Hasidic Foundation. Book of Longsuffering [Hebrew]. Brooklyn: Moriah Offset, 1976.

This ethical text from the Bratzlaver Hasidic tradition mixes interpretations of biblical and rabbinic passages with homiletical stories and exhortations. Central themes include simplicity of living and faith, dependence upon God alone, domestic tranquility and the raising of children, care of orphans, coping with disease and distress, aiding the poor, the needy, and welcoming guests, and the ethical value of studying Torah.

236 Bulka, Reuven. "Hasidism and Logotherapy: An Encounter through Anthology," in Mystics and Medics: A Comparison of Mystical and Psychotherapeutic Encounters, 104-118. New York: Human Sciences Press, 1979.

Bulka provides a fascinating comparison between ideas and values expressed in Hasidic literature (using Newman's Hasidic Anthology) and in the Logotherapy writings of Viktor Frankl. Bulka is not impartial but is a vigorous proponent of both Logotherapy and traditional Judaism. Despite his enthusiasm the critical reader might comment that the values adduced are rather simplistic and general.

237 Dan, Joseph. "Introduction." In The Teachings of Hasidism, 1-36. Edited by Joseph Dan with the assistance of Robert J. Milch. New York: Behrman House Publishing Company, 1983.

In the introduction to this excellent English language anthology Dan suggests that the most important element in Hasidic teaching is not the lore and stories but the moral guidebooks and sermonic literature associated with it. Dan notes that Hasidism rejects the cosmic mysticism of the kabbalah and puts in its place the faith in the zaddik, the Hasidic leader, and communal loyalty. Important texts by Hasidic moralists are included.

238 Faierstein, Morris. "Hasidiana Americana: A Survey of American Literature on Hasidism." Conservative Judaism 35 (1982): 66-74.

This essay looks at the way popular literature and theology has understood Hasidism. The writings of Abraham Heschel, Elie Wiesel, and Samuel Dresner are examined. The author notes the appeal of the Hasid as a Jewish model for American Jews. Hasidism is often used as an ethical example, a symbol of the interplay of religion and morality in Jewish life. The social concerns of both Heschel and Wiesel are reflected in the way in which they retell Hasidic stories.

239 Friedman, Maurice. "Hasidism and Contemporary Man," in Touchstones of Reality: Existential Trust and the Community of Peace, 143-181. New York: E.P.Dutton and Company, 1974.

Friedman, the foremost interpreter of Martin Buber and a graceful writer, interprets Hasidism with ethical sensitivity and clear moral concerns. He relies upon Martin Buber's tales of the Hasidim and his interpretation of Hasidism to demonstrate the Hasidic ideal of community. On the basis of this ideal he argues that Hasidism teaches contemporary human beings the value of social loyalty and faithfulness through community. Friedman's transformation of story into social vision is a model of how Jewish mystical writings can be utilized in contemporary Jewish ethical reflection.

240 Greeves, Zeev. <u>Hasidic Conduct Literature as an Expression of Ethics</u>. Thesis submitted to the Senate of the Hebrew University. Jerusalem: Hebrew University, 1979.

This scholarly work contends that Hasidic moral teachings were directly responsible for the spread and popularity of Hasidism, especially the type created by Rabbi Nahman of Bratzlav. He traces the development of these books which offered pithy guidance to Hasidim from Dov Baer, the major organizer of the Hasidic movement through the period of Rabbi Nahman. He claims that this literature resolves the tension that can exist between a spiritual quest for self-perfection before God and the demand for social reform. This type of study demonstrates the place of Hasidic ethics in the Jewish moral tradition.

241 Heschel, Abraham Joshua. <u>A Passion for Truth</u>. New York: Farrar, Straus, and Giroux, Inc., 1973.

Heschel, a popularizer of Hasidism, investigates how a moral teacher must stand in tension with the status quo. He suggests an affinity between the Christian theologian Soren Kierkegaard and the Hasidic master Rabbi Mendel of Kotsk. In the course of showing that both were iconoclasts who sought to revitalize the tradition of which they were a part he provides a background on early Hasidism and its ethics (the Baal Shem Tov and his first followers) and the moral teachings of the later masters. This book is a useful contribution to ecumenical ethics.

242 Kuperstok, Nathan. "Extended Consciousness and Hasidic Thought." In <u>Mystics and Medics: A Comparison of Mystical and Psychotherapeutic Encounters</u>, 87-97. Edited by Reuven Bulka. New York: Human Sciences Press, 1979.

As with many of the essays in Bulka's anthology (see 102) this is a fervent defense of traditional Judaism using modern categories. The point that Kuperstok argues is that contemporary people need to go beyond linear thinking to experience the mystic dimension of reality. Hasidism provides an opportunity within the framework of traditional Judaism for just that extension of consciousness that is necessary today. The essay is rather simplistic and popular but is a good example of how contemporary traditional Jews show the relevance of their beliefs to the needs and concerns of people in the world today.

243 Mintz, Jerome. "Ethnic Activism: The Hasidic Example." <u>Judaism</u> 28 (1979): 449-464.

Mintz's study notes that the American context affords Hasidism, for the first time a political forum in which to put their ideas into practice. Although the essay is focused on America the same dynamics can be witnessed in Israeli Hasidism and as such is a valuable sociological study. It can also be found in Bulka (102), 225-241.

244 Nadler, Allan. "Piety and Politics: The Case of the Satmar Rebbe." Judaism 31 (1982): 135-152.

Nadler explores the adaptation of Hasidism to modernity and examines how the Satmar Rebbe became involved in politics from pietistic motivation. This is worth reading as a present day example of Hasidic ethics as applied to a specific social situation.

245 Nathan, of Nemirov. Rabbi Nahman's Teachings. Trans. by Aryeh Kaplan. n.p.: n.d.

This translation of a major Bratzlaver Hasidic text is annotated with particular reference to contemporary ethical and moral questions. Of significance is the discussion of the relationship between ethics and Judaism. Judaism, it is contended, is not an ethics. Ethics is secular; Judaism is a revealed religion in which God's word and not philosophical virtues provide the basis for human action. The work is recommended both as a classical text in Jewish ethics and as an example of how classical works continue to have modern significance.

246 Rotenberg, Mordecai. Dialogue with Deviance: The Hasidic Ethic and The Theory of Social Contraction. Philadelphia: Institute for the Study of Human Issues, 1983.

Rotenberg's sociological approach makes a rather tendentious theory of Jewish ethics of particular interest. This study attempts to provide a comprehensive theory of Jewish ethics through a study of certain themes found predominantly in Hasidism. Rotenberg suggests that Hasidism presents the paradigm case of Jewish ethics as "alter-centered." By this he means that the individual attains personal salvation through working for the good of others and of the community. He seeks to prove this point by analyzing certain Hasidic stories, tales by the Hebrew writer Agnon, and by looking at certain midrashic material. He contends that the mystic idea of "tzimtzum" or the contraction of God at creation is a symbol of that personal self-contraction that ethics demands. His ideas are stimulating, his contrast between the Protestant Ethic and the Hasidic Ethic is certain to be controversial, and his writing is engaging. The argument, however, suffers from being ad hoc rather than grounded in academic study of Hasidism.

247 Schiller, Mordechai. "Some Thoughts on Hasidism." Tradition 19 (1981): 99-109.

Ethics and Hasidism are closely related in the modern mind and Schiller takes that into account in his explanation of its appeal. He contends that modern Jews have become disenchanted with modernity. They are seeking self-transcendence and are disillusioned with a materialistic culture. The "non-linear" thinking espoused by Hasidism offers an alternative to modern materialism and its lack of morality. This article is not so much an analysis of a phenomenon as a persuasive polemic intended to show the validity and attractiveness of a traditional morality through references to Hasidism.

248 Schochet, J. Immanuel. "The Philosophy of Lubavitch Activism." Tradition 13 (1972): 18-35.

Schochet suggest that Lubavitch Hasidism is active in its attempt to return Jews to their roots and their tradition because of a piety that contents that loving others means bringing them into the midst of society. This dramatic love of neighbor is suggested here as the theological basis for the active involvement of Lubavitch Hasidism in communal life. This article is less scholarship than datum for understanding American Jewish ethics.

249 Wiesel, Eli. Somewhere-A Master: Further Hasidic Portraits and Legends. Trans. by Marion Wiesel. New York: Summit Books, 1982.

The ethical relevance of this collection of Wiesel's retelling of Hasidic tales is clear in the emphasis he places upon community. The leaders who are the heroes of his stories here always play a role in forming, maintaining, and creating communal life. Their sayings and stories show the relationship between the leader and the community, and for Wiesel, demonstrate the moral interdependency of the individual and the group. The entire book can be seen as an essay in the necessity for the individual to contribute to the group and the significance of the group as a basis for individual life.

250 Wineman, Aryeh. "Torah into Prayer: 'Leqqutei Tifillot'." Conservative Judaism 35 (1982): 43-49.

This scholarly article focus on how Rabbi Nahman of Bratzlav's disciple Rabbi Nathan transformed his master's teachings into prayers. Wineman finds in this process an ethical principle -- the distinction between study and prayer is blurred. There is an obscuring of the word of God to human beings and the response of human beings to God. Wineman surveys a number of basic teachings and subjects and points to the difference in nuance between the expression of these ideas as teachings and as prayers.

MODERNITY AND ETHICS: GENERAL APPROACHES

251 Agus, Jacob Bernard. "Three Pathways from a Tradition-centered to a Humanistic Ethic," in The Vision and The Way: An Interpretation of Jewish Ethics, 220-251. New York: Frederick Ungar Publishing Company, 1966.

This illuminating chapter in Agus' survey (see 002) provides useful background for the transition from premodern to modernity. Agus sketches the trends in contemporary Jewish ethical thinking and offers a summary of views important for understanding modern Jewish ethics. Agus traces the development of a modern Jewish approach to ethics through the fifteenth century Italian Jewish poet-philosopher Leone Ebreo (Judah Abrabanel) through the secularist Baruch Spinoza to Moses Mendelssohn.

252 Agus, Jacob Bernard. "The Vision and the Way in the Nineteenth Century" in The Vision and The Way: An Interpretation of Jewish Ethics, 253-320. New York: Frederick Ungar Publishing Company, 1966.

This chapter in Agus' survey (see 002) is indispensable for comprehending the themes of contemporary Jewish moral writings. The issues of the modern period as developed after the challenge of Enlightenment had established the framework of discussion are suggested in relationship to a number of modern Jewish ethicists: Hermann Cohen, Moritz Lazarus, Ahad HaAm, Hasidism, Samuel David Luzzatto, Israel Salanter, Martin Buber, and Franz Rosenzweig among others. While Agus sees each of these thinkers as part of a great dialogue of Jewish ethics, each thinker was propounding not a pluralism but an independent view of Judaism. Agus' synthesis is attractive, but it is his own and not the vision of the thinkers he studies.

253 Ahren Yitzhak and Porter, Jack Nusan. "Martin Buber and the American Jewish Counter Culture." Judaism 29 (1980): 332-339.

This study notes the influence of Martin Buber on American Jews in the Jewish Counter Culture. Perhaps the most important insight is that Buber's attractiveness lies in his rejection of an external Jewish "norm" that permits ethics and morality to be subjective rather than absolute. This attractiveness in Buber's thought for modern Jews, however, may be a philosophical liability. The ethical appeal of Buber should be noted as an important element in his popularity among contemporary Jews.

254 Berenbaum, Michael. The Vision of the Void: Theological Reflections on the Works of Elie Wiesel. Middletown: Wesleyan University Press, 1979.

This study explores the way Elie Wiesel and Richard Rubenstein recast Jewish ethics in the light of the Nazi Holocaust. While both affirm humanity in the face of human destructiveness, Rubenstein argues for a new realism while Wiesel stimulates a modern moral consciousness by reference to the absence of any moral sensitivity in the face of the Holocaust. This book should be read as an illuminating study of literature in its role as shaper of ethical values. Compare 270 and 294.

255 Berkovits, Eliezer. Faith After the Holocaust. New York: Ktav Publishing House, 1973.

Berkovits considers the two major events in modern Jewish history, the Nazi slaughter of six million Jews and the creation of the State of Israel as evidence that the modern age is bereft of ethical restraint. He argues that the moral principles needed in modern life can be found only in Jewish life and teachings. For important criticisms of this work see Fox (268) and Katz (281).

256 Berkovits, Eliezer. Major Themes in Modern Philosophies of Judaism. New York: Ktav Publishing House, 1974.

The various essays in this collection provide a traditionalist critique of various alternative types of Jewish thinking. Hermann Cohen, Martin Buber, Franz Rosenzweig, and Mordecai Kaplan, and Abraham Heschel are considered and their views and Jewish theology are reviewed. Many sections of these essays are of interest to those studying modern Jewish ethics.

257 Bourel, Dominique. "Exigencies du Liberalism de Mendelssohn." Recherches de Science Religieuse 66 (1978): 517-532.

Bourel considers whether Mendelssohn's view of Judaism, with its emphasis on universal ethics, its liberalism, and its defense of Jewish practice was a compromise to the needs of his times. Bourel studies Mendelssohn's apologetic writings, his antipathy towards Spinoza, and his attitude toward the Enlightenment. She concludes that his was an honest and legitimate presentation of Judaism, making no concessions to modernity.

258 Branson, Roy. "The Individual and the Commune: A Critique of Martin Buber's Social Philosophy." Judaism 24 (1975): 82-96.

Branson suggests the Buber's social thought is limited to a criticism of I-It existence and an emphasis on the corporate I-Thou. This approach, he contends, overlooks the necessity for power in establishing social justice. Ethics demands a double consciousness: of the need for social structures and of the corruption of the individual by sin. Buber is criticized for failing to recognize these realities of communal institutions that leads him into a naive and unrealistic ethics. Branson overlooks Buber's recognition of the need for institutions as well as the realism that always tempered his Zionism.

259 Breslauer, S.D. "Modernizing Jewish Ethics." Encounter 43 (1982): 143-156.

This essay is focused on the way selected contemporary Jewish thinkers reevaluate Jewish parochialism, view of human nature, and hope for social progress in the light of two modern events: the Nazi slaughter of six million Jews and the establishment of the State of Israel.

260 Cohen, Hermann. Reason and Hope: From the Jewish Writings of Hermann Cohen. Trans. by Eva Jospe. Bnai Brith Jewish Heritage Classics. New York: W.W.Norton and Company, 1971.

This judicious selection and translation of Hermann Cohen's writings on Jewish themes reveal his ethical analysis of Judaism and German culture, of the Hebrew prophets and the messianic ideal, of Zionism, and of the self. Judaism, for Cohen, was representative of both religion and ethics and was not important "merely" for its ethical monotheism but as an exemplar of religious ethics generally.

261 Cohen, Hermann. Religion of Reason, Out of the Sources of Judaism. Trans. by Simon Kaplan. New York: Frederick Ungar Publishing Company, 1972.

This translation of Cohen's mature thinking is an excellent introduction to his view of Judaism as an exemplar of ethical monotheism. It shows how ethics dominated his view of Judaism. The book is a compendium of expositions of moral teachings concerning compassion, reconciliation, and messianism. Cohen's view has been criticized as lacking in Jewish content but the moral seriousness and Jewish passion that animates his concerns are clearly evident.

262 De Greef, J. "Ethique, Reflexion, et Historie Chez Levinas." Revue Philosophique Louvain 67 (1969): 431-460.

This essay suggests that for Levinas ethics takes precedence over metaphysics, morality over ontology. He suggests that Levinas considers ethics a historical category that has its own, nonphilosophical reality. This emphasis on the historical has often been associated with Judaism and is not new with Levinas. It is curious to see the same themes reoccuring in Jewish thinkers who have been influenced by differing traditions -- Kantian, Existentialist, Phenomenological, and Hegelian. Whether this commonality represents a Jewish consensus can, of course, be disputed.

263 Deitrich, Wendel. "The Idea of Messianic Mankind in Hermann Cohen's Later Thought." Journal of the American Academy of Religion 48 (1980): 245-258.

Deitrich notes that Cohen's thought rejects the idea of personal, individual immortality. The promise of immortal life, however, becomes an ethical concept for Cohen. Humanity as a messianic ideal will perpetuate and continue the highest human values. It is in the unity of humanity, achieved through imitation of the divine unity, that true immortality is possible -- an ethical immortality as humanity reaches its moral goals and thereby gives everlasting life to those who sought the ethical ideal.

264 Downing, Christine R. "Guilt and Responsibility in the Thought of Martin Buber." Judaism 18 (1969): 53-63.

Since Buber's ethics are focused on the I-Thou relationship both guilt and responsibility can be reduced to whether one is open to such relationship and enters authentically into such relationship. Downing criticizes the vagueness implicit in such a view of guilt and responsibility. The actual writings of Buber, however, suggest that he understood guilt and responsibility in very concrete, detailed ways.

265 Ebbinghaus, J. "Deutschum und Judentum bei Hermann Cohen." Kant-Studien Deutsch 60 (1969): 84-96.

Ebbinghaus explores the relationship Cohen establishes between Judaism and Germanism. He looks at the way Cohen sought to reconcile the two traditions and demonstrate their identity. He notes that Cohen's view of Jewish ethics and his emphasis on its universalism was influenced by his dedication to the German ideal.

266 Edel, Abraham. "Some Current Trends in Ethical Theory." Journal of the Central Conference of American Rabbis (1968): 50-62

This survey of modern ethical theory begins by looking at Kant's demands for moral autonomy and suggests that the search for moral rules in modern philosophical ethics has led to an uncertainty about the absolute nature of religious regulations. This is a clear analysis of the philosophical problem that has shaped liberal Judaism. It is reprinted in Silver (126), 9-28.

267 Fackenheim, Emil L. "Idolatry as a Modern Possibility," in Encounters Between Judaism and Modern Philosophy: A Preface to Future Jewish Thought, 171-198. New York: Basic Books Inc., 1973.

Fackenheim rejects those thinkers who insist that idolatry is a modern temptation when understood not as a literal worship of pagan gods but as the substitution of some subsidiary value for the divine will. While Will Herberg and Abraham Heschel may extend the concept of idolatry to include ethical pluralism Fackenheim sees this as the result of the influence of Christian theology. He suggests that Jewish thinkers return to the more literal understanding of idolatry found within the tradition itself.

268 Fox, Marvin. "Law and Ethics in Modern Jewish Philosophy: The Case of Moses Mendelssohn." Proceedings of the American Academy for Jewish Research 43 (1976): 1-14.

The modern problem within which Jews must wrestle, Fox declares, is that of justifying a parochial legal system while declaring ethics a universal, human phenomenon. Moses Mendelssohn sought to solve this dilemma by stressing that Judaism is a revealed legislation not a revealed ethics. Ethics are universal, but Judaism has a special mode of training in order to attain those ethics. Fox rejects this dichotomy between law and ethics that was accepted by many modern Jewish thinkers who followed Mendelssohn.

269 Fox, Marvin. "Review Essay: Berkovits' Treatment of the Problem of Evil." Tradition 14 (1974): 116-124.

Fox analyzes Berkovits' investigation of belief in God after the Holocaust (see 255). He questions the argument for the necessity of evil on the basis of God's self-restraint and raises the objection that if the ethical ideal is imitation of God then human beings should imitate such restraint. If value comes from the deeds of God then a God beyond values cannot be acceptable.

270 Friedman, Maurice. "Elie Wiesel: The Job of Auschwitz," in The Hidden Human Image: A Heartening Answer to the Dehumanizing Threats of Our Age, Delta Book, 106-134. New York: Dell Publishing Company, 1974.

The thought of Elie Wiesel is an important aspect of contemporary Jewish ethics (see Berenbaum, 254, and Roth, 294). Friedman suggests that his thought represents the ethical stance of the survivor who struggles with and against God.

271 Gordis, Robert. "A Basis for Morals: Ethics in a Technological Age." Judaism 25 (1976): 20-43.

Gordis finds American civilization suffering from a crisis of ethical nihilism. He claims that while science can improve human knowledge and provide the raw material for ethics, only a transcendent source of value can offer the perspective from which a morality based on scientific evidence can be developed. Gordis suggests that Jewish sources provide that transcendent basis. Judaism, in his view, has a firm grasp upon natural law; in the decalogue, Leviticus 19, Micah, and the conception of Noahide morality Judaism suggests a universal ethical standard. Gordis utilizes Jewish sources creatively, but might be accused of stretching the tradition of universalism too broadly.

272 Goren, Arthur A., ed. Dissenter in Zion: From the Writings of Judah L. Magnes. Cambridge: Harvard University Press, 1982.

This anthology of writings reveals the radical pacifism and ethical views of this unique type of Zionist. Judah L. Magnes, a Reform rabbi, spiritual Zionist, and educator, was dedicated to a rebirth of Jewish religious and ethical values. He was more a moral thinker than a political figure and this collection of his work shows him in that role.

273 Guibal, Francis. "Une Religion D'Adultes." Esprit 9 (1980): 157-165.

See the annotation at 045.

274 Heilprin, Irving. "The Claim of Responsibility in Malamud's The Assistant." Conservative Judaism 29 (1975): 63-67.

This analysis of Malamud's novels turns into a discussion of the basic ideas in Jewish ethics. Heilprin sees Malamud as an interpreter of the moral and ethical values in Judaism. His heroes suffer for the Law; they learn that it is good to sacrifice oneself for others. This ethical sensitivity is, according to Heilprin, rooted in Jewish tradition, and he suggests that novelists like Malamud are the exponents of that tradition in the modern context.

275 Henning, Gunther. Philosophie des Fortschritts: Hermann Cohens Rechtfertingung. Munich: Wilhelm Goldmann Verlag, 1972.

Hermann Cohen's philosophy emphasized optimism and hopefulness for the future. Henning examines Cohen's idea of "progress" within the context of a Marxist analysis of society. While religion is not subservient to ethics in Cohen's thought, messianic hope does tend to reinforce bourgeois ethics. This view of ethical monotheism is fascinating although the Marxist analysis is somewhat forced since Cohen was as much a critic of emancipated Jewish social life as a supporter of it.

276 Jonas, Hans. Philosophical Essays: From Ancient Creed to Technological Man. Englewood Cliffs, New Jersey: Prentice-Hall, 1974.

This collection of essays contains a number of reflective studies on the problems confronting modern religious individuals. Whether studying Gnosticism, technology, or the way in which religious values have shaped modern Western culture Jonas is provocative and stimulating. Among the important essays dealing with modernity are "Jewish and Christian Elements in Philosophy: Their Share in Shaping the Modern Mind," pp. 21-44 and "Contemporary Problems in Ethics from a Jewish Perspective," pp. 168-182, also found in Journal of the Central Conference of American Rabbis (1968): 27-39, and in Silver (126), 27-38.

277 Jospe, Eva. "Hermann Cohen's Judaism: A Reevaluation." Judaism 24: (1976): 461-472.

Cohen's perspective on Judaism has relevance for modern Jews even if his reduction of the variety of Judaism to one category -- ethical monotheism -- may be limiting. Jospe suggests that in the moral chaos of modernity Cohen's goal orientation, messianic humanism, and ethical seriousness are important contributions. Jospe argues that Cohen can still offer guidance to modern Jews. Reading this essay will demonstrate how Jews have struggled with religious ethics in the modern period. It is reproduced as the introduction to 260.

278 Kaplan, Edward. "Martin Buber and the Drama of Otherness: The Dynamics of Love, Art and Faith." Judaism 27 (1978): 196-206.

This essay argues that while Buber's ethics seems to lie in the inclusive unity of the I-Thou relationship this emphasis may be misleading. Buber makes otherness his central category. The ethical imperative is to affirm the authenticity and independence of the other. Buber's ethics, aesthetics, and religious views are focused around the key concern of allowing the other to remain a unique, irreducible reality that cannot be dissolved into the self.

279 Kaplan, Simon . "Introduction." In Hermann Cohen, Religion of Reason, Out of the Sources of Judaism, xi-xxii. Trans. by Simon Kaplan. New York: Frederick Ungar Publishing Company, 1972.

This perceptive introduction to Hermann Cohen's major work on Jewish religion and ethics summarizes the prominent themes in it. Kaplan stresses the dialectic between philosophy and religion, between reason and piety. He suggests that for Cohen revelation initiates a process of ethical reflection rather than supplies a set of conclusions. Since the goal of religious living is ethical self-perfection Cohen stresses the eternal task of human life rather than any detailed maxims.

280 Katz, Robert L. "Martin Buber and Psychotherapy." Hebrew Union College Annual 46 (1975): 413-431.

Katz argues that Buber's contribution to ethics lies in his view of human nature and psychology. Buber sees the human being as "present" with the ethical "duty" of including the other within the self and of including oneself in the other. Katz considers this insight of ethical value in contrast to other theorists who claim that this view lacks the detail and realism needed in a modern morality.

281 Katz, Steven. Post-Holocaust Dialogues: Critical Studies in Modern Jewish Thought. New York: New York University Press, 1983.

Katz reviews the position of the major Jewish thinkers of modern times -- Buber, Berkovits, Rubenstein, and Ignaz Maybaum and concludes that Kantian ethics has had a deleterious influence on all modern Jewish thinkers and suggests that the dichotomies between the individual and society and between authority and autonomy are misleading ones. Insofar as Cohen and Buber, for example, remain within the Kantian framework they are unable to grasp the basis of Jewish ethics; insofar as they have liberated themselves from that framework they move towards a new understanding of Judaism. Katz raises controversial issues about major Jewish thinkers and provides a critical analysis of perplexing issues in modern Jewish thinking. Naturally moral reflection as focused on the problem of law and autonomy and on the problem of evil raised by the Nazi Holocaust is central to both the thinkers he reviews and his discussion of them. Compare 255, 268.

282 Kegley, Charles W. "Martin Buber's Ethics and the Problem of Norms." Religious Studies 5 (1969): 181-194.

Kegley wonders if Buber's rejection of philosophical and ethical systems as vain attempts to find universal categories is a strength or weakness since the personal approach Buber espouses confuses ethical reflection by exaggerating the uniqueness of each moral situation. Rather than subjective response some objective criteria is needed in ethical decision making.

283 Kluback, William. Hermann Cohen: The Challenge of a Religion of Reason. Brown Judaica Studies 53. Chico: Scholars Press, 1984.

This extended study of Hermann Cohen's evolution from a Kantian to a Jewish view of the virtues and ethics traces Cohen's development and shows how he eventually makes Isaiah 53 and the virtue of compassion the central aspect of his thought. This scholarly analysis presents a helpful contrast between Cohen's ethical optimism and Christian ethical pessimism.

284 Knoff, Josephine Z. "The Ways of Mentschlekhayt: A Study of Morality in Some Fiction of Bernard Malamud and Philip Roth." Tradition 13 (1973): 67-84.

Knoff analyzes the ethical spirit animating the fiction of two Jewish writers and suggests that they draw their moral conviction from the Jewish tradition. She discovers the ethical impulses in their writings as a subconscious drawing on Jewish resources for a moralization of modernity. This essay shows how Jewish ethics has assumed the form of literature in modern writings.

285 Lawton, Philip W. Jr. "A Difficult Freedom." Tijdschrift Voor Filosophie 37 (1975): 681-691.

Lawton suggests the centrality of ethics in Levinas' view of Judaism. The Jew according to Levinas is to provide the model of moral responsibilty that will be the basis for human unity in justice. Dialogue can occur only when people meet and adhere truthfully to their basic principles rather than agree out of indifference to basic beliefs. The ideas of Levinas are interpreted here as a call for meaningful interfaith discussion, discussion that goes beyond surface agreements to essential differences of worldview.

286 Levinas, Emmanuel. "Aimer La Thora Plus Que Dieu," in Difficile Liberte: Presence Du Judaism, 189-193. 2nd edition. Paris: Albin Michel, 1976.

Levinas is not only a modern philosopher but also reflects critically on Jewish thinkers in the contemporary period. This essay begins by reflecting on modern Jewish thought and some responses to the Holocaust. It continues by stressing the need for pious humility as well as ethical dignity in human life. Compare 067-070 and 288.

287 Levinas, Emmanuel. "La Pensee Juive Aujourdui," in Difficile Liberte: Presence Du Judaism, 209-218. 2nd edition. Paris: Albin Michel, 1976.

This essay is both an exercise in critical analysis and an interpretation of Jewish ethics. Levinas stresses that Judaism establishes the ethical link between human beings. He sees the State of Israel and the kibbutz experiment in particular as a link with prophetic ethics. This review of modern Jewish thinkers is also a statement of belief in Jewish ethical ideals.

288 Levinas, Emmanuel. "To Love the Torah More than God." Trans. by Harriet A. Sugarman and Richard I. Sugarman, with a commentary by Richard I. Sugarman. Judaism 28 (1979): 216-223.

See annotation at 068.

289 Levine, Norman. "The Tragedy of Bourgeois Cosmopolitanism: On Martin Buber's Politics." Judaism 30 (1981): 427-433.

Buber's politics is derived from ethical universalism that, according to Levine, skewed its emphasis from political reality to culture. Such an ethics is impossible since it undermines the seriousness of parochial, particularistic interests. These interests are the basis of politics and Buber's cosmopolitanism is a vestige of the bourgeois class system that he sought to transform. Compare the Marxist analysis of Hermann Cohen in 275.

290 McCollester, Charles. "The Philosophy of Emanuel Levinas." Judaism 19 (1970): 344-354.

Levinas is interpreted as a moral philosopher who criticizes modern philosophy for separating itself from its religious roots. Philosophy, he suggests, begins in the moral experience and can only understand itself by reference to that experience. Judaism offers contemporary thinkers a means of transcending the dialectic of history and thereby of coming to terms with the meaning of justice and ethics. McCollester is clearly more impressed with Levinas' moral seriousness and his view of Judaism as a religion of ethics than with the phenomenological philosophy and metaphysics that undergirds this moral approach.

291 Novak, David. "Universal Moral Law in Hermann Cohen." Modern Judaism 1 (1981): 101-117.

After reviewing various theories of the Noahide laws in Judaism Novak concentrates on Cohen's presentation of them. Novak notes Cohen's objections to Moritz Lazarus and his use of Kantian ethics. This is a valuable study in the ethics of law and the Noahide codes as well as a historical review of Cohen and his view of Jewish ethics.

292   Rosenfeld, Leonora Cohen. " The Judaic Values of a Philosopher: Morris Raphael Cohen." Jewish Social Studies 42 (1980): 189-202.

Morris Raphael Cohen's views are presented as exemplifications of his Jewish values. There is actually little distinctively "Jewish" about Cohen's philosophy, but the article is valuable in showing how secular Jewish thinkers maintained their connection with and roots in the Jewish community.

293   Rotenstreich, Nathan. From Mendelssohn to Rosenzweig: Jewish Philosophy in Modern Times. New York: Holt, Rinehart, and Winston Company, 1968.

The first chapters of this book look at ethics and the basis for modern Jewish religion. Rotenstreich analyzes liberal thinkers like Hermann Cohen and Moritz Lazarus and traditionalists like Samuel David Luzzatto. After Cohen, however, he sees the emphasis shift from ethics to the ontological. This interpretation, however, misses much of the moral seriousness that not only Buber but also Leo Baeck and Franz Rosenzweig shared.

294   Roth, John K.   A Consuming Fire: Encounters with Elie Wiesel and the Holocaust.   Atlanta: John Knox Press, 1979.

Roth argues that Wiesel's novels helps Jews focus on new moral questions raised by the twin events of the Holocaust and the modern State of Israel. He perceives the humanistic element in Wiesel and interprets it as an ethical challenge. Compare 254 and 270.

295   Schwarzschild, Steven S. "The Tenability of Herman (sic!) Cohen's Construction of the Self." Journal of the History of Philosophy 13 (1975): 361-383.

In a technical but valuable study Schwarzschild shows how Cohen's view of the self, as set out in his Religion of Reason is parallel to that of more modern thinkers -- Erik Erikson, Sartre, Strawson, and Husserl. Cohen's emphasis upon God as the source of the ethical correlation whereby a self comes into being is stressed. Cohen's philosophy is presented as a major statement of individualism and ethical responsibility.

296   Schweid, Eliezer. "Hermann Cohen as a Biblical Exegete." [Hebrew] Daat 10 (1983): 93-122.

Schweid investigates the method Cohen uses to make the Bible a suitable resource for philosophy. Cohen's stress on ethics, Schweid suggests, makes the Bible a fertile philosophical resource for him.

297 Schweid, Eliezer. "The Status and Value of the Individual in Spinoza." [Hebrew] Daat 11 (1983): 91-102.

Schweid notes that while Maimonides view of self-perfection demands social involvement Spinoza's individualistic approach concentrates on free thought and enlightened self-interest. That view, by removing social concern, set the stage for modern secular ethics.

298 Sole, Moshe Zeev. "Moritz Lazarus: The Ethics of Judaism," in On the Essence of Judaism [Hebrew], 100-104. Jerusalem: Keriyat Sefer, 1969.

Sole is not unsympathetic with Lazarus and points out how he turned from summarizing Jewish ethics to discussing the major concepts in Jewish ethical reflection. While Lazarus was not alone in his emphasis on the ethical in Judaism -- this was a hallmark of the Jews of the German Enlightenment -- he was unique in emphasizing the divine source of Jewish ethics. Theocratic values rather than personal autonomy was for him the basis of Jewish ethics even though ethics as such was autonomous and did not depend upon theology or law. In this way Lazarus was more traditional than many of his contemporary Jewish thinkers.

299 Strauss, Leo. "Introductory Essay." In Hermann Cohen, Religion of Reason, Out of the Sources of Judaism, xxiii-xxxviii. Trans. by Simon Kaplan. New York: Frederick Ungar Publishing Company, 1972.

Strauss sees Cohen's goal as that of harmonizing culture and Torah. This task, however, is a modern one and in view of Cohen's own sense of continuity with medieval Jewish thought must be questioned. Strauss interprets Cohen's identification of Jewish law with the moral law as one consequence of his approach. Some aspects of Cohen's philosophical work, according to Strauss, are superior to and more self-consistent than his interpretation of Judaism.

300 Ucko, Sinai. "Compassion: Remarks on Herman Cohen." [Hebrew] Iyyun 20 (1969): 23-28.

Ucko notes that Hermann Cohen's view of Judaism has not been as influential as some thinkers expected and reviews Cohen's work to correct this lack. He claims that Cohen is close to the traditionalist thinker Samuel David Luzzatto. He also claims that Cohen goes beyond the "dialogic" philosophers who do not fully explore the theological roots of the I-Thou relationship. Cohen, however, by emphasizing compassion shows that I-Thou meeting depends upon humanity's creation in the image of God, and image which provides the commonality binding all people together. This is claimed to be a distinctly religious and Jewish viewpoint.

301 Vogel, Manfred. "The Concept of Responsibility in The Thought of Martin Buber." Harvard Theological Review 63 (1970): 159-182.

Vogel shows that Buber raises the question of moral responsibility in two ways: what is my duty and to whom is my duty. The answer to the first is that my duty is responsiveness and it is addressed to the other in the I-Thou relationship. He criticizes this view as a weakening of moral norms.

302 Worob, Avraham. "Buber's Concept of the Self," in Duties of the Mind: Essays on Jewish Philosophy, 1-39. Edited by Nova Worob. Spring Valley: Shaare Emet, 1975.

Worob suggests that Buber's view of the self and its ethical task is related to Jewish mystical teachings. The Lurianic myth of sparks needing redemption, of the Shekinah (God's indwelling presence) sorrowing in exile, and of the importance of ethical obligations to others are adduced to show Buber's rooting in Jewish tradition. While Buber is clearly a self-consciously Jewish thinker his debt to the tradition is more intuitive than this essay suggests.

303 Wyschogrod, Edith. Emmanuel Levinas: The Problem of Ethical Metaphysics. The Hague: Martinus Nijhoff, 1974.

This detailed study of Levinas, his Kantian themes, his roots in Husserl and phenomenology, and his theory of ethics, devotes an entire chapter to Judaism and ethics, "Philosophy and the Covenant." While admitting that "Levinas refrains from the use of religious language" Wyschogrod decodes his thought using copious material from talmudic and rabbinic literature. Levinas, according to Wyschogrod, sees Judaism as a "counter current" to modernity. She shows how Judaism can integrated Kantian autonomy while being heteronomous; for Levinas Jewish "heteronomy" is awareness of the suffering of others and the will to respond to that suffering. Ritual is central as a means of inculcating that discipline that ethics demands. Wyschogrod analyses Levinas' view of atonement and the way in which he supports it by using talmudic texts.

304 Wyschogrod, Edith. "Martin Buber and the No-Self Perspective." In History, Religion, and Spiritual Democracy: Essays in Honor of Joseph L. Blau, edited by Maurice Wohlgelernter, 130-150. New York: Columbia University Press, 1980.

Buber's view of the self is contrasted with that in Zen Buddhism, a contrast of interest precisely because Buber used Zen stories to illustrate ideas about Hasidism. His rejection of Zen is, for Wyschogrod, connected with his

antipathy to Nietzsche whose anthropology he accepts while
condemning his rejection of values. In Buber's rejection of
the no-self on the one hand and of Nietzsche on the other
Wyschogrod finds his ethics: he affirms the self but not the
will to power that removes the self from its true goal--
that of encounter of the Thou. Buber's thinking can be
understood, then, as ethical even when it seems theological.

305 Yaffe, Martin D. "Liturgy and Ethics: Hermann Cohen
and Franz Rosenzweig on the Day of Atonement." Journal of
Religious Ethics 7 (1979): 215-228.

This careful study compares the interpretation each of these
thinkers gave to the ritual of the Day of Atonement. For
Cohen the ritual symbolized ethical integrity. Atonement is
an ethical act of return to moral living. For Rosenzweig it
means a return to faith, a redirection of the will to
religious goals. Clearly Yaffe means to indicate the type
of difference to which Rotenstreich points (293). Cohen
marks the culmination of the identification of Judaism with
ethics and Rosenzweig begins a concentration on the ontology
of being a Jew. These thinkers show a continuity of ethical
concern between the rationalist and existentialist
traditions in Judaism.

306 Zac, Sylvain. "Essence du Judaisme et Liberte de
Conscience." Les Nouveaux Cahiers 34 (1973): 14-29.

Mendelssohn's view of the "essence of Judaism" is useful in
determining the shape of modern Judaism. His view of
universal ethics and the necessity for liberty of conscience
in allowing different traditions to point the way to that
ethics can establish the positive value of both religion in
general and Judaism particularly.

MODERNITY AND JEWISH ETHICS: LIBERAL OPTIONS

307 Borowitz, Eugene B. Choices in Modern Jewish Thought: A
Partisan Guide. New York: Behrman House Publishing Company,
1983.

This survey of Jewish thought during the modern period
that incorporates much of an earlier book A New Jewish
Theology in the Making (Philadelphia: Westminster Press,
1968) dwells at length at the ethical interpretation of
Jewish religion in Cohen and Leo Baeck. Borowitz seeks to
show how a liberal form of Judaism can be faithful to both
covenant theology and ethical autonomy.

308 Borowitz, Eugene B. Reform Judaism Today III: How We
Live. New York: Behrman House Publishing Company, 1978.

See the annotation at 028.

309 Borowitz, Eugene B. "The Autonomous Jewish Self."
Modern Judaism 4 (1984): 39-56.

Borowitz restates his view that the central concern of liberal Jews has been a reconciliation of the autonomous ethical self with the authentic Jewish tradition. He surveys liberal thinkers -- Hermann Cohen, Martin Buber, Mordecai Kaplan -- to see how they resolve the dilemma of personal ethical responsibility and a communally created Jewish order of living.

310 Brusin, David. "The God of Mordecai Kaplan." Judaism 29 (1980): 209-220.

Brusin interprets Kaplan's naturalism as a means of emphasizing the imitation of God. Kaplan's theology is thus an ethics of action, a means of demonstrating the practical application of theoretical ideas. Brusin characterizes Kaplan's theology as a liberal Jew's interpretation of Micah's command to "love mercy, do justice, and walk humbly with God." Kaplan's theology is, thus, reinterpreted as an ethical interpretation of Jewish religion.

311 Ellenson, David. "Emil Fackenheim and the Revealed Morality of Judaism." Judaism 25 (1976): 402-413.

Ellenson reviews Fackenheim's confrontation with Kantian ethics and suggests that the liberal assumption of the primacy of autonomy is problematic. He analyzes the problem of interpreting Abraham's willingness to sacrifice Isaac and looks at that story in the tradition of existential Jewish philosophy. He notes that Fackenheim, like others who reject or wrestle with Kant, makes moral worth dependent upon independent ethical decision making and suggests limitations in that view. This essay investigates Fackenheim's approach and challenges his view by emphasizing the duties of covenant.

312 Fackenheim, Emil L. God's Presence in History: Jewish Affirmations and Philosophical Reflections. New York: New York University Press, 1970.

Fackenheim intimates a new turn in liberal Jewish thinking, drawing on the midrash and tradition to confront the Holocaust and the modern State of Israel. He discovers a new ethical demand addressed to the modern Jew: survival is an ethical necessity not only for the sake of Jews but for the sake of humanity.

313 Fackenheim, Emil L. Quest For Past and Future: Essays in Jewish Theology. Bloomington: Indiana University Press, 1968.

This collection of essays presents a liberal interpretation of Jewish theology and ethics. Fackenheim struggles with the ethical and theological questions of being a Jew in the modern world. See 355, 435, 493, 584, 627, 649. The most impressive essay is a confrontation with Kant (pp. 204-228) and is an expansion of his earlier "The Revealed Morality of

Judaism: A Confrontation with Kant." in Rediscovering Judaism: Reflections On a New Theology, edited by Arnold Jacob Wolf, (Chicago: Quadrangle Books, 1965), pp. 51-75. This classic study of moral obligation and liberal Judaism is an important contribution to contemporary ethics. It is reprinted in Kellner (111) pp. 61-83, and as "Abraham and the Kantians: Moral Duties and Divine Commandments," in Encounters Between Judaism and Modern Philosophy: A Preface to Future Jewish Thought (New York: Basic Books, Inc., 1973), pp. 9-29.

314 Fackenheim, Emil L. To Mend the World: Foundations of Future Jewish Thought. New York: Schocken Books Inc., 1982.

The title of this work reveals Fackenheim's debt to Jewish mysticism. The mystical idea that Jewish living can bring tikkun or mending to the world leads Fackenheim beyond liberal thinkers from Spinoza through Franz Rosenzweig to a new sense of Jewish moral obligation. He argues that the modern obligation for the Jew is that of survival, not for parochial interests but for moral reasons. Jewish safety is morally required for the welfare of humanity. See also 492.

315 Guttmann, Alexander. "The Moral Law as Halacha in Reform Judaism," in Studies in Rabbinic Judaism, 175-183. New York: Ktav Publishing Company, 1976.

Guttmann argues that the term halakha developed as a description of particular Jewish practices evolved after the biblical period. This is a provocative challenge to Reform Jews to cease using the term "moral law" as a substitute for halakha because such usage is a misuse of a historical category. The essay is reprinted in Reform Judaism: A Historical Perspective, Essays From the Year books of the Central Conference of American Rabbis, edited by Joseph L. Blau (New York: Ktav Publishing Company, 1973), 336-347.

316 Kraut, Benny. From Reform Judaism to Ethical Culture: The Religious Evolution of Felix Adler. Monographs of the Hebrew Union College 5. An I. Edward Kiev Library Foundation Book. Cincinnati: Hebrew Union College Press, 1979.

Kraut argues that the Ethical Culture Movement was not an outgrowth of Reform Judaism, but that even its founder, Felix Adler recognized that his ideas entailed a break with traditional Judaism. He foresaw his universalistic movement as a replacement for traditional religions of all sorts, even though his earliest followers were drawn from Reform Judaism. His ethical concerns and activist stance, however, deeply influenced the Reform Jewish Movement and its own moral activities.

317 Lubarsky, Sandra D. "Ethics and Theodicy: Tensions in Emil Fackenheim's Thought." Encounter 44 (1983): 59-72.

Emil Fackenheim's work needs careful study and Lubarsky's comments are lucid and helpful. She notes the various ways in which Jewish thinkers have responded to the Nazi Holocaust. She investigates Fackenheim's response in particular and finds that he has presented a new view of God and a new understanding of the divine-human relationship. She criticizes this view and suggests that the same presence of God in the realm of ethics is appropriate in history. Relationship involves limitations, and Fackenheim is criticized for not having focused on the human limitations in the divine-human encounter. Had Fackenheim remained true to relational theology and ethics, Lubarsky suggests, he could have seen God's presence at Auschwitz as that demanding mutuality and relationship from human beings even when most difficult.

318 Meyer, Michael A. "Problematics of Jewish Ethics." Journal of the Central Conference of American Rabbis (1968): 63-74.

Meyer surveys the problems of developing a liberal Jewish ethics. He looks at nineteenth and twentieth century Jewish thinkers who face the issues of acculturation, universalism, and maintaining continuity with the Jewish past. While rejecting the views of Moritz Lazarus he affirms the position of Hermann Cohen. The modern liberal Jew, he suggests, can find much of value in Cohen's messianic outlook. This essay is reprinted in Silver (126), 111-129.

319 Samuelson, Norbert. "Can Democracy and Capitalism Be Jewish Values?: Mordecai Kaplan's Political Philosophy." Modern Judaism 3 (1983): 189-215.

Samuelson notes that Kaplan focused on "factors of crisis" as a means of coping with the problems of modern Judaism. This led to his reconstruction of such concepts as the chosen people, salvation, and Torah. The political organization of society -- capitalism and democracy -- also needed to be integrated into Jewish theology. Kaplan noticed that time spent on earning a living exceeded that spent on the traditional mitzvoth or commandments. Samuelson suggests that Kaplan makes the notion of economic goods a moral good in his restructuring of Judaism. Mitzvah, thereby, coincides with the ethical activities that Jews in fact pursue.

320 Samuelson, Norbert. "Revealed Morality and Modern Thought." Journal of the Central Conference of American Rabbis (1969): 18-30.

Samuelson begins his review of liberal Jewish ethics by asking general philosophical questions. He questions the verifiability of the relationship between God and the collective personality of Israel. The major part of the essay, however, is a review of Fackenheim's view of Kant (see 313) He considers autonomy less essential for morality than relationships between persons. A self-contradictory moral demand, he claims, is one that if fulfilled destroys the possibility of relationship. That view refutes both the problem and the solution offered by Fackenheim. In the face of the argument that morality depends upon an ethics of relationship rather than autonomy Fackenheim could only respond that he is arguing from the standpoint of the actor, not from an external moral standpoint abstracted from the real situation. The individual is responsible for decision making and cannot be held responsible for incidental results of that decision. The moral question raised by Kant is that of "the perfectly good will" and not of "the perfectly good act." When that distinction is recognized then the criticism that Fackenheim ignores the morality of relationship misses the mark. See the reprinting of this essay in Silver (126), 131-150 and in Kellner (111), 84-99.

321 Scult, Mel. "The Sociologist as Theologian: The Fundamental Assumptions of Mordecai Kaplan's Thought." Judaism 25 (1976): 345-352.

Scult maintains that Kaplan viewed religion as concerned with morality and self-perfection. His restructuring of Judaism sought to make its tradition more capable of enabling Jews to reach those aims. He reinterpreted Jewish religion as an instrument for cultivating values and perfecting the self.

322 Swyhart, Barbara Ann. "Reconstructionism: Hokhmah as an Ethical Principle." Judaism 24 (1975): 436-445.

Kaplan's work is interpreted as an "ethical reshaping" of Judaism. He saw his task as discovering the central values of American life and translating them into Jewish categories. Democracy was thus translated into the category of covenant. The basic religious principle according to Swyhart was "wisdom" (in Hebrew hokhmah) that is the source of values accessible to all rational beings rather than revelation.

TRADITIONAL RESPONSES TO MODERNITY

323 Bulka, Reuven. Different Paths, Common Thrust: The Shoalogy of Berkovits and Frankl." Tradition 19 (1981): 322-339.

Bulka interprets both Berkovits and Frankl as authentically Jewish responses to the Holocaust. In contrast to Richard Rubenstein (see 591, 592) these thinkers represent traditional Judaism and its affirmation of life and God's goodness. In contrast to Emil Fackenheim (see 312-314) they do not see the Holocaust as a transitional event needing a new type of Judaism. While Berkovits is unaware of his similarity to Frankl, and in fact rejects Frankl as a secularist, Bulka is convinced that both share what might be called a traditionalist perspective on the Holocaust.

324 Harris, Monford. "The Theologico-Historical Thinking of Samuel David Luzzatto." Jewish Quarterly Review, n.s., 52 (1962): 216-244, 309-334.

Harris looks at Luzzatto's defense of Judaism as both universalistic (following the model of Abraham) and particularistic (following the model of Moses). He contrasts Luzzatto, the traditionalist, with the ethics of Buber or the Reform leaders. His basic concern was neither progress or reason but love of Judaism. His aim was not to demonstrate the common human element in Jewish religion but rather the uniqueness of Israel's faith. This he discovered in an ethics of love, compassion, and sympathy in contrast to Spinoza's ethic.

325 Hartman, David. "Soloveitchik's Response to Modernity: Reflections on 'The Lonely Man of Faith'," in Joy and Responsibility: Israel, Modernity and the Renewal of Judaism, 198-231. Jerusalem: Ben-Zvi Posner, 1978. Publication of the Shalom Hartman Institute for Judaic Studies.

The traditionalist response of Soloveitchik's existentialism is placed in historical perspective. Buber, Fackenheim, Heschel and other recent Jewish writers are analyzed in contrast to Soloveitchik. Hartman notes that contemporary Jewish thinkers are uneasy with the halakhic sensibility.

326 Kasher, Naomi. "Leibowitz's View of Religion in Relationship to Kantian Ethics." In Sefer Yeshiyahu Leibowitz: A Collection of Essays on his Thought and in his Honor [Hebrew], edited by Asa Kasher and Jacob Levinger, 21-34. Tel Aviv: Tel Aviv University Student Association, 1977.

Kant can be utilized, with changes, by traditional Jews. Yeshiyahu Leibowitz provides one example of such utilization. There are profound similarities and differences between Kant and Leibowitz. Leibowitz does not see Judaism as a means to an end but as categorically universal. Mitzvoth are interpreted as ethical imperatives that apply to all Jews universally and are thus autonomously accepted by each Jew as an act of reason. Leibowitz's traditionalism takes Kant's categories and transfers them to Jewish religious categories.

327 Kurzweil, Z'vi. "Universalism in the Philosophy of Rabbi Joseph B. Soloveitchik." Judaism 31 (1982): 459-471.

This essay examines major themes in Soloveitchik's exposition of the two types of human character and suggests that his central values are are precisely those at the heart of secular western culture: creativity, originality, spontaneity, authenticity. Soloveitchik, then, not only widens the Jewish ideal to include these values but imputes to humanity as a whole the alienated condition indicated by the theological category of exile. This essay demonstrates how contemporary Orthodox Jewish thought draws from and works with elements in contemporary non-Jewish thought. Kurzweil concludes that in his confrontation with modernity Soloveitchik has reinforced universalism while working to restore the balance between it and <u>halakhic</u> life.

328 Levi, Zeev. "Judaism and Humanistic Values." In <u>Sefer Yeshiyahu Leibowitz: A Collection of Essays on his Thought and in his Honor</u>, edited by Asa Kasher and Jacob Levinger [Hebrew], 119-127. Tel Aviv: Tel Aviv University Student Association, 1977.

See the annotation at 066.

329 Levitz, Irving. "Crisis in Orthodoxy: The Ethical Paradox." In <u>Dimension of Orthodox Judaism</u>, edited by Reuven Bulka, 380-386. New York: Ktav Publishing House, 1983.

There has been a contemporary revival of traditional Jewish life that is both promising and challenging to contemporary Orthodox Judaism. This analysis of contemporary Jewish action and theory shows a dichotomy between deed and preaching. Religious self-righteousness leads to practical immorality. Orthodox Jews are urged in this article to live up to their own commitments. This essay shows both self-criticism and the continuation of the "reproof" genre of Jewish moral writing.

330 Margolies, Morris. <u>Samuel David Luzzatto: Traditionalist and Scholar</u>. New York: Ktav Publishing House, 1979.

Margolies sees Luzzatto's ethics as the key to his ability to reconcile modernity and traditional Judaism. He suggests that by distinguishing between Judaism, that emphasizes kindness and righteousness, and Greek thought, that emphasizes intellectual attainments, Luzzatto found the way in which Judaism could contribute to the modern world. This is clearly an advocate position but does introduce the reader to a fascinating modern Jewish thinker.

331 Motzkin, Aryeh, Leo. "Spinoza and Luzzatto: Philosophy and Religion." <u>Journal of the History of Religion</u> 17 (1979): 43-51.

This basically expository article explains Luzzatto's opposition to Spinoza. This opposition was based, according to the author, on Luzzatto's view that philosophy, derived from the Greeks, could only provide rational and intellectual stimulation. Pity and compassion derive from religion and therefore ethics must depend upon religion rather than philosophy for guidance. Luzzatto's complaint against Spinoza was thus an ethical one and his defence of Judaism lay in its deep morality.

332 Niewohner, Frederich. "Isaac Breuer und Kant: ein Beitrag zum Thema: Kant und Das Judentum." Neu Zeitschrift fur Systematische Theologie und Religionsphilosophie 17 (1975): 142-150; 19 (1977): 172-185.

Usually Kant is associated with the liberal Jewish thinkers. Niewohner's informative article shows how a Neo-Orthodox Jewish leader used Kant as a means of confirming the ontological priority of Torah categories. Torah in this philosophy is said to provide the "a priori" categories by which all of reality is to be understood.

333 Rosenberg, Shalom. "The Position of Religious Ethics." In Sefer Yeshiyahu Leibowitz: A Collection of Essays on his Thought and in his Honor [Hebrew], edited by Asa Kasher and Jacob Levinger, 138-145. Tel Aviv: Tel Aviv University Student Association, 1977.

See the annotation at 084.

334 Rosenblum, Noah H. Luzzatto's Ethico-Psychological Interpretation of Judaism: A Study in the Religious Philosophy of Samuel David Luzzatto. New York: Yeshiva University Press, 1965.

This examination of Luzzatto shows his ethical concerns, provides a useful biographical sketch, and suggests how his moral philosophy enabled him to unite modernity and Judaism. It is an extended study that demonstrates how he developed an ethical interpretation of Judaism not only out of the sources of Judaism but out of the needs and situation of a traditionalist caught in a changing world.

335 Schwarzbach, Bertram E. "Halakah et Values Seculaires la Philosophie Religieuse de Y. Leibowitz. Les Nouveaux Cahiers 16 (1980): 30-42.

Leibowitz is shown to struggle with science, biblical fundamentalism, and the need for transforming Jewish law in a modern Jewish state. His difference from the liberals and Reform Jews is stressed; nevertheless he seeks to establish a new, vital, and compelling halakhic world. A renovated Jewish law will be able to cope with both the problems and the opportunities of modernity. His emphasis upon revelation as working through halakha rather than directly through the Bible permits him a flexibility when grappling with modernity.

336 Shapiro, David. "The World Outlook of Rabbi Kook." In Samuel K. Mirsky Memorial Volume: Studies in Jewish Law, Philosophy, and Literature, edited by Gersion Appel, Morris Epstein, and Hayim Leaf, 75-100. Jerusalem: Sura Institute for Research; New York: Yeshiva University Press, 1970.

After summarizing Kook's outlook Shapiro notes that for Kook secular values are insufficient to motivate ethics. Kook claims that secularity lacks depth and that morality can only be rooted in God. Judaism, according to this view, has a universal significance in being able to redeem the world from evil. This approach is a common one in traditional defenses of Jewish ethics. Shapiro's clear style contributes to the value of the essay. This article is reprinted in Shapiro (125), 285-315.

337 Soloveitchik, Joseph B. "On the Love of Torah and the Redemption of the Religious Spirit," in In Aloneness, In Togetherness: A Selection of Hebrew Writings, 401-433. Edited by Pinchas Peli. Jerusalem: Orot, 1976.

Soloveitchik confronts the issues and problems of living as a traditional Jew in the modern world. He distinguishes between the State of Israel as a theological necessity and the government of Israel as a practical reality. He looks at the revival of religious interest and the life of the Orthodox Jew.

338 Worob, Avraham. "The Guide to the Repentant," in Duties of the Mind: Essays on Jewish Philosophy, edited by Nova Worob, 52-58. Spring Valley: Shaare Emet, 1975.

Worob draws on medieval and early modern authors, including Maimonides, Bachya, Salanter, and the Shulhan Arukh, in order to guide modern Jews back to their tradition. This is a modernized handbook for morality addressed not to those within the tradition but to those struggling to regain it.

3
Issues in Jewish Ethics

HALAKHA, AGGADAH, AND JEWISH ETHICS

339 Agus, Jacob Bernard. "Faith and Law," in Dialogue and Tradition: The Challenges of Contemporary Judeo-Christian Thought, 427-444. New York: Abelard-Schuman Publishing Company, 1971.

Agus argues that both law and faith, inner response and external directives are needed in human religious life. This type of reconciliation of the two modes of religious action is typical of Jewish thinkers. The problem of justifying a religion of law while espousing the depth-religious nature of Judaism is presented because Judaism sees the performance of mitzvoth, of commanded deeds as the basic mode of entering into relationship with God.

340 Agus, Jacob Bernard. "A Theological Foundation for the Halacha." Judaism 29 (1980): 57-63.

This essay is part of a response to a challenging statement by Robert Gordis (see 361). For Agus the halakha is a response to the duality of life as related to the duality of the divine interaction with the world. Agus presents his basic approach here but concisely focused on the issue of the dynamic nature of halakha. This essay is reproduced in Agus (001), 195-202.

341 Agus, Bernard Jacob. "The Virtue of Obedience," in The Vision and the Way: An Interpretation of Jewish Ethics, 92-127. New York: Frederick Ungar Publishing Company, 1966.

This chapter (see 002) surveys the give and take between autonomy, heteronomy, and theonomy (the rule of God) in Judaism. This is a judicious look at the traditions of sage, mystic, and rationalist in the Jewish legal tradition and their ethical implications. The question of the place of law in Judaism and its relationship to pietist faith is discussed.

342 Amiel, Moshe Avigdor. "Social Justice, Legal Justice and Our Justice." In <u>Between Man and His Fellow: Treatises on Human Relations in Judaism</u> [Hebrew], 3-83. Translations and Collections From Israel's Wisdom. Jerusalem: Mossad Harav Kook, 1975.

See the annotation at 020.

343 Appel, Gersion. "A Rational Conception of Mitzvot." In <u>Samuel K. Mirsky Memorial Volume: Studies in Jewish Law, Philosophy, and Literature</u>, edited by Gersion Appel, Morris Epstein, and Hayim Leaf, 21-33. Jerusalem: Sura Institute for Research; New York: Yeshiva University Press, 1970.

See the annotation in 189.

344 Artz, Raphael. "Imperative and Conscience in Jewish Law: An Interview with Raphael Artz." In <u>The New Jews</u>, edited by James A. Sleeper and Alan L. Mintz, Vintage Books, 144-151. New York: Random House Inc., 1971.

Artz considers Jewish observance as a means of creating personal holiness. He notes the difference between observing the commandments and enhancing the beauty of them; that latter has become a major aim of his work, he says. This aim influences many Jews who make the law more than mere obedience to an external authority and rather an extension and expansion of their selfhood. He sees his view of the commandments as part of a program that will reaffirm the key values in Judaism and recommend a positive program of Jewish existence.

345 Berkovits, Eliezer. <u>God, Man and History: A Jewish Interpretation</u>, 99-114. 3rd Printing. New York: Jonathan David Publishing Company, 1979.

This reprinting of a classic statement of Jewish theology is an extraordinary interpretation of Jewish law. The idea of revelation is the pivotal concept around which an investigation of ethics, the holy deed, theology, and the Jewish people is organized. <u>Halakha</u> is the central category in Judaism for Berkovits, and he explains it as a means of relationship whereby individuals confront God and discover their ethical task. See particularly pp. 99-114 and below entries 421, 422.

346 Berkovits, Eliezer. "Authentic Judaism and the Halakha." <u>Judaism</u> 19 (1970): 66-76.

This clear and dynamic defense of traditional Jewish ethics examines the "ethos of the <u>halakha</u>" and concludes that authentic Judaism is filled with humanitarian, ethical considerations. Berkovits uses traditional ethical categories to show how Jewish law measures up to them rather than claim that the <u>halakha</u> is itself the essence of morality. The essay is reprinted as "The Centrality of the Halakha," in Neusner (121), 63-72.

347 Bleich, J. David. "Halakha as Absolute." Judaism 29 (1980): 30-37.

In response to the challenge by Robert Gordis (see 361) Bleich asserts that halakha is an absolute value of its own. He claims that it is not dominated by an independent ethical principle that regulates its development but is rather an expression of an inherent ethical impulse. While this is a consistent traditionalist position it should be contrasted with that of Berkovits (345, 346) who insists on maintaining a difference between halakha and the ethics involved in it.

348 Bokser, Ben Zion. "The Struggle for Change." Judaism 29 (1980): 43-48.

Bokser introduces a note of caution into the discussion of change and development in halakha by suggesting that not every conflict between morality and law can be resolved. Only some, certainly suggestive, cases demonstrate the primacy of ethics. As a traditionalist within Conservative Judaism he recognizes that some changes are necessary; he also demands that they be made with care. Compare 361 and the other references to this discussion found there.

349 Borowitz, Eugene B. Reform Judaism Today III: How We Live. New York: Behrman House Publishing Company, 1978.

See the annotation at 028 and 308 and compare with 309.

350 Breslauer, S. Daniel. "'I and Thou' and Jewish Ritual," in The Chrysalis of Religion: A guide to the Jewishness of Buber's "I and Thou", 68-97. Nashville: Abingdon Press, 1980.

Although ostensibly devoted to the problem of ritual this chapter provides a vivid summary of Buber's view of Jewish law. Buber is contrasted to Samson Raphael Hirsch and Franz Rosenzweig as one modern alternative to traditional views of the halakha and its ethics. Buber's view of halakha as a moral teaching rather than a dogmatic legalism is discussed at length.

351 Bulka, Reuven. "The Role of the Individual in Jewish Law." Tradition 13/14 (1973): 124-136.

Bulka is at his strongest when discussing psychology; this essay in Jewish theology is a bit general and weak. In discussing the meaning of halakha and Jewish law Bulka stresses the humanistic element within it. He sees it as a means of eliciting the best within an individual and thus as an aid in personal development. Traditional law is thus more than legalism; it stimulates moral growth.

352 Bulman, Nachman. " Reason, Emotion, and Habit in the training of a Torah Personality." In Building Jewish Ethical Character, edited by Joseph Kaminetsky and Murray I. Friedman, 28-37. New York: The Fryer Foundation, 1975.

While traditionalist in focus this article is a serious grappling with human nature, Judaism, and the teaching of Torah. The tension between musar ethics and halakhic rigor is recognized but the former is presented as a call for rigorous self-immersion in the halakhic literature. The author considers this call particularly relevant in the modern world. The dichotomy between ethics and law is thus overcome since ethical ideals arise out of familiarity with the legal tradition.

353. Dorff, Elliot. "The Interaction of Jewish Law and Morality." Judaism 26 (1977): 453-466.

Elliot Dorff, a Conservative Jewish theologian, contends that there is no ethic independent of the halakha. He suggests that the reality of morality is established by the legal obligations of the halakha and therefore no ethics independent of that law is possible. This is an important challenge to much of modern Jewish ethical thought.

354 Elkins, Dov Peretz. "A New Meaning for Mitzvah," in Humanizing Jewish Life, 210-213. New York: A.S. Barnes and Company, 1976.

This theological interpretation of mitzvah is a challenging contention that Jewish law must be rooted in morality. The central concept of mitzvah, according to Elkins, needs a new interpretation other than a heteronomous law imposed on the individual. Elkins suggests such a new interpretation-- mitzvah refers to "the fulfillment of the growth needs, health needs, and higher needs" of human beings.

355 Fackenheim, Emil L. "The Dilemma of Liberal Judaism," in Quest for Past and Future: Essays in Jewish Theology, 130-147. Bloomington: Indiana University Press, 1968.

Fackenheim suggests that the problem of the law as commandment is the central problem facing the liberal Jew. The two must be distinguished in his view. The law discloses only itself, the commandment discloses its giver as well. Because obedience to the commandment is motivated by a desire to enter into relationship with the commander it includes both a religious and ethical component.

356 Fox, Marvin. "Law and Ethics in Modern Jewish Philosophy: The Case of Moses Mendelssohn." Proceedings of the American Academy for Jewish Research 43 (1976): 1-14.

See the annotation at 268.

357 Fox, Marvin. "On the Rational Commandments in Saadiah's Philosophy: A Re-examination." Proceedings of the Sixth World Congress of Jewish Studies 3, edited by Avigdor Shinan, 33-43. Jerusalem: World Union of Jewish Studies, 1977.

See the annotation at 170.

358 Galston, Miriam. "The Purpose of the Law According to Maimonides ." Jewish Quarterly Review, n.s., 69 (1978): 27-51.

See the annotation at 171.

359 Gewirtz, Leonard, "The Innovations of Modern Orthodoxy." Sh'ma 14 (1983): 20-21.

This defense of Orthodoxy against the charge that it has become stagnant and has lost the dynamic quality of traditional Judaism claims that it has indeed made dramatic changes in modern times. The attitudes toward Zionism, the use of a sermon, and the confrontation of modern science and halakha are cited as evidence that Orthodoxy has not abandoned the principles of growth and development. The response of Robert Gordis (364) shows the value of the short, direct, and focused format of Sh'ma.

360 Gordis, Robert. "Authority in Jewish Law." In Conservative Judaism and Jewish Law, edited by Seymour Siegel and Elliot Gertel, 47-78. Studies in Conservative Jewish Thought 1. New York: The Rabbinical Assembly of America, 1977.

Gordis updates, for this volume, a survey of Conservative Jewish views on the authority of Jewish law. He focuses on the importance of moral ideals as standards and on the practical ways of implementing these standards.

361 Gordis, Robert. "A Dynamic Halakha: Principles and Procedures of Jewish Law." Judaism 28 (1979): 263-282.

This challenging and controversial article claims that Jewish law advances and changes because of new ethical insights. Gordis cites examples from Jewish tradition to support his claims: the laws of inheritance, of the rebellious son, of monogamy, all underwent modification to meet the changed ethical awareness that had developed. He suggests that other changes are now needed because of a modern moral awareness. See the discussion in 340, 347, 348, 390.

362 Gordis, Robert. "The Ethical Dimension in the Halakhah." Conservative Judaism 26 (1972): 70-74.

Gordis, focusing on articles by Seymour Siegel (410), endorses the claim that Jewish law is a responsive, developing entity that is shaped by the moral and ethical value-concepts of Judaism. He chooses examples that demonstrate how the halakha is a process in which ethical values and concerns shape the direction of growth.

363 Gordis, Robert. "The Halakha: Past, Present, Future: A Reply to the Responses." Judaism 29 (1980): 85-109.

This article responds to criticism called forth by 361. Gordis remarks that the two extremes -- Orthodox and Reform Judaism -- are united in rejecting his view of the halakha. The Orthodox Jew claims that halakha never changes and should not change now; the Reform Jew charges that halakha never changes and therefore should be entirely rejected.

364 Gordis, Robert. "The Innovations of Modern Orthodoxy." Sh'ma 14 (1983): 21-22.

Gordis repeats his interpretation of Judaism as an evolving religious system. He charges that the substance of Judaism should change to more fully approximate its ethical ideals, but that modern Orthodoxy has not made such changes. A polemical tone in both this and the preceding entry lend a passion to the exchanges in Sh'ma and should be read with this in mind.

365 Greenberg, Simon. "Ethics and Law in Judaism," in The Ethical in the Jewish and American Heritage, 157-218. Moreshet 4. New York: The Jewish Theological Seminary of America, 1977.

This comprehensive study analyzes the principles of Jewish law and focuses on specific issues: women, family life, civil law, and the Sabbath. An earlier version of this work is "Ethics, Religion, and Judaism I," Conservative Judaism 26 (1972): 85-126. See the full annotation at 010.

366 Guttmann, Alexander. "The Moral Law as Halakha in Reform Judaism." In his Studies in Rabbinic Judaism, 175-183. New York: Ktav Publishing House, 1975.

See the annotation at 315.

367 Halivni, David Weiss. "Can A Religious Law be Immoral?" In Perspectives on Jews and Judaism: Essays in Honor of Wolfe Kelman, edited by Arthur A. Chiel, 165-170. New York: Rabbinical Assembly of America, 1978.

This seminal article argues against the view that there is an independent ethos that can determine whether a religious law is moral or not. Halivni insists that the talmudic view identifies God's will and morality. The halakha is itself the basis for determining what is and what is not moral. The idea of conflict between ethics and Torah is, traditionally, an absurdity.

368 Hartman, David. "Halakha as a Ground for Creating a Shared Spiritual Language." Tradition 16 (1976): 7-40.

This article moves quickly from an analysis of covenant community as understood by Joseph Soloveitchik to call for a common Jewish religious language. It suggests that halakha can provide that language since the meaning if not the details of the commandments represent universal ethical values. Hartman confronts those thinkers who, like Yeshiyahu Leibowitz, disagreed with him and stimulated considerable debate (see 380, 388, 416). See also Hartman (047), 130-161.

369 Hartman, David. "Risk and Uncertainty in Halakha," in Joy and Responsibility: Israel, Modernity, and the Renewal of Judaism, 93-129. Publication of the Shalom Hartman Institute for Judaic Studies. Jerusalem: Ben Zvi Posner.

Hartman combines philosophical sophistication and traditionalism to present a view of halakha drawing insights from both traditional and liberal thinkers. Torah is understood in the context of existential anxiety.

370 Herzog, Isaac. Judaism: Law and Ethics. New York: Soncino Press, 1974.

This collection of essays demonstrates by its comprehensive and inclusive scope the interaction of law and ethics, commandment and morality. See 051, 141, 142, 174.

371 Jacobs, Louis. "Halakha and History: Separate Realms." Sh'ma 13 (1983): 124-125.

Jacobs suggests that Judaism is not "panhalachism." There are separate realms for history and for halakha so that obedience to law and recognition of change go together.

372 Jung, Leo. "Keddusha-Holiness," in Between Man and Man, 62-68. 3rd enlarged edition. New York: Board of Jewish Education Press, 1976.

Jung claims that the halakha entails going beyond the law to the ethical duty of foregoing one's legal advantage for the sake of the other. Ethics is higher than the law not because it is more lenient than it but because it is more demanding. This reverses the contention that Judaism is a religion of law and demonstrates that it demands an ethical standard far higher than mere legalism. See 058 and pp. 167-173 of the Hebrew version.

373 Kadushin, Max. "Halakha and Aggadah: Jewish Law and Concretizing Jewish Value Concepts." In Conservative Judaism and Jewish Law, edited by Seymour Siegel and Elliot Gertel, 217-236. Studies in Conservative Jewish Thought 1. New York: The Rabbinical Assembly of America, 1977.

See the discussion at 143 since this represents a selection from pp.59-93 of that entry.

374 Klein, Isaac. "An Approach to Halakha," in Responsa and Halakhic Studies, 128-134. New York: Ktav Publishing House, 1975.

Klein, an articulate Conservative Jew, distinguishes between aggadah and halakhah by calling the former the emotional motivation for ethical behavior and the latter the concrete details of behavioral norms. His essay demonstrates traditionalist thinking in Conservative Judaism and its theological basis for affirming halakhah as independent of external ethical considerations.

375 Konvitz, Milton R. "The Rule of Law: Torah and Constitution," in Judaism and the American Idea, 53-68. New York: Schocken Books Inc., 1980.

Konvitz provides a clear, persuasive argument to show that the principles governing Jewish law and American government are remarkably similar. One such principle that Konvitz sees as central in both traditions is the refusal to bow before power; secular leadership is to be governed by the law and not to dominate this. This principle was threatened in both Jewish history and recent American history, and Konvitz defends its utility and philosophical importance.

376 Konvitz, Milton. "Law and Morals." Conservative Judaism 23 (1969): 44-71.

This thoughtful essay notes that morality in Judaism was the province of the priest -- who delineated what could be done -- and the prophet -- who demanded what ought to be done. It reviews biblical concepts and passages distinguishing between specific moral injunctions and general guidelines, while maintaining that in Judaism morality, law, and religion were never separate. He reinforces this view by studying Greek thought from Plato through Aristotle and finding the same sense of the law as, ideally, identical with moral wisdom.

377 Korn, Eugene B. "Ethics and Jewish Law." Judaism 24 (1975): 201-214.

Korn looks at the question raised by Plato's Euthyphro of whether the good is good because God prefers it or whether God prefers the Good because it is good and concludes that Judaism acknowledges certain moral principles that are independent of Jewish law. Some controversial cases such as capital punishment are examined in the light of this conclusion and the essay ends by considering the ethical meaning of Abraham's willingness to sacrifice his son.

378 Lamm, Norman, "Scholarship and Piety," in Faith and Doubt: Studies in Traditional Jewish Thought, 212-246. New York: Ktav Publishing House, 1971.

See the annotation at 225.

379 Landman, Leo. "Law and Conscience: The Jewish View." Judaism 18 (1969): 17-29.

This important study of social ethics focuses on civil disobedience but also examines the relationship of concrete law to a so-called "higher law" of morality and is therefore relevant here. The problem of such a "higher law" of conscience is that it differs from person to person. It is unreliable since it depends on the individual's capacity for accepting it and cannot be legislated as social law.

380 Leibowitz, Yeshiyahu. "Practical Commandments, " in Judaism, the Jewish People, and the State of Israel [Hebrew], 13-36. Tel Aviv: Schocken Books Inc., 1976.

This excellent essay by a major Israeli scholar contends with the meaning of the commandments, the question of autonomy, the relationship between ethics and divine legislation. It argues that there is only a religious rationale for Jewish living: the commandments cannot be rationalized on psychological, philosophical, or sociological grounds; this view has aroused admiration and disagreement among Leibowitz's critics.

381 Leibowitz, Yeshiyahu. "For its own sake and not for its own sake," in Judaism, the Jewish People, and the State of Israel [Hebrew], 311-314. Tel Aviv: Schocken Books Inc., 1976.

This short essay continues the themes of the previous entry. The mitzvoth or commandments are parochial: they are specifically addressed to the Jewish people. Leibowitz raises the question of whether Jewish law can be understood as universal or as particularistic and insists that the commandments cannot be interpreted as a universal ethics.

382 Leibowitz, Yeshiyahu. "What is biblical ethics to a Jew?," in Judaism, the Jewish People, and the State of Israel [Hebrew], 350-357. Tel Aviv: Schocken Books Inc., 1976.

This exchange of letters with an Israeli educator explains why Jewish teaching (the Torah) is important even if it does not provide new information. Torah is a guide and a means to religious experience. It is not, according to Leibowitz, a source of human knowledge, but rather Jews are dependent upon revelation to develop ethical awareness.

383 Leiser, Benton M. "Rely on Tradition it Transcends Itself." Sh'ma 5 (1975): 302-303.

This essay, reflecting the informal approach of Sh'ma, suggests that halakha is in fact representative of an independent morality. As such it has no need of the radical revision of either Reform or Conservative Judaism.

384 Lichtenstein, Aaron. The Seven Laws of Noah. New York: Rabbi Jacob Joseph School Press, 1981.

See the annotation at 149.

385 Lichtenstein, Aharon. "Does Jewish Tradition Recognize an Ethic Independent of Halakha?" In Modern Jewish Ethics: Theory and Practice, edited by Marvin Fox, 52-88. Columbus: Ohio State University Press, 1975.

This essay combines scholarly knowledge and sensitivity to moral issues. Lichtenstein examines the meaning of both morality and law seeking to find if the phrase "beyond the line of the law" (see 133) suggests an ethic independent of the halakha. He sees in this phrase a recognition that the laws of Judaism have their force and motivation in the divine origin ascribed to them. Since this motivation implies more than legalism it makes an ethics inherent in religious sensitivity. This essay is reprinted in Kellner (111), 102-113.

386 Loewe, Raphael. "Potentialities and Limitations of Universalism in the Halakha." In Studies in Rationalism: Judaism and Universalism, edited by Raphael Loewe, 115-150. London: Routledge and Kegan Paul Ltd., 1966.

This perceptive essay focuses on two questions: is every Jew necessarily included in "the world to come" as the Talmud states and as Jewish philosophers were at pains to rationalize and how does Judaism and its law apply to non-Jews? Loewe surveys the Noahide laws in rabbinic and medieval Jewish literature and discovers an ambiguity that he says is the mark of distinction between a self-consciously "Jewish" thinker and a modern humanist.

387 Marmur, Dov. "In the Light of the Torah," in Beyond Survival: Reflections on the Future of Judaism, 117-155. London: Darton Longman and Todd Ltd., 1982.

In a popular but seriously considered study of Jewish law Marmur focuses on the tension between "ought" and "can" in Jewish life. He suggests that Jewish law makes action -- especially at home -- a central ethical category. Judaism is, thus, a deed-oriented religion that considers moral action rather than faith primary. This is a valuable liberal interpretation of Torah.

388. Marx, Tzvi. "A Rejoinder to a Rejoinder on 'Halakha as a Ground for Creating a Shared Spiritual Language.'" Tradition 18 (1979): 99-110.

This article defends the position of David Hartman (369) against the criticism of Solomon Spiro (416). Marx contends that only a more pluralistic response to the variety of Jewish options is practical in the Israeli context. A messianic hope that eventually all Jews will follow halakha and thus have a traditional commonality is, he contends, unrealistic and therefore supports Hartman's suggestions as a welcome opportunity for pluralistic dialogue. The controversy demonstrates tensions within Orthodox Judaism and it conception of halakha and ethics.

389 Meltzer, Yehuda. "Ethics and Halakha Once Again" [Hebrew]. Iyyun 26 (1978): 256-264.

Meltzer, discussing the implications of Leibowitz' view of law and ethics (see 380-382), suggests that the moral justifications for halakha are often overlooked. The conclusion he draws is that while theoretical discussions may resolve the question of ethics and halakha the practical decisions facing the believing Jew are difficult particularly in the areas in which morality and halakha seem farthest apart.

390 Mihaly, Eugene. "Halakha is Absolute and Passe." Judaism 29 (1980): 68-75.

Mihaly, as spokesman for a liberal interpretation of Reform Judaism, argues that halakha cannot accommodate the ethical advances of modern times. The energies and creativity of Jews, he suggests, should go towards evolving a viable ethics. While "fundamentalist" Jews criticized Robert Gordis for emphasizing the dynamics of Jewish law too much, Mihaly criticized him for being too traditionalist (see 361 and the references there).

391 Milishanski, Jacques K. "The Essence of the Halakha," in Studies in Hebrew Law and Lore: Values and Evaluations [Hebrew], Part 1, 205-223. Jerusalem: Neuman Press, 1976.

This detailed analysis of Jewish law and ethics traces the roots of halakhic authority to revelation and divine legislation. Halakha itself is presented as the concretization of the idea of commandment.

392 Neusner, Jacob. "Belief and Behavior: Correspondences," in Understanding Jewish Theology: Classical Issues and Modern Perspectives, 105-106. New York: Ktav Publishing House, 1973.

This brief introduction to Shapiro's essay (407) suggests that matters of belief influence behavior and behavior shapes belief. This interrelationship reveals the moral force of the halakha in Jewish religion. The nexus of obedience to the Law and personal moral response is delineated clearly and sharply in short compass.

393 Neusner, Jacob. "Does Torah Mean Law?" In Judaism and Ethics, edited by Daniel Jeremy Silver, 153-160. New York: Ktav Publishing House, 1970.

This article, one of the least recent included in this volume, distinguishes between "nomos" as conventional law and "logos" as the cosmic order of the universe. Neusner examines the Christian dichotomy between law and love in contrast to both the rabbinic mode of thinking and to "nomos" as used in Greek philosophy. Students of both philosophy and ethics will find this essay of value.

394 Novak, David. "Law and Theology in Judaism."
Tradition 13 (1972): 77-94.

This discussion of halakha, aggadah, and ethics discusses the thinkers like Max Kadushin, Abraham Heschel, and Joseph B. Soloveitchik who seek to define a Jewish ethic that is either halakhic or aggadic or a complex organism uniting the two. Novak himself argues that the relationship between the two is like that between form and substance. Halakha provides the substance, aggadah the moral framework within which the halakha develops. The essay is reprinted in Novak (074), 1-14.

395 Novak, David. "Transcending Denominational Labels."
Sh'ma 13 (1983): 120-121.

In this short, suggestive, and passionate piece Novak contends that it is the approach to halakha and not institutional affiliation that divides Jewish thinkers. Some affirm that halakha never changes, some make ethical principles the criteria of change, and some look for internal halakhic criteria for change.

396 Novak, David. "Universal Moral Law in Hermann Cohen."
Modern Judaism 1(1981):101-117.

See the annotation in entry 291.

397 Petuchowski, Jakob J. "Plural Models within the Halakha."
Judaism 19(1970): 77-89.

This useful essay, reproduced in Bulka (102), 149-162, looks at Louis Jacobs as an example of an enlightened Orthodox Jew who interprets halakha as a process rather than as a set of conclusions. As a Reform Jew Petuchowski defends such a position as compatible with both liberal ethics and traditional Judaism. See also 423.

398 Petuchowski, Jakob J. "Problems of Reform Halacha."
In Contemporary Reform Jewish Thought, edited by Bernard Martin, 105-122. Chicago: Quadrangle Books, 1968.

Petuchowski shows how a liberal thinker can still affirm halakha. He contends that even a Reform approach must be based upon obedience to divine commandments.

399 Plaut, W. Gunther. "The Halacha of Reform." In Contemporary Reform Jewish Thought, edited by Bernard Martin, 88-104. Chicago: Quadrangle Books, 1968.

This alternative to Petuchowski (398) views halakha as a subjective response to divine law and defines the law as moral imperatives. Although many traditionalists feel that such a definition obscures the true meaning of halakha, this view is popular among liberal thinkers who affirm God as giver of the moral law but reject the details of halakha.

400 Rabinovitch, Nahum L.   "Halakha and Other Systems of Ethics: Attitudes and Interactions." In Modern Jewish Ethics: Theory and Practice, edited by Marvin Fox 89-102. Columbus: Ohio State University Press, 1975.

See the annotation at 081.

401 Rabinovitch, Nahum L. "The Law in Rabbinic Judaism." The Greek Orthodox Theological Review 24 (1979): 301-307.

This valuable introduction to traditional Jewish ethics argues that Torah is a blueprint for imitating God, for animating social change, and for actualizing individual potential; it is the concrete working out of the demand to imitate the divine.

402 Rackman, Emanuel. "The Categorical Ethical Thrust of Halacha." Sh'ma 10 (1980): 94-95.

Rackman argues that Kant's "categorical imperative" is too restricted to fully encompass the variety of human moral experience. Jewish morality, however, because it is both autonomous and theonomous is able to encompass the entire range of human morality.

403 Rosenthal, Erwin J. "Torah and 'Nomos' in Medieval Jewish Philosophy." In Studies in Rationalism: Judaism and Universalism, edited by Raphael Loewe, 215-230. London: Routledge and Kegan Paul Ltd., 1966.

See the annotation at 178.

404 Ross, Jacob Jacob. "Morality and the Law." Tradition 10 (1968): 5-16.

In a popular presentation Ross suggests that Torah is really the perfect codex of both law and morals, unchanging and eternal. His argument includes a review of the halakhic process and its theological underpinnings and thus is a valuable introduction to traditional Jewish ethics. Many readers, however, may object to the dogmatic way the author avoids many of the philosophical problems of his position.

405 Scherman, Nosson. "Intellectual Honesty About Halacha." Sh'ma 13 (1983): 121-124.

In a brief, passionate if informal, article Scherman rejects the idea that Jewish law should respond to evolving moral values and argues that halakha is a religious category that cannot be molded to fit human needs.

406 Schwartzbach, Bertram E. "Halakha et Values Seculaires: La Philosophie Religieuse de Yishiyahu Leibowitz." Les Nouveaux Cahiers 16 (1980): 30-42.

See the annotation at 335.

407 Shapiro, David S. "The Ideological Foundations of the Halakha," in Studies in Jewish Thought 1, 122-144. Studies in Judaica. New York: Yeshiva University Press, 1975.

Shapiro argues that the concept of imitatio Dei is the ethics of the halakha that makes it distinctly Jewish. The universal ethical meaning of halakha, he suggests, can be found in the Noahide laws. This essay is reproduced without footnotes in Neusner (121), 107-120; See 392.

408 Sherwin, Byron. "Law and Love in Jewish Theology." Anglican Theological Review 64 (1982): 454-466.

This polemical, but informative, defense of Judaism suggests that Jewish law is a means of awakening an ethical love of others. The commonly assumed dichotomy between law and love, according to Sherwin, is untenable.

409 Sidorsky, David. "The Autonomy of Moral Objectivity." In Modern Jewish Ethics: Theory and Practice, edited by Marvin Fox, 153-173. Columbus: Ohio State University Press, 1975.

This serious analysis of the desire to retain moral autonomy while affirming tradition suggests that religious and secular justification for moral decisions are different. After surveying the most recent trends in moral philosophy Sidorsky finds a new orientation beyond linguistic philosophy that looks more positively on religious ethics.

410 Siegel, Seymour. "Ethics and the Halakhah." In Conservative Judaism and Jewish Law, edited by Seymour Siegel and Elliot Gertel, 124-131. Studies in Conservative Jewish Thought 1. New York: The Rabbinical Assembly of America, 1977.

This article whether by itself or as a contribution to an important anthology is an important reflection on the interaction of law and ethics that reviews historical halakhic changes and calls for modern changes as well. This reproduces his "Ethics and the Halakhah," in Conservative Judaism 25 (1971): 33-40.

411 Siegel, Seymour. "The Meaning of Jewish Law in Conservative Judaism: An Overview and Summary." In Conservative Judaism and Jewish Law, edited by Seymour Siegel and Elliot Gertel, xiii-xxvi. Studies in Conservative Jewish Thought 1. New York: The Rabbinical Assembly of America, 1977.

Introducing an important anthology Siegel stresses the idea of covenant and argues that it includes an evolutionary sense of the interaction of ethics and law. He concludes that this view demands a type of religious pluralism that embraces both tradition and modernity.

412 Simon, Ernst. "Law and Observance in Jewish Experience." In Tradition and Contemporary Experience: Essays on Jewish Thought and Life, edited by Alfred Jospe, 221-238. New York: Schocken Books Inc., 1970.

This careful article finds halakha to be "demanding and commanding but not despotic." Jewish law is portrayed as the framework within which personal moral decisions are to be made, a framework that is historical since it spans generations and is nontotalitarian since it includes variations. It is reprinted in the same volume as the previous entry, pages 237-253.

413 Soloveitchik, Aaron. "Law and Morality in Modern Society." In Building Jewish Ethical Character, edited by Joseph Kaminetsky and Murray I. Friedman, 19-27. New York: The Fryer Foundation, 1975.

This devotional article advocates Torah study as the best training in ethical behavior. Arguing that law and morality are intrinsically united, this articulate statement of traditional Judaism rejects altering halakha for the sake of "ethics." It is clearly not meant as a philosophical refutation of the primacy of ethical law but as an insider's statement of the way in which Torah can be identified with ethics as its ultimate expression.

414 Spero, Shubert. "Morality and Halakha," in Morality, Halakha, and the Jewish Tradition, 166-200. The Library of Jewish Law and Ethics 9. New York: Ktav Publishing House and Yeshiva University Press, 1983.

This essay in Spero's book (016) is a good introduction to the theoretical issues involved in studying the relationship between law and morality in the halakha. Spero surveys the sources of Jewish moral teaching and discovers that the most important component in the Torah is its moral awareness.

415 Spero, Shubert. "Systematic Aspects of Jewish Morality," in Morality, Halakha, and the Jewish Tradition, 275-334. The Library of Jewish Law and Ethics 9. New York: Ktav Publishing House and Yeshiva University Press, 1983.

In this section (of 016) Spero shows the technical methods of Jewish law as applied to Jewish moral decision making. The wealth of practical examples makes this a valuable survey of the actual ethics of the halakha.

416 Spiro, Solomon J. "Halakha as a Ground For Creating a Shared Spiritual Language: Rejoinder." Tradition 16 (1977): 50-57.

This response to David Hartman's call (369) to make halakha an inclusive ideological category acceptable to both observant and non-observant stimulated controversy (see 388 and 417).

417 Spiro, Solomon J. "A Rejoinder to Tzvi Marx." Tradition 19 (1981): 35-41.

Spiro laments in response to Tzvi Marx (388) that isolation seems to be the only strategy that has succeeded in preserving the Jewish people and Jewish religion. He decries the "falling away" from traditional halakhic observance by many modern Jews. He reiterates his contention that Jewish ethics and morality are only possible if the rigor of Jewish law is upheld.

418 Stitskin, Leon. "Witnessing and Personal Religious Experience." In Issues in the Jewish-Christian Dialogue: Jewish Perspectives on Covenant, Mission, and Witness, edited by Helga Croner and Leon Klenicki, A Stimulus Book 108-133. Studies in Judaism. New York: Paulist Press, 1979.

This is a careful argument that while made from a traditional perspective takes philosophical concerns seriously. Stitskin notes the tension between a heteronomous revealed law and autonomously chosen personal values and claims that in Judaism commandment is a pedagogic vehicle for a person's individual ethical discoveries. Commandment, he suggests, is only a tool whereby an affirmation of transcendent values is made possible through action in this mundane world. Understood in that way Jewish law is a means to personal moral affirmation.

419 Twersky, Isadore. "Religion and Law." In Religion in a Religious Age, edited by S. D. Goitein, 69-77. Cambridge, Massachusetts: Association for Jewish Studies, 1974.

In a scholarly and fascinating article Twersky analyzes the way in which the oral law developed in Jewish life. He suggests that study of the written law and of its oral interpretation was used as a confirmation of faith and religion. Law was a means by which faith was strengthened.

420 Weinberg, Jacob S. "Mitzvos as 'Springboards' for Ethical Behavior." In Building Jewish Ethical Character, edited by Joseph Kaminetsky and Murray I. Friedman, 73-76. New York: The Fryer Foundation, 1975.

This didactic essay, best read as an address to the already committed, argues for the pedagogical value of the commandments. Because they teach trust in God and prepare a person for a relationship with the divine obedience to them leads Jews to ethical and moral behavior. Halakhah, is thus an indirect method of moral education.

421 Wurzburger, Walter S. "Covenantal Imperatives." In Samuel K. Mirsky Memorial Volume: Studies in Jewish Law, Philosophy and Literature, edited by Gersion Appel, Morris Epstein, and Hayim Leaf, 2-12. Jerusalem: Sura Institute of Research; New York:Yeshiva University Press, 1970.

This valuable essay contrasts Kant and Judaism using even liberal thinkers like Buber and Rosenzweig. It defends traditional Judaism, in contrast to Kant, because it rests on a set of covenantal imperatives that are a set of deeds that lead the individual to a relationship with God. This essay has recently been reproduced in The Jacob Dolnitsky Memorial Volume: Studies in Jewish Law, Philosophy, Literature, and Language, edited by Morris Casriel Katz (Skokie: Hebrew Theological College, 1982), 247-254.

422 Wurzburger, Walter S. "Law as the Basis of a Moral Society." Tradition 19 (1981): 42-54.

This valuable defense of law as the basis of morality. presents a cogent argument for an ethics of rules rather than merely principles. Morality needs authority to be an effective normative guide. Wurzburger contends that only a transcendent authority can provide the legitimacy that an ethical system needs. The argument presented shows why contemporary society may need the structure of religious law even while it advocates personal conscience.

423 Wurzburger, Walter S. "Plural Models and the Authority of Halakhah." Judaism 20 (1971):390-395.

This response to Jakob Petuchowski (See 397) suggests that while the halakhah is not monolithic it cannot accommodate all systems of Judaism. Reform Jewish practice and theory cannot fall within the unity of even the most pluralistic halakhah. This essay is reproduced in Bulka (102), 162-168.

THEOLOGICAL CONCEPTS AND JEWISH ETHICS

424 Agus, Jacob Bernard. "Revelation as Quest: A Contribution to Ecumenical Thought." Journal of Ecumenical Studies 9 (1972): 217-230.

This helpful article surveys the entire range of Jewish ethical literature and reaffirms Agus' contention that Jewish ethics is dialectical. It shows this ethical dialectics in particular relationship to the idea of revelation. It is reproduced in Agus (001), 43-62.

425 Agus, Jacob Bernard. "The 'Yes' and The 'No' of Revelation," in The Jewish Quest: Essays on Basic Concepts of Jewish Theology, 77-86. New York: Ktav Publishing House, 1983.

In this valuable essay Agus compares different religious experiences of revelation and suggests that the ethical implication of the concept is that of removing two idolatries: that of human pride and that of pietistic dogmatism. The ideal of tikkun olam or improvement of the world is the true focus of the idea of revelation for Agus and he reviews a variety of Jewish precedents to demonstrate his point.

426 Belkin, Samuel. "Man as a Temporary Tenant." In
Judaism and Human Rights, edited by Milton R. Konvitz, 251-
258. Bnai Brith Heritage Classics. New York: W.W. Norton
and Company, 1972.

This impressive study of Jewish anthropology and theology of
creation suggests that one purpose of the commandments is to
limit human pride. They teach Jews to acknowledge that
human beings are neither complete masters of the world or of
themselves. Instead human beings have moral obligations as
tenants in God's created world.

427 Berkovits, Eliezer. "Creation and Value," in God, Man
and History: A Jewish Interpretation, 66-74. 3rd Printing.
New York: Jonathan David Publishers, 1979.

Berkovits investigates the meaning of creation and contrasts
it with merely considering God as the primary cause. That
difference is a difference in valuation and thus suggests a
difference in ethical obligation on the part of human beings
to whom the world has been entrusted. The idea of God as
creator is thus the foundation for an ecological ethics.

428 Berkovits, Eliezer. "Divine Law and Ethical Deed," in
God, Man and History: A Jewish Interpretation, 99-114. 3rd
Printing. New York: Jonathan David Publishers, 1979.

In this helpful study of the relationship between reason and
revelation Berkovits suggests that the Torah is the revealed
tool by which the divided self is enabled to choose the good
and reject evil. The discipline provided by revelation is
said to create a habit of moral response that is then put
into practice.

429 Breslauer, S. Daniel. "Creation and Process: Halakhah
and the Natural Order," in A New Jewish Ethics, 25-46.
Symposium series 9. New York: Edwin Mellen Press, 1983.

This liberal approach to Jewish law highlights the problem
of natural processes and discusses Jewish theology and
observance (in particular the Sabbath) in relationship to
the natural order and human responsibility to it. It
considers questions of bioethics as well as of ecology and
insists that the ethical elements in a Jew's response to
modernity arise from taking theology seriously.

430 Carmell, Aryeh and Cyril Domb, ed. Challenge: Torah
Views on Science and its Problems. New York: Feldheim
Publishing Company, 1976.

See the annotation at 108.

431 Cohen, Jack C. "Towards a Theology of Ethics." In
Faith and Reason: Essays in Judaism, edited by Robert Gordis
and Ruth B. Waxman, 290-297. New York: Ktav Publishing
House, 1973.

This argument for a naturalistic ethics seeks to derive religious morality from a theological statement. An investigation of religious ethics, it contends, suggests that people mean by God a guarantor of transcendent ethics, not a supernatural being. The normal understanding of theology is thus reversed; language about God becomes indirect language about human responsibilities.

432 Dressler, Eliyahu. "The Attribute of Mercy," in *Strive for Truth: Michtavme Eliyahu, the Selected Writings of Eliyahu Dressler*, 46-77. Trans. by Aryeh Carmell. New York: Feldheim Publishing Company, 1978.

Dressler's *musar* meditation considers the attribute of mercy ascribed to God. God allows even the wicked the opportunity to fulfill their desires. After considering the pietistic conclusion is the acknowledgment that whatever God does is done for the best. Theology, here, leads to a revision of the ethical ideal of reward and punishment as well as to a reinterpretation of the value of morality in human action.

433 Etkin, William. "The Religious Meaning of Contemporary Science." In *Challenge: Torah Views on Science and its Problems*, edited by Aryeh Carmell and Cyril Domb, 30-40. New York: Feldheim Publishing Company, 1976.

This fundamentalist and uncritical essay holds that both religion and science share certain common beliefs. Since both presume an ordered world of predictability, it is argued, both share a faith in a trustworthy creator.

434 Etzion, Itzhak Raphael. *The Unity of God as a Principle of Judaism and as the Basis of Jewish Morality* [Hebrew]. The Principles of Judaism in Israel's Thought 2. Jerusalem: Pardes Hana, 1969.

Etzion's popular presentation of Jewish philosophical and theological ideas suggests the relationship between monotheism and morality. It surveys both Jewish and non-Jewish philosophy, the major themes of Jewish ethics, and the relationship between them and Jewish theology.

435 Fackenheim, Emil L. "Can There be Judaism Without Revelation?" In his *Quest for Past and Future: Essays in Jewish Theology*, 66-82. Bloomington: Indiana University Press, 1968.

This early essay by Fackenheim claims that revelation affirms the relevance of this particular person, this particular place, and this particular time and is therefore an essential element in any ethics. Without revelation a moral deed is only an instance of a universal principle; with revelation a moral deed expresses the doer's uniqueness.

436 Freudenstein, Eric G. "Ecology and the Jewish Tradition." *Judaism* 19 (1970): 406-414.

This examination of the relationship between theology and
the ethical issue of ecology suggests that a theory of
creation is an impetus to ecology. It investigates biblical
and rabbinic texts that seem to indicate a concern for the
environment. Because creation is valued by God it must be
respected by human beings. The essay is reproduced in
Konvitz (115), 265-274.

437 Friedman, Maurice. "Science and Scientism," in The
Hidden Human Image: A Heartening Answer to the Dehumanizing
Threats of Our Age, a Delta Book, 31-65. New York: Dell
Publishing Company, 1974.

Friedman uses the Psalms, Hasidic tales, and the thought of
Martin Buber to confront modern thinking about human
domination over nature and control of the natural order. In
a compelling analysis of human nature he considers the
ethical task to be responding to the environment as a
fellow creature of God so that technology becomes a means
of relating to the world.

438 Gendler, Everett. "On the Judaism of Nature." In The
New Jews, edited by James A. Sleeper and Alan L. Mintz,
Vintage Books, 233-243. New York: Random House Inc., 1971.

Gendler, in an impressive minority statement, sets about
reclaiming the Jewish appreciation of nature through the use
of traditional rituals, modern poetry, and rabbinic
quotations. He contends Jews today must reestablish their
ties with nature. Unlike many other Jewish thinkers he
affirms nature without fear of the temptation to paganism.

439 Goldman, Morris. "Man's Place in Nature." Tradition
10 (1968): 100-115.

This treatise on the need for religious rather than secular
morality claims that only the former guarantees against an
exploitation of nature. On another level, however, it is a
fundamentalist rejection of the evolutionary theory. The
former theological argument is powerful and persuasive; the
polemical rejection of evolution is less so.

440 Gordis, Robert. "A Basis for Morals: Ethics in A
Technological Age." Judaism 25 (1976): 20-43.

See the annotation at 271.

441 Granatstein, Melvin. "Theodicy and Belief." Tradition
13 (1973): 36-47.

The philosophical question of whether faith can be verified
is raised in this article only to be dismissed as irrelevant
because Jews know God through the commandments and no
through miracles. Theology, according to this Orthodox
defense, is less determinative of belief than the experience
that comes from moral and halakhic action.

442 Greenberg, Simon. "A Revealed Law: Torah MiSinai, The Divine Origin of Jewish Law." In Conservative Judaism and Jewish Law, edited by Seymour Siegel and Elliot Gertel, 176-193. Studies in Conservative Jewish Thought 1. New York: The Rabbinical Assembly of America, 1977.

This defense of revelation should be read in conjunction with Greenberg's other works (010, 044). It demonstrates how belief in God shapes an entire pattern of human behavior and therefore has ethical implications.

443 Helfund, Jonathan I. "Ecology and the Jewish Tradition: A Postscript." Judaism 20 (1971): 330-335.

Helfund responds to the article by Eric Freudenstein (see 436) and adds details to show that Jewish law prevents causing the extinction of a species since that would impair the divine plan. This "postscript" adds further arguments to show that Torah law is ecologically aware of the need for preservation and conservation.

444 Hirsch, Samson R. "Do Not Destroy." In Judaism and Human Rights, edited by Milton R. Konvitz, 259-264. Bnai Brith Heritage Classics. New York: W.W. Norton and Company, 1972.

Hirsch, an early neo-Orthodox leader in Germany, explained the moral significance of the prohibition on destroying trees during times of war. The inclusion of this essay in a contemporary collection dedicated to Jewish ethics shows the continuing concern with demonstrating the ethical relevance of traditional Judaism.

445 Jacobs, Louis. "Creation," in A Jewish Theology, 93-113. New York: Ktav Publishing House, 1973.

Louis Jacobs argues against the need for a literal acceptance of the details of the biblical creation story. Instead its significance is that God as creator has established a purpose and meaning to the world. The moral implication of creation is that human beings have a special task and responsibility towards the natural world.

446 Jonas, Hans. "Technology and Responsibility: Reflections on the New Tasks of Ethics," in Philosophical Essays: From Ancient Creed to Technological Man, 3-20. Englewood Cliffs: Prentice-Hall Publishing Company, 1974.

Hans Jonas has evolved a theology that takes the modern challenge seriously and his work must be considered as seminal. In this essay Jonas looks at human capabilities for controlling and shaping life from the Greek period through the present and concludes that the greater power now available through technology should be tempered by a greater sense of responsibility. See also 276.

447 Kaplan, Asa. "Fundamental Assumptions for Discussions on Religion and Science." Trans. by Lawrence Kaplan. Tradition 10 (1968): 87-99.

This interesting specimen of traditional thought seeks to defend Jewish thought without rejecting the findings of natural science. Its naive approach may leave many readers unconvinced.

448 Klein, Isaac. "Science and Some Ethical Issues, " in Responsa and Halakhic Studies, 159-175. New York: Ktav Publishing House, 1975.

Klein responds to the moral dilemmas raised by the advances of modern science and suggests that science has set new problems to which it has not provided solutions. Judaism, however, has in his view an ethical system able to solve these dilemmas since it is a tradition rooted in God's command to the creatures to improve creation.

449 Klein, Isaac. "The Word of God," in Responsa and Halakhic Studies, 176-186. New York: Ktav Publishing House, 1975.

Klein, a traditionalist Conservative Rabbi whose reflections on theology and ethics are important for his movement, sees revelation as a central religious category that responds to the three challenges facing the modern Jew: definition of status, the meaning of prophecy and its power to motivate devotion to religious values, and adherence to halakha. That concept is central, in his view, because it provides the underpinning of both practical observance and theoretical self-understanding.

450 Lamm, Norman. "Ecology in Jewish Law and Theology," in Faith and Doubt: Studies in Traditional Jewish Thought, 162-185. New York: Ktav Publishing House, 1971.

Lamm's theological perspective on Jewish ethics emphasizes that humanity's commanding role in the world brings with it responsibility for the natural order. The Sabbath is interpreted as a continual reminder that not progressive technology but cooperation with the divine purpose is the human task. This essay notes the prohibition against destruction and suggests that human beings may build, change, produce and create but do not hold title to the natural creation.

451 Lamm, Norman. "The Religious Implications of Extraterrestrial Life," in Faith and Doubt: Studies in Traditional Jewish Thought, 107-160. New York: Ktav Publishing House, 1971.

This extended essay considers more than just the question of extraterrestrial life. It questions whether the Bible must be taken as a literal blueprint of the creative process and rejects such a literalism. It suggests that the aim is to show that God has a purpose in bringing life into being and that there are moral implications in the act of creation. The moral responsibility of human creativity is emphasized.

452 Levinas, Emmanuel. "La Revelation Dans La Tradition Juive." In La Revelation, 57-77. Brussells: Faculty of the the University of Saint Louis, 1977.

Levinas interprets revelation as an ethical category that demands not only a relationship to the divine, but also social responsibility to other people and obedience to ritual instructions. The value of this essay is enhanced by his contrast between Greek and Jewish views of revelation that focuses on the ethical dimension in the latter.

453 Levy, Leo. "Science in Torah Life." In Challenge: Torah Views on Science and its Problems, edited by Aryeh Carmell and Cyril Domb, 94-100. New York: Feldheim Publishing Company, 1976.

This quaint and engaging traditional argument notes that scientific experimentation and the use of scientific discoveries is part of the ideal life of the Jew. It argues that since a scientific profession leaves time for studying Torah it should be a preferred Jewish occupation.

454 Lubarsky, Sandra D. "Ethics and Theodicy: Tensions in Emil Fackenheim's Thought." Encounter 44 (1983): 59-72.

This essay while focused on theodicy demonstrates how a serious consideration of God's nature affects every aspect of theological thinking. See the full annotation at 317.

455 Matt, Heskel J. "Man's Choice and God's Design." Judaism 21 (1972): 211-221.

This popular essay dealing with the problem of human freedom and the divine plan for creation suggests that while experience shows human behavior shaped by social conditioning, physical and mental capacities, and other environmental factors, these can all be reduced to divinely established elements within our context.

456 Novak, David. "A Theory of Revelation," in Law and Theology in Judaism, 2nd series, 1-27. New York: Ktav Publishing House, 1976.

Novak suggests that while revelation is often considered authoritarian because it imposes its behavioral norms upon people such norms are necessary for true freedom. All learning, he contends, involves both authority and personal choice. He concludes that in the light of medieval Jewish thought the antinomianism of many Jewish existentialist thinkers is both theologically suspect and pedagogically self-defeating.

457 Orbach, William. "The Four Faces of God: Towards a Theology of Powerlessness." Judaism 32 (1983): 236-247.

Orbach draws upon the insights of process theology to suggest that God is in process, an idea he sees anticipated by the Jewish mystics. He uses the paradigm of a God in process as the basis for a Jewish ethics that is both responsive to modernity and true to the tradition.

458 Plaut, Gunther. "God and the Ethical Impulse." In Judaism and Ethics, edited by Daniel Jeremy Silver, 215-225. New York: Ktav Publishing House, 1970.

Plaut roots Jewish ethics in the exodus experience, in the love of the stranger, and in imitation of the divine. He suggests that the basic commandments including the doing of justice are based upon an imitation of God's graciousness to humanity. Jewish ethics is, thus, less a demand for blind obedience to legal prescriptions than a response to the divine call for human moral responsibility. This is a persuasive theology of Jewish ethics.

459 Rabinovitch, Nahum L. "Torah and Science: Conflict or Complement" In Challenge: Torah Views on Science and its Problems, edited by Aryeh Carmell and Cyril Domb, 40-52. New York: Feldheim Publishing Company, 1976.

Rabinovitch provides a careful examination of Jewish philosophy to demonstrate a division between scientific and religious knowledge that is still not a conflict. Religious ethics, from this perspective, adds what science cannot provide on its own -- a structure of meaning to guide the usage of potentially dangerous knowledge.

460 Rabinovitch, Nahum L. "Torah and the Spirit of Free Inquiry." In Challenge: Torah Views on Science and its Problems, edited by Aryeh Carmell and Cyril Domb, 54-67. New York: Feldheim Publishing Company, 1976.

Rabinovitch affirms that Jewish ethics is an intellectual system, a mode of worship, and a rule of conduct and involves three human responses: reason, devotion, and morality, each of which must be used in making a moral decision. The essay is particularly useful in giving concrete examples of how such decisions are made when confronted with scientific theories.

461 Rackman, Emanuel. "Theocentricity in Jewish Law." In Essays on the Occasion of the Seventieth Anniversary of the Dropsie University, 1909-1979, edited by Abraham I. Katsh and Leon Nemoy, 371-382. Philadelphia: Dropsie University Press, 1979.

Rackman traces Jewish norms to the idea of God's creation of humanity in the divine image. There is a curious correspondence between the Reform rabbi Gunther Plaut (458) and the modern Orthodox rabbi Emmanuel Rackman since both emphasize the theological nature of Jewish ethics and the rooting of morality in imitation of the divine.

462 Radkowsky, Alvin. "The Relationship Between Science and Religion." In Challenge: Torah Views on Science and its Problems, edited by Aryeh Carmell and Cyril Domb, 68-92. New York: Feldheim Publishing Company, 1976.

Radkowsky argues that since God is the source of all knowledge there is only mutual illumination and not contradiction between science and religion and draws parallels between the findings in both. This article stresses the Jewish affirmation of science as a tool in fulfilling the task assigned by God to human beings.

463 Reines, Chaim Zeev. "Judaism's Relation to Animals," in Essays and Investigations in Jewish Ethics and Law [Hebrew], 40-44. Jerusalem: Rubin Mass Company, 1972.

According to Reines Judaism resists totemism that attributes special powers to the animal world and technology that reduces animals to their usefulness for human beings. Judaism respects the life of animals. Reines claims that Judaism has, thereby, offered an advanced ethics as appropriate today as in ancient times.

464 Ross, Jacob Joshua. "Anthropocentricity and Theocentricity." In Sefer Yeshiyahu Leibowitz: A Collection of Essays About his Thought and in his Honor [Hebrew], edited by Asa Kasher and Jacob Levinger, 56-65. Tel Aviv: Tel Aviv Student Association, 1977.

Ross illuminates the theocentricity of Isaiah Leibowitz as a reaction to modernity's focus on human beings but then analyzes other thinkers who focus on humanity rather than God. He concludes that both foci are needed since a theocentric focus provides motivation; an anthropocentric focus gives direction to human service. This analysis demonstrates the ethical dimension in the way a religion understands both the divine and the human.

465 Roth, Sol. Science and Religion Studies in Torah Judaism. New York: Yeshiva University Press, 1967.

This serious consideration of the scientific method and the discoveries of science looks at a variety of Jewish thinkers and considers the problem of scientific determinism. It finally concludes that determinism is not an ethical problem since it is used in science only as a postulate and not as a constitutive principle.

466 Schneersohn, Menachem M. "A Letter on Science and Judaism." In Challenge: Torah Views on Science and its Problems, edited by Aryeh Carmell and Cyril Domb, 142-149. New York: Feldheim Publishing Company, 1976.

This famous open letter by the Lubavitch Rebbe (a Hasidic master holding sway in Brooklyn, New York) contrasts science which deals only with theory and Torah which deals with absolute truth. In a clever and persuasive move the Rebbe suggests that scientists oppose the Bible not because it is false but because its truth undermines their own sense of ingenuity and therefore are suspect.

467   Schulweis, Harold M. "The Ambiguous Uses of Divine Personality. In Perspectives on Jews and Judaism: Essays in Honor of Wolfe Kelman, edited by Arthur A. Chiel, 373-381. New York: Rabbinical Assembly of America, 1978.

Schulweis, in a clear and methodical essay, notes that God's essence is mysterious and in the context of the biblical covenant the attributes of God are meant to indicate both mystery and morality. From the moral standpoint, however, God's personality must be accessible if it is to be morally compelling. Dialogic covenant must at least reveal the basis for ethical behavior. Schulweis finally concludes in a unique response to the problem of evil that in a post-Holocaust world either the divine personality or divine morality must be rejected.

468   Schulweis, Harold M.   "Theological Modesty and the Idea of Divine Perfection." Judaism 24 (1976): 489-493.

This brief essay is a rewarding study and critique of Jewish theological speculation. Theologians attempt to discern the moral intention of God; Schulweis considers the efforts of Martin Buber and Soren Kierkegaard to unravel the mysteries of the story of the binding of Isaac and the testing of Abraham. He concludes that the idea of divine perfection is a limitation of human speculation and should encourage theological modesty. This modesty may have an ethical corollary -- human self-limitation because the divine stature is far greater than that of any human being.

469   Schwarzschild,, Steven S. "Do Noachides Have to Believe in Revelation?" Jewish Quarterly Review, n.s., 52 and 53 (1962): 297-308; 30-65.

The first of these essays is concerned with the medieval period and moves from Maimonides to Moses Mendelssohn. The second is focused on the modern period with particular emphasis on Hermann Cohen. The central issue is whether a righteous non-Jew is expected to be righteous on the basis of the revelation to the Jewish people. Schwarzschild notes that there are differing views in Jewish sources as to what is required of the Noahide reflected in the variety of sources and interpretations of this tradition.

470   Shapiro, David S.   "God, Man, and Creation." Tradition 15 (1975): 25-47.

This rich exploration of Jewish theology and practice suggests that God's relationship with creation is a paradigm for the human relationship to the world. More specifically God's covenant with nature implies specific responsibilities for human action. Ecology is a mundane and natural concern; Torah elevates it into a means of imitating God. This use of the natural order as a means of forging a link between humanity and God is illustrated in a variety of Jewish religious principles: the principle that "derech eretz," or the way of the land, preceeds Torah law, the celebration of the holiday of booths as both a harvest festival and a reminder of Israel's history, and the Noahide covenant that suggests that there is a natural law that is transfigured in the Sinai covenant.

471 Shapiro, David S. "God, World, and Man." Tradition 14 (1974): 37-47.

Shapiro takes the creation of the universe as the foundation for the concept of a moral purpose in the universe. Morality understood this way means an active involvement in the world, a life of imitation of the positive attributes of the divine. God's relationship to the creation provides the paradigm for the individual Jew's relationship to the world. Human virtues, then, come from imitation of God, precisely in God's role as creator of the world. Understood this way creation is not only a doctrine of theology but also a fundamental principle of Jewish ethics.

472 Soloveitchik, Aaron. "The Fire of Sinai." In Building Jewish Ethical Character, edited by Joseph Kaminetsky and Murray I. Friedman, 11-18. New York: The Fryer Foundation, 1975.

See the annotation at 091. Note in particular the way in which a traditional Jewish presentation considers revelation and ethics inherently intertwined.

473 Spero, Shubert. "Selfhood and Godhood in Jewish Thought and Modern Philosophy." Tradition 18 (1980): 160-171.

Spero, in a thoughtful reflection on contemporary thought that makes ample use of traditional Jewish writings, comments on the double nature of theology's moral implication. On the one hand knowing more about the divine gives an insight into human moral responsibility. On the other hand knowing more about the self leads to insight about God. The double concern for imitation of God and the divine image within humanity points to a double emphasis in Jewish ethics: human beings have the moral capacity to know the right and the good but they need to awaken the potential within them to follow the moral path. The essay is particularly impressive because of its use of modern thought.

474 Vogel, Manfred. "L'homme et la Creation Selon la Tradition Religieuse du Judaism." Sidic 11 (1978): 4-24.

Vogel uses the story of creation to contend that history and not nature is the primary category in Jewish thought. While using biblical and talmudic sources his main concern is philosophical. His clearly existentialist leanings emphasize relationship as the basic human responsibility that he interprets as an imitation of the divine relationship to creation.

475 Wechsler, Harlan J. "The Artisan's Touch: Jewish Ethics and The Doctrine of Creation." Conservative Judaism 28 (1974): 54-60.

This popular but enjoyable essay contrasts the biblical creation story to other Ancient Near Eastern Myths and claims that the Bible provides for human dignity by the concept of imitation of the divine creativity. The issue of creation and its meaning is transformed into a discussion of human dignity and its root in a view of divine activity.

JUDAISM AND SOCIAL ETHICS

476 Agus, Jacob Bernard. "The Covenant Concept: Particularistic, Pluralistic, or Futuristic." Journal of Ecumenical Studies 18 (1981): 217-230.

Since the concept of covenant is the central category in Jewish social thinking, this excellent study is required reading for an understanding of Judaic social ethics. Covenant, Agus claims, need not be an exclusivist concept. The polarities of religious experience, knowledge and ignorance, universalism and particularism, faith and event, need not be kept as alternatives. Because here are a variety of covenants described in the Hebrew Scriptures and the rabbinic sages affirmed a universal revelation of ethics and of faith covenant, this excellent historian of Jewish thought suggests, in an inclusive idea. See also Agus (001), 62-76.

477 Agus, Jacob Bernard. "A Jewish View of World Community," in The Jewish Quest: Essays on Basic Concepts of Jewish Theology, 112-146. New York: Ktav Publishing House, 1983.

Agus surveys the views of Philo, Hillel, and Maimonides. He notes that the divine enters into universal history through creation, redemption, and revelation and concludes that Jewish philosophers have a world perspective. His theory of Jewish ethical dialectics thus leads to an ecumenical social vision.

478 Atlas, Samuel. "Dina D'Malkhuta Delimited." Hebrew Union College Annual 46 (1975): 269-288.

Atlas analyzes the concept of "The law of the land is law" and suggests that its purpose is to delimit the area in which force can prevail. This cautionary article alerts liberals of the limits beyond which this concept cannot be pushed as a guide for contemporary relationships between religion and the state. For other treatments of this same principle see 484, 491, 509. 510, 521, 527.

479 Bergman, Samuel Hugo. "Can Transgression Have an Agent: The Law of the State and the Conscience of the Individual," in The Quality of Faith: Essays on Judaism and Morality, 13-23. Trans. by Yehudah Hanegbi. Jerusalem: World Zionist Organization, 1970.

See the annotation at 132 and compare with 487, 497, 505, 507, 511, 521.

480 Bergman, Samuel Hugo. "The Humanism of the Covenant," in The Quality of Faith: Essays on Judaism and Morality, 64-89. Trans. by Yehudah Hanegbi. Jerusalem: World Zionist Organization, 1970.

Bergman emphasizes that Judaism is a religion of community and covenant rather than of the solitary individual. Its vision is that of messianic community rather than of individual redemption. Social action is thus covenantal action based upon the divine concern for human interrelationships. See 005; the essay appears on pages 63-80 of the Hebrew version.

481 Berkovits, Eliezer. "Ethics and Majority." Sh'ma 6 (1976): 121-122.

In a popular but valuable essay on the relationship of religion and politics Berkovits suggests that the claim to speak for a majority is, by its very nature, a sign that the speaker cannot be trusted and should not be trusted. The Israeli attempt to legislate morality is as suspect as the American "silent majority." Berkovits insists that ethics and religious authority must be kept separate.

482 Blanchard, Tzi. "Our Social Concerns Have a Jewish Ground." Sh'ma 5 (1975):300-302.

This essay written from a musar standpoint argues that Jews have a religious obligation to be involved in social concerns. While traditional Judaism has often remained outside of the political mainstream, this article argues for a moral imperative that drives religious Jews to transform the social order. This defense of traditional Jewish activism is an important representative of a modern mood among Orthodox Jews.

483 Bleich, J. David. "Jews and the State: Halakha is Our Guide." Sh'ma 5 (1975): 310-312.

Bleich contends, in a brief but valuable restatement of an Orthodox position, that in the West ethics has been left to personal decision where as in Judaism morality has been legislated for the common good. While admitting that this legislation was meant for Jews alone he contends that the contemporary Jew has a task of teaching and persuading non-Jews as well.

484   Blidstein, Gerald J.   "A Note on the Function of 'The Law of the Kingdom is Law' in the Medieval Jewish Community." Jewish Journal of Sociology 15 (1973): 213-219.

This study of "the law of the kingdom is law" looks particularly at its diaspora relevance. It responds to earlier work by Leo Landman and focuses on the meaning that can be derived from the way Jews utilized the concept of accepting secular legislation. Blidstein finds it more revealing of intraJewish relationships than of Jewish - non-Jewish relationships. This point of view should be compared with that expressed in 478, 491, 509, 510, 520, 527.

485   Borowitz, Eugene B.   "Judaism and the Secular State." The Journal of Religion 48 (1968): 22-34.

Borowitz suggests, in a cogent statement of liberal Jewish thought, that Jews have an ambivalent attitude towards the idea of the state. The essay includes a study of biblical, talmudic and medieval concepts focusing on the twin ideas of "the law of the land" and "exile."

486   Branson, Roy.   "The Individual and the Commune: A Critique of Martin Buber's Social Philosophy." Judaism 14 (1975): 82-96.

See the annotation at 258.

487   Braude, Samuel G.   "Civil Disobedience and the Jewish Tradition." In Judaism and Ethics, edited by Daniel Jeremy Silver, 229-239. New York: Ktav Publishing House, 1970.

Braude investigates the roots of Jewish social protest in a comprehensive examination of the biblical prophets, the talmudic principle of "the law of the land is law," and the tradition of martyrdom when it is demanded concluding that the basic principle is Jewish loyalty. See also 479, 484, 497, 506, 508, 511, 521.

488   Cohen, David.   "The Relevance of Torah to the Social and Ethical Issues of Our Time." In Building Jewish Ethical Character, edited by Joseph Kaminetsky and Murray I. Friedman, 47-60. New York: The Fryer Foundation, 1975.

This polemic of militant orthodox Judaism against secularism suggests that only Torah solutions are true answers to contemporary problems.

150 BIBLIOGRAPHICAL SURVEY

489 Cohen, Martin A. "The Mission of Israel After Auschwitz." In Issues in the Jewish-christian Dialogue: Jewish Perspectives on Covenant, Mission, and Witness, edited by Helga Croner and Leon Klenicki, A Stimulus Book, 157-180. Studies in Judaism. New York: Paulist Press, 1979.

Cohen argues in a thoughtful, post-Holocaust theological context, that the corporate well-being of the people of Israel has always been a central ethical concern in Judaism. He claims that this social dimension in Jewish ethics is essential in the post-Holocaust era because the corporate life of the Jewish people has been radically threatened.

490 Cohon, Samuel S. "The Universal and the Particular in Judaism." In Faith and Reason: Essays in Judaism, edited by Robert Gordis and Ruth B. Waxman, 311-318. New York: Ktav Publishing House, 1973.

This affirmation of both the particularism and universalism of Judaism interprets Jewish religion as an organic complex of spiritual values that integrate particular identity and universal concern. It warns Jews to maintain the dialectic of particularism and universalism and affirm universal concern even when protecting national survival.

491 Faber, Salamon. "On The Principle of Dina de-Malkhuta." Judaism 26 (1977): 117-122.

This is a review of Shilo's study of the concept of "The law of the land" (see 527). Faber suggests that a moral concern underlies this principle. Jews are to accommodate to the changing nature of society and their environment; this principle allows for such adaptation and illustrates the dynamics of Jewish religion. See 478, 484, 487, 509, 510, 520, 527.

492 Fackenheim, Emil L. "History, Rupture, and 'Tikkun Olam': From Rosenzweig Beyond Heidegger," in To Mend the World: Foundations of Future Jewish Thought, 147-314. New York: Schocken Books Inc., 1982.

This excellent review of modern Jewish social thought surveys modern Jewish thought and explains how Jews reentered history as a social and political group. The repoliticalization of the Jewish people as a moral necessity in modern times expresses, for Fackenheim, the concrete realization of covenant society.

493 Fackenheim, Emil L. "Religious Responsibility for the Social Order," in Quest for Past and Future: Essays in Jewish Theology, 188-194. Bloomington: University of Indiana Press, 1968.

This serious theological investigation of the roots of Jewish concern for social structure claims that Judaism does not separate religious and social responsibility. The will of God has as its main goal the transformation of human life, the bringing of the Kingdom of God on earth, and is therefore social and messianic in its impetus. The essay is reproduced in Silver (126), 241-248.

494 Fenster, Myron. "New Directions in Jewish Social Ethics: More Concern, Less Doctrine." Conservative Judaism 24 (1970): 58-61.

Fenster responds to the contention of Seymour Siegel that Jews should turn to a more conservative politics (see 528). He points to the history of Jewish involvement in liberal causes, the example of Elie Wiesel in the contemporary period, as examples of Jewish concern for universal rights in contrast to reactionary and repressive conservative politics. This contrast suggests to him that Jews should be wary of conservatism.

495 Friedman, Maurice. "The Community of Otherness and the Covenant of Peace," in The Hidden Human Image: A Heartening Answer to the Dehumanizing Threats of Our Age, a Delta Book, 358-371. New York: Dell Publishing Company, 1974.

Friedman argues for a new type of world community that, inspired by biblical and Hasidic precedent, would be bound together by common aims but free enough to encourage individual distinctiveness. This approach offers a modern alternative that is hopeful, humanistic, and deeply Jewish.

496 Gilbert, Arthur. "The Meaning and Purpose of Jewish Survival." In Judaism and Ethics, edited by Daniel Jeremy Silver, 315-326. New York: Ktav Publishing House, 1970.

Gilbert, a Reconstructionist Jewish thinker, urges that ethics be based not upon supernaturalism but upon an evaluation of human needs. He argues that this approach was valid in the past and, in the modern period, he contends that Jewish peoplehood provides a transcendent ideal that can animate a social ethics.

497 Gottleib, Dale. "Collective Responsibility." Tradition 14 (1974): 48-65.

Gottlieb remarks that the ethical test comes when values collide and that in Judaism the conflict is resolved in accordance with social responsibility. This Orthodox viewpoint is argued with illustrations from traditional Jewish law and practice.

498 Greenberg, Moshe. "Rabbinic Reflections on Defying Illegal Orders: Amasa, Abner, and Joab." Judaism 19 (1970): 30-37.

499 Hirsch, Richard G. "Social Values in Judaism and their Realization in the Reform Movement." Journal of the Central Conference of American Rabbis 18 (1971): 36-46.

Hirsch traces the emphasis that Reform Judaism has placed upon social action as well as the traditional basis for that emphasis. He suggests that the commitment of the movement has been vague and inactive. He calls for greater practical involvement in social issues. This is an interesting rebuke to the Reform Movement from one of its own leaders.

500 Hirsch, Richard G. "Toward a Theology for Social Action." In Judaism and Ethics, edited by Daniel Jeremy Silver, 249-261. New York: Ktav Publishing House, 1970.

Hirsch suggests that Jewish tradition, despite its variety and diversity, can provide concrete examples to guide moral decision making. He rejects "situation ethics" as vague, aggadic, and lacking the normative structure needed to give direction to social reform. Although a liberal Jew Hirsch issues a call for a more responsibly traditional theology of Jewish social concern.

501 Hochbaum, Jerry. "Community Action for Orthodoxy: Priorities and Perspectives." Tradition 11 (1971): 83-91.

This brief a challenge to contemporary Orthodoxy Judaism from within claims that the modern age presents Jews with an opportunity to put their religious ethics into practice, but it must be used wisely. He suggests some principles to be used in establishing those priorities and calls for a new type of leadership to reflect the revived interest in politics animating many traditional Jews.

502 Israel, Richard D. "Jewish Tradition and Political Action." In Tradition and Contemporary Experience: Essays on Jewish Thought and Life, edited by Alfred Jospe, 189-204. New York: Schocken Books Inc., 1970.

In a fascinating and self-critical essay Israel notes the association of Jews and political liberalism and suggests that among the variety of factors involved in it is enlightened self-interest. More Jews became active in civil causes out of this motive than out of traditional Jewish values. He considers such motivation highly unstable and encourages the check of traditional values. This essay should be read for its double concern with social responsibility and traditional Jewish mores.

503 Jung, Leo. "The Sense of Responsibility," in Between Man and Man, 159-176. 3rd enlarged edition. New York: Board of Jewish Education Press, 1976.

Jung, an example of a traditional Jew who espouses national patriotism, lists the various duties and obligations of the Jew from private duties to obligations towards family, community, and nation. He considers patriotism a religious duty towards one's nation and political responsibility a Jewish commandment. See 056; the essay can be found on pp.113-125 of the Hebrew version.

504 Kaplan, Mordecai. The Religion of Ethical Nationhood: Judaism's Contribution to World Peace. New York: Macmillan Publishing Company, 1970.

See the annotation at 058.

505 Kellner, Menahem Marc. "Should Government Legislate Halakhah." Sh'ma 5 (1975): 298-300.

Kellner insists that the basis of Jewish ethics is the imitation of God. The only key to such imitatio dei, however, is the halakha. Applying that principle he offers a good restatement of Jewish thinking about law, ethics, and social legislation. This short article demonstrates both clear theoretical thinking and its application to a modern social dilemma facing contemporary Jews.

506 Kimmelman, Reuven. "The Rabbinic Ethics of Protest." Judaism 19 (1970): 38-58.

See the annotation at 144 and compare 487, 497, 498, 506, 508, 511, and 521.

507 Konvitz, Milton R. "Judaism and the Democratic Ideal," in Judaism and the American Idea, 69-90. New York: Schocken Books Inc., 1980.

Konvitz offers a rather broad picture of the "democratic ideal" but one that is representative of the thought of many American Jews. He suggests parallels between prophetic social and ethical ideals and democratic values. The ideals of social and economic equality are present in both systems of thought. The conception of a law-centered society is also common to Judaism and democracy.

508 Konvitz, Milton R. "Individual Conscience and Group Consciousness in Israel and in the Diaspora." Judaism 20 (1971): 153-166.

Konvitz considers the tension between personal conscience and group consciousness. He suggests that Jewish nationalism and Jewish religion are interrelated and that affirm equally individual conscience and social solidarity. The article is reprinted in Konvitz (655), 139-159. See also 487, 497, 498, 506, 508, 511, and 521.

509 Landman, Leo. "A Further Note on 'The Law of the Kingdom is Law.'" Jewish Journal of Sociology 17 (1975): 37-41.

Landman remarks on his own earlier work and that of others that indicate that the principle that "the law of the kingdom is consider as Torah law" is primarily a diaspora concept. This study is important not only because it expands views earlier expressed but it also responds to criticism those views received. Landman examines the medieval literature to find evidence for his contention. He notes that Jews always distinguished between what was acceptable under that principle and what was not. His findings should be compared with that of other scholars in entries 478, 484, 491, 520, and 527.

510 Landman, Leo. "Dina d'Malkhuta Dina: Solely A Diaspora Concept." Tradition 15 (1975): 89-96.

The debate about the extent of the application of the principle that Jews must accept the law of the land as Torah law is reviewed. Landman reiterates his belief that it applies only in the diaspora and is a means of coming to terms with a non-Jewish government. The Jewish kings were always bound by Torah law alone. The State of Israel, on this reasoning, should be governed by Torah law and not by "the law of the land."

511 Landman, Leo. "Law and Conscience: the Jewish View." Judaism 18 (1969): 17-29.

See the annotation at 379 and 487, 497, 498, 506, 508.

512 Levenson, Jon D. "Poverty and the State in Biblical Thought." Judaism 25 (1976): 230-241.

Levenson examines the "ethical codes" of the Hebrew Scriptures: Deuteronomy and Leviticus in particular. He discovers that they were usually ideal and not put into practice. While acknowledging that it would be impossible to transplant ethical values from the biblical setting into contemporary life he suggests that the codes do provide a modern paradigm. Ethics may well outstrip reality. An ethical demand may seem exaggerated and impossible and still be a moral necessity despite realistic expectations.

513 Lipman, Eugene. "The Mission of Israel and Social Action." In Judaism and Ethics, edited by Daniel Jeremy Silver, 263-269. New York: Ktav Publishing House, 1970.

Lipman identifies the commandments as Israel's attempts to fulfill the mission of Torah through concrete deeds in society and personal experience. He reviews various theories of Judaism but finds them lacking a compelling rationale for social action. He studies the theories of Martin Buber and Mordecai Kaplan in particular but concludes that the philosophy of Second Isaiah, an expectant and active messianic hope, is the best basis for social ethics.

514 Marmur, Dov. "The Jew and the State." In his Beyond Survival: Reflections on the Future of Judaism, 160-165. London: Darton Longman, and Todd Ltd., 1982.

This interesting if unscholarly essay remarks upon the "creative maladjustment" of the Jew to life in the exile. It suggests that Jewish social consciousness is aroused by the psychological alienation that exile creates. The Jew is ambivalent to the state and seeks to transform reality into the messianic ideal.

515 Mintz, Jerome R. "Ethnic Activism: The Hasidic Example." Judaism 28 (1979): 449-464.

See the annotation at 243.

516 Polish, David. "Judaism and Human Rights." Journal of Ecumenical Studies 19 (1982):40-50.

See the annotation at 079.

517 Polish, David. "Pharisaism and Political Sovereignty." Judaism 18 (1969): 415-422.

Polish notes that the early rabbis accepted political domination and suggests that the messianic vision they affirmed was part of a program to make political dependency more acceptable. His view of Post-Biblical Jewish politics as accommodation should be compared to other essays on the subject (see 487, 497, 498, 506, 508, 511, and 521).

518 Priest, James Eugene. Governmental and Judicial Ethics in the Bible and Rabbinic Literature. New York: Ktav Publishing House and Malibu: Pepperdine University Press, 1980.

See the annotation at 155.

519 Rabinkov, Zalman Baruch. "The Individual and the Community in Judaism." In Between Man and His Fellow: Treatises on Human Relationships in Judaism [Hebrew], 85-110. Trans. by Tzvi Bar-Meir. Translations and Collections From Israel's Wisdom. Jerusalem: Mossad Harav Kook, 1975.

See the annotation at 080.

520 Rakefet-Rothkoff, Aaron. "The Law of the Land in Halakhic Perspective." Tradition 13 (1973): 5-23.

This article pays particular attention to the problem of Jewish collaboration with an unjust government. The point is made that injustice of the land is not acceptable. In the case of war a preventative, just war is acceptable and draft evasion is not to be countenanced by Jewish authorities. This essay should be compared to entries 478, 484, 491, 509, 510, and 527.

521 Rosenthal, Gilbert S. "Civil Disobedience." Conservative Judaism 22 (1968): 39-47.

This is a very general and not well developed survey of Jewish thinking about relationships between Jews and established governments. Rosenthal touches all the important points -- biblical precedence, historical examples, the principle of the law of the land, medieval thought about monarchy. His conclusions, however, should be contrasted with those of thinkers represented in entries 487, 497, 498, 506, 508, and 511.

522 Rotenstreich, Nathan. "Universalism and Particularism." In Proceedings of the Jerusalem Colloquium of Religion, Peoplehood, Nation and Land, edited by Marc H. Tanenbaum and R.J.Zwi Werblowsky, 19-30. Truman Research Institute Publication 7 Jerusalem: Hebrew University of Jerusalem, American Jewish Committee, Israeli Interfaith Committee, 1970.

This serious and erudite essay argues that universalism is untenable except as an abstract idea. Since human creativity demands specific, concrete realization, the national institutions of state, law, and history in general are contributions to humanity as a whole. Jewish social ethics, therefore, consists as much in what Jews do specifically as Jews in building a Jewish community as in what they do for humanity as a whole.

523 Roth, Sol. The Jewish Idea of Community. New York: Yeshiva University Press, 1977.

This informative, if idealized and polemical, investigation of the idea of community in Judaism focuses on sanctification by separation from the non-Jewish world. This particularist perspective is defended as a moral affirmation of covenant. See in contrast Shatz, (526).

524 Samuelson, Norbert M. "Can Democracy and Capitalism be Jewish Values? Mordecai Kaplan's Political Philosophy." Modern Judaism 3 (1983): 189-215.

See the annotation at 319.

525 Schwarzschild, Steven S. "On The Theology of Jewish Survival." In Judaism and Ethics, edited by Daniel Jeremy Silver, 287-314. New York: Ktav Publishing House, 1970.

Schwarzschild makes a cogent protest against "Israeli triumphalism" by arguing that Jewish survival is for the sake of covenant existence, not for political expedience. He suggests that an ethical approach to the Arab nations will symbolize this type of covenantal ethics in opposition to chauvanistic politics. Jewish survival, on this reading, is not an ethical value by itself but only becomes moral through a specific conception of the purpose of Jewish life and of the continued existence of the Jewish people.

526 Shatz, David. "The Jewish Idea of Community." Tradition 17 (1978): 122-129.

In a lengthy review of Sol Roth's book (see 523) Shatz affirms Jewish universalism. Community is more ethical and less particularistic than Roth would have it, he claims. The religious command to love of neighbor is not merely emotive but action oriented. Such actions, he suggests, can be directed to the non-Jew as well as to the Jew.

527. Shilo, Schmuel. Dina DeMalkutha Dina: The Law of the Land is Law [Hebrew]. The Institute for Research in Jewish Law Publication 5. Jerusalem: Jerusalem Academic Press, 1974.

This survey of the development of the idea of "the law of the land is law" from its talmudic origins through its development in medieval and modern times concludes that the principle was never applied uncritically as a general formula. Each case was investigated to see if it fell under the appropriate legal and ethical categories to be included as a true "law of the land." As conditions changed so the way in which earlier texts were understood also changed. Shilo demonstrates that the application of a legal principle may involve considerable ethical reflection. See the considerable discussion in entries 478, 484, 491, 509, 510, and 520.

528 Siegel, Seymour. "New Directions in Jewish Social Ethics: A Case for Traditional Conservatism." Conservative Judaism 24 (1970): 55-64.

Siegel questions the association of Jews with liberal causes. The idea of covenant law seems to him an indication that political authority is important since human sinfulness is said to require the restraint and control of a strong central government. He advances both the principle of dina d'malchuta dina "the law of the kingdom is law," and the reliance on messianic hope rather than political activism as proof that Jewish politics is basically conservative. See the response by Fenster, (494).

529 Silver, Daniel Jeremy. "Beyond the Apologetics of Mission." In Judaism and Ethics, edited by Daniel Jeremy Silver, 327-338. New York: Ktav Publishing House, 1970.

Silver contends that the functional questions of Jewish survival are practical and immediate. The theological justification of that survival are merely afterthoughts. Jews should not rush to legitimize their survival through theology. An exaggeration of the mission and meaning of Israel can lead to disillusionment. This view should be contrasted with Schwarzschild, (525).

530 Soloveitchik, Joseph B. "The Community." Tradition 17 (1978): 7-24.

This traditional argument suggests that in Judaism the individual and society are inseparable. Community is understood as essential and ontological a reality as the individual person. God created Jewish community at Sinai and thereby gave it an independent existence. Community implies joint responsibility for causing suffering, pain, or affliction to another.

531 Soloveitchik, Joseph B. "On the Love of Torah and the Redemption of the Religious Spirit," in In Aloneness, In Togetherness: A Selection of Hebrew Writings [Hebrew], 401-433. Edited by Pinchas H. Peli. Jerusalem: Orot, 1976.

These essays by an important Orthodox thinker explore the relationship between the Jew and the State of Israel as a Jewish land and as a secular government.

532 Twersky, Isadore. "Some Aspects of the Jewish Attitude Towards the Welfare State," in Studies in Jewish Law and Philosophy, 108-129. New York: Ktav Publishing House, 1982.

In a learned and insightful essay Twersky surveys Jewish social ethics from talmudic aggada through the halakhic injunctions of Maimonides and the Shulhan Arukh. He notes that a providential view of history did not entail a quietism but rather an active concern for the poor that made social action a collective responsibility. There is precedent, he concludes, within Judaism for declaring that the state has responsibility to provide for all its members.

533 Weinstein, Deena and Michael A. Weinstein. "Jewish Ethics: The Tension Between Particularism and Universalism." Listening 14 (1979): 6-12.

See the annotation at 097.

534 Wiesel, Elie. Legends of Our Time. New York: Holt, Reinhart and Winston Inc., 1969.

In a fascinating combination of traditional style and contemporary sensitivity Wiesel returns to the persona of being his grandfather's grandchild. Approaching social ethics from the perspective of a Holocaust survivor he tells stories of both the past and present in order to stress the obligations owed by the living to the dead.

535 Wiesel, Elie. One Generation After. Trans. by Lily Edelman and the Author. New York: Random House Inc., 1972.

This moving narrative told with stylistic grace is focused on the modern period and on social ethics. Wiesel continues the reflection on contemporary events and stories as begun in the earlier entry. He records meetings with Soviet Jews, Marranos, and Israelis. In each case his unique perspective on social ethics, that of a survivor with a humanistic mission, is clearly evident.

4
Themes in Jewish Ethics

THE LOVE COMMANDMENT AND SELF-SACRIFICE

536 Agus, Jacob Bernard. "Polarity in Jewish Ethics." Sh'ma 7 (1977): 115-117.

See the annotation at 019.

537 Blidstein, Gerald. "The non-Jew in Jewish Ethics." Sh'ma 7 (1977): 37-39.

Blidstein's claim that the non-Jew is given rights in Judaism involves a study of "charity," that is of a legislated moral obligation extending to all human beings. This response to Schwarzschild's article on Jewish ethics (see 089) is part of a valuable debate in contemporary Jewish ethics.

538 Brickner, Balfour. "Silent Hate is Also a Sin." Sh'ma 9 (1979): 113-115.

In a short, nontechnical note Brickner claims that suspicion and "silent hate" is as much a contradiction of the love commandment as is action.

539 Daub, David. "Limitations on Self-Sacrifice in Jewish Law and Tradition ." Theology 72 (1969): 291-304.

This historical study is also helpful in gaining perspective on Jewish views of self-sacrifice (see 546, 549, 550, 553). Daub notes the safeguards against such action as well as the permission to practice it in cases of extreme danger to Jewish belief and religious life. He claims that the primacy of life is the basic rule of Jewish ethics.

540 Dove, Y. "Kindliness." In Building Jewish Ethical Character, edited by Joseph Kaminetsky and Murray I. Friedman, 259-264. New York: The Fryer Foundation, 1975.

See the annotation at 032.

160 BIBLIOGRAPHICAL SURVEY

541 Dressler, Eliyahu. "The Discourse on Lovingkindness: Or Giving and Taking," in <u>Strive for Truth: Mitchtavme Eliyahu, the selected writings of Eliyahu Eliezer Dressler</u>, 118-158. Trans. by Aryeh Carmell. New York: Feldheim Publishing Company, 1978.

This extended <u>musar</u> discourse encompasses all elements of human living: character traits, love -- as it applies to neighbor, sexuality, and family -- perfecting the world, loving of God, are all related to the choice between being a taker or a giver. The keystone of lovingkindness, Dressler argues, is making this particular choice. Jewish tradition, he suggests, is on the side of being a giver. This study shows the importance of love in all its aspects to Jewish ethical thinking.

542 Fisch, Harold. "A Response to Ernst Simon." In <u>Modern Jewish Ethics: Theory and Practice</u>, edited by Marvin Fox, 57-61. Columbus: Ohio State University Press, 1975.

The dialogue between Ernst Simon and Harold Fisch is an important example of differing Jewish ethical perspectives. Fisch rejects the view that the central ethical principle in Judaism is that of loving the neighbor (see Ernst Simon's original statement in entry 559). He raises five objections: the demand to the love the neighbor is not unique, other commands than that of love apply to relationships with the neighbor; love commandments involve reciprocity and not merely a onesided outpouring of affection, the difference between "hesed" (loving as expressed in deeds of kindness) and "ahavah" (love as an affection) needs to be made clear, and finally there is no Jewish ethics independent of or outside of <u>halakhic</u> action.

543 Gifter, Mordecai. "Ahavas Chesed." In <u>Building Jewish Ethical Character</u>, edited by Joseph Kaminetsky and Murray I. Friedman, 219-223. New York: The Fryer Foundation, 1975.

See the annotation at 039.

544 Harvey, Warren Zev. "Love: The Beginning and End of the Torah." <u>Tradition</u> 15 (1976): 5-22.

See the annotation at 048.

545 Himmelfarb, Milton. "The Ethics of Jewish Self-Defense." <u>Sh'ma</u> 7 (1977): 89-90.

This article continues the debate sparked by Steven Schwarzschild (See 089 and the annotation there) and suggests that Schwarzschild's demands for universalism are unrealistic and therefore against Jewish interests. The theme of love of the other in relationship to self-concern is developed as a basis for Jewish ethical thought. The vigor of the debate demonstrates its importance in contemporary Jewish ethical thinking.

546 Jacobs, Louis. "Greater Love Hath No Man...The Jewish Point of View of Self-Sacrifice." In Contemporary Jewish Ethics, edited by Menahem Marc Kellner, 175-183. Sanhedrin Jewish Studies. New York: Sanhedrin Press, 1978.

In a seminal study of self-sacrifice Louis Jacobs argues against "Jewish realism" and notes the biblical exaltation of the sacrifice of one's own life for the sake of principle and for the sake of others. He suggests that while law can only point to legal requirements; saintliness goes beyond the letter of the law and has its own obligations. Compare 539, 549, 550, 553.

547 Jung, Leo. "The Program of Kindness," in Between Man and Man, 34-43. 3rd enlarged edition. New York: Board of Jewish Education Press, 1976.

This fascinating example of a traditional Jew's program of moral action is an inspirational rather than critical program. Jung suggests that an individual's life as well as the life of others involved will benefit from following the directives of Jewish morality. See also 056; the essay is found on pp. 142-144 of the Hebrew version. It should also be compared to a companion article, "The Love of Grace," found on pp. 69-73 and in Hebrew 173-176 that also emphasizes love as a basic element in Jewish ethics.

548 Klausner, Joseph. "Christian and Jewish Ethics." In Faith and Reason: Essays in Judaism, edited by Robert Gordis and Ruth B. Waxman, 100-114. New York: Ktav Publishing House , 1973.

See the annotation at 059.

549 Petuchowski, Jakob J. "The Limits of Self-Sacrifice." In Modern Jewish Ethics: Theory and Practice, edited by Marvin Fox, 103-118. Columbus: Ohio State University Press, 1975.

Petuchowski seems to agree that radical ethics is a modern rather than a traditional Jewish standpoint. The law does limit the extent to which an individual should go in love of others and in self-sacrifice. He is, however, persuaded by Louis Jacobs (entry 546) that morality can go beyond the law since communal self-interest often takes precedence over the instinct for individual survival. This debate demonstrates the complexity of both the principle of love and demands for self-sacrifice in Judaism. Compare 539, 550, 553.

550 Pines, Shlomo. "Two Who Walk in the Desert," in Studies in the History of Jewish Philosophy: The transmission of Texts and Ideas [Hebrew], 9-11. Jerusalem: Bialik Institute, 1977.

See the annotation at entry 153.

162 BIBLIOGRAPHICAL SURVEY

551 Plishkin, Zelig. Love Your Neighbor: You and Your Fellow Man in the Light of Torah. Brooklyn: Aish HaTorah, 1977.

See the annotation at 013.

552 Rackman, Emanuel. "The Centrality of the Concept of Chesed." In The Jacob Dolnitsky Memorial Volume: Studies in Jewish Law, Philosophy, Literature, and Language, edited by Morris Casriel Katz, 44-50. Hebrew Section. Skokie: Hebrew Theological College, 1983.

See the annotation at 082.

553 Reines, Chaim Zeev. "The Self and the Other in Rabbinic Ethics." In Contemporary Jewish Ethics, edited by Menahem Marc Kellner, 162-174. Sanhedrin Jewish Studies. New York: Sanhedrin Press, 1978.

This successful mixture of scholarship and popular appeal criticizes the view that Judaism is more realistic that Christianity and argues that there are certain moral imperatives in Judaism that do lead to the idea of self-sacrifice, even though there is a strong tradition that insists upon emphasizing the self. The moral demand to go beyond the requirements of the law when the honoring of human beings demand it, he claims, implies self-sacrifice in certain situations. Compare 539, 546, 549, 550.

554 Samuelson, Norbert. "The Ethics of Preferring One's Own." Sh'ma 7 (1977): 41-42.

See annotation at 087 and the references at 089.

555 Schwarzschild, Steven S. "The Question of Jewish Ethics Today II." Sh'ma 7 (1977): 118-124.

This article continues the on-going discussion of the question of martyrdom and self-sacrifice. The debate of whether parochial or universal values is central in Judaism and the place of survival in the Jewish ethical system is equally crucial. The various positions involved in this discussion need careful scrutiny (see the original article in 089 and the references there).

556 Shapiro, David S. "The Concept of 'Chesed' in Judaism," in Studies in Jewish Thought 1, 98-121. Studies in Judaica. New York: Yeshiva University Press, 1975.

This masterful analysis of an ethical principle explains that love in Judaism implies imitation of the divine. More specifically it entails a creative preservation of the world. Shapiro demonstrates the interconnection between religious belief and ethical living. The use of biblical and talmudic sources enriches this essay.

557 Shatz, David. "The Jewish Idea of Community." Tradition 17 (1978): 122-129.

See the annotation at entry 526.

558 Sherwin, Byron. "Law and Love in Jewish Theology." Anglican Theological Review 64 (1982): 454-466.

See the annotation at 408.

559 Simon, Ernst. "The Neighbor Whom We Shall Love." In Modern Jewish Ethics: Theory and Practice, edited by Marvin Fox, 29-56. Columbus: Ohio State University Press, 1975.

This important study of the command to love the neighbor discusses whether the neighbor means only a Jew or whether it includes the non-Jew. It focuses on the talmudic debate on whether love of neighbor or the divine image within each human being is the basic ethical principle and concludes that only a sensitivity to the universal importance of each human being can entitle a Jew to claim that Israel's God is the God of all humanity. This article emphasizing universalism and the centrality of the love commandment sparked considerable debate (see Fisch 542 and the various entries associated with 089).

560 Spero, Shubert. "The Self and the Other," in Morality, Halakha, and the Jewish Tradition, 201-235. The Library of Jewish Law and Ethics 9. New York: Ktav Publishing House, 1983.

This part of Spero's book (see 016) is a valuable summary of the issues involved in Jewish ethical thought. The chapter explores the ethical demands upon an individual to move from selfish concern to consideration of others and the arguments concerning the love commandment, the limitations on self-sacrifice, the demand for martyrdom, and the individual's duties toward the community of Israel. Spero provides an encyclopedic view of the sources and their interpretations.

561 Weber, Stanley G. "Another Perspective on Jewish Ethics." Sh'ma 7 (1977): 48-49.

See the annotation at 096.

562 Wyschogrod, Michael. "The Particularism of Jewish Ethics." Sh'ma 7 (1977): 39-40.

See the annotation at 099.

HUMAN DIGNITY AND THE DIVINE IMAGE IN HUMANITY

563 Altmann, Alexander. "Homo Imago Dei in Jewish and Christian Theology." Journal of Religion 48:3 (1968): 235-259.

See the annotation at 131.

564 Buber, Martin. "Imitatio Dei." In Contemporary Jewish Ethics, edited by Menahem Marc Kellner, 152-161. Sanhedrin Jewish Studies. New York: Sanhedrin Press, 1978.

Buber's classic contrast between Greek Philosophy, Christianity, and Judaism claims that Greek Philosophy is abstract, Christianity too concrete, but Judaism seeks to "perfect our unique selfhood." The Jew, Buber claims clearly reading his "I-Thou" philosophy back into Jewish tradition, walks in divine ways by responding to the experience of God. See also 576.

565 Damiel, Yitzhak. "On Faith in Man and its Meaning," in Faith In Man and What Is Beyond It [Hebrew], 7-27. Tel Aviv: Mahberot L'Safrut, 1968.

See the annotation at 031.

566 Friedman, Maurice. "Jesus: Image of Man or Image of God," in Touchstones of Reality: Existential Trust and the Community of Peace, 182-204. New York: E.P.Dutton and Company, 1974.

Friedman reviews his encounter with the New Testament and suggests in an important statement of one Jewish view of Jesus that in the distinction between apocalyptic and prophetic religion lies the difference between Christianity and the Jewish religion of Jesus. He affirms the latter as an image of humanity, a basis for human dignity. He fails to find within Pauline Christianity and equally compelling image of human life.

567 Harvey, Warren Zev. "Holiness: A Command to Imitatio Dei." Tradition 16 (1977): 7-28.

This competent summary of Jewish views of holiness and imitation of God has a popular style and clear expression. It suggests that the moral imperative for human life is imitating divine actions but distinguishes between the moral imperative to walk in God's ways and the religious imperative to become holy. Both, however, are interrelated as the foundation of the Jewish directive for human living.

568 Heschel, Abraham Joshua. "The Sacred Image of Man," in The Insecurity of Freedom: Essays on Human Existence, 150-167. New York: Schocken Books Inc., 1972.

This essay focuses on Judaism's view of humanity as created in the image of God and explores the ethical implications of that view. Heschel's creative theological argument is that being human involves both the dignity of being created in the divine image and the recognition of limitations. He suggests that biology has reduced the image of humanity to zoological terms, a reduction that he considers moral suicide. See also 052, 053.

569 Jacobs, Louis. "The Doctrine of the Divine Spark in man Jewish Sources." In <u>Studies in Rationalism: Judaism and Universalism</u>, edited by Raphael Loewe, 87-114. London: Routledge and Kegan Paul Ltd., 1966.

This scholarly reflection on a central religious and moral concept compares Jewish, Hindu, and Muslim views of the divine spark within humanity as well as Hasidic and non-Hasidic interpretations of it. It concludes that this view of God is closely tied to the meaning of human selfhood.

570 Karff, Samuel E. "Man's Power and Limits in a Technological Age." <u>Judaism</u> 23 (1974): 161-173.

This passionate plea for religious humility suggests that in an age in which human beings have attained control over their environment they must wrestle with both a sense of their power and their impotence. The modern age requires both humility and recognition of human potential. The Jewish tradition stresses the balance between these two positions and therefore is of particular use in the contemporary crisis.

571 Konvitz, Milton R. "Human Dignity: From Creation to Constitution-A Philosophy of Human Rights From the Standpoint of Judaism." In <u>Essays on the Occasion of the Seventieth Anniversary of the Dropsie University(1909-1979)</u>, edited by Abraham I. Katsh and Leon Nemoy, 297-306. Philadelphia: Dropsie University Press, 1979.

Konvitz explores the theological basis for the idea of human dignity, its rooting in the biblical creation story, its development in rabbinic literature, its emphasis in medieval pietistic literature and claims that the same spirit animated the framers of the American constitution. The essay is reproduced in Konvitz (655), 33-51.

572 Konvitz, Milton R. "Man's Dignity in God's World," in <u>Judaism and Human Rights</u>, 27-32. Bnai Brith Jewish Heritage Classics. New York: W.W.Norton and Company, 1972.

In a short but valuable survey of Jewish anthropology Konvitz reviews the sources of the idea of human dignity in Judaism in the Bible, in Hasidism and in modern thinkers like Abraham Isaac Kook. He remarks on the need for a double criteria that emphasizes both humility and dignity. This statement of belief demonstrates how classical religious ideas are applied to contemporary ethical issues.

573 Lamm, Norman. "Notes on the Concept of <u>Imitatio Dei</u>." In <u>Rabbi Joseph H. Lookstein Memorial Volume</u>, edited by Leo Landman, 217-229. New York: Ktav Publishing House, 1980.

In a scholarly review of mystical and <u>musar</u> literature Lamm contrasts the idea of impersonating God with the concept of imitating divine morality. This work can be used as an academic complement to more theological studies.

574 Linzer, Norman. The Nature of Man in Judaism and Social Work. New York: Commission on Synagogue Relations, 1978.

This ambitious philosophical work explores the way in which both Judaism and social work oppose the presumptions of a pessimistic, materialistic, and limited modern conception of being human. The views of Jewish thinkers -- Heschel, Soloveitchik, Cynthia Ozick -- are used to stress the dual nature of being human, the lifestages through which a person progresses, and the means of coping with good and evil. The concepts of sin, repentance, and the holy sparks within each soul are discussed as well as the details of Jewish religious observance.

575 Lopian, Eliyahu. "The Power of Human Nature and the Function of Suffering," in Lev Eliyahu: A Collection of Talks, 34-40. Trans. by B.D.Klein. Jerusalem: Kalman Pinski, 1975.

This homiletical piece graphically describes the evil against which each person must struggle. Suffering is interpreted as part of this struggle in a traditionalist, and well written, statement of religious anthropology. The essay "Man's Grandeur and Degradation," pp., 90-99, is an equally representative statement of traditional Jewish views of human nature emphasizing the duality of human potential.

576 Shapiro, David S. "The Doctrine of the Image of God and Imitatio Dei," in Studies in Jewish Thought 1, 25-43. Studies in Judaica Series. New York: Yeshiva University Press, 1975.

Shapiro's valuable essay notes that imitation of God as a religious act, as well as a moral one, is part of Jewish tradition. Through imitation of the transcendent qualities of the divine a human being learns moral humility. The Sabbath is taken as the primary example of such imitation that leads to humility and that gives expression to both ethical values and the need for holiness.This essay provides a counterpoint to Buber's contribution to the interpretation of the concept of imitation of God (see 564). It is more traditional in its orientation, use of sources, and final conclusions than Buber's idiosyncratic approach. Both essays are reproduced in Kellner (111), 127-151.

577 Shapiro, David S. "The Meaning of Holiness in Judaism," in Studies in Jewish Thought 1, 63-97. Studies in Judaica Series. New York: Yeshiva University Press, 1975.

This article presents historical and philosophical evidence in a clear and precise way. It is an exemplary study of

Jewish moral concepts regarding the image of God. Shapiro argues that the imitation of God means following in the ways of the halakha. God's justice and mercy are the basis upon which human beings construct the kingdom of heaven on earth. In view of this human task Shapiro notes that the kabbalah and Maimonides contend that human virtue strengthens the divine presence in the world. By imitating God's moral qualities humanity makes the world more moral. This active ethics is contrasted with the idea of imitation of God in both Greek philosophy and Eastern religious traditions.

578 Soloveitchik, Joseph B. Halakhic Man, trans. by Lawrence Kaplan. Philadelphia: Jewish Publication Society of America, 1983.

See the annotation at 092.

579 Soloveitchik, Joseph B. In Aloneness, In Togetherness: A Selection of Hebrew Writings [Hebrew]. Edited by Pinchas H. Peli. Jerusalem: Orot, 1976.

Not only does this anthology include the classic essay on Halakhic man, but a number of other significant studies. In one Soloveitchik examines the difference between Sabbath and the major holidays, on the one hand, which are obvious in their holiness and the New Moon celebration, on the other, which has a concealed holiness. He then shows how the same distinction holds true for human qualities. Human dignity and human ethics are often best served in quiet, unobvious ways.

580 Soloveitchik, Joseph B. "Majesty and Humility." Tradition 17 (1978): 25-37.

See the annotation at 093.

FREE WILL, EVIL, AND JEWISH ETHICS

581 Agus, Jacob Bernard. "Freedom and Determination," in The Vision and the Way: An Interpretation of Jewish Ethics, 199-219. New York: Frederick Ungar Publishing Company, 1966.

This useful introduction to the question of freedom and determinism relates the issue to differing evaluations of human worth in Judaism. Because the human being is both dust and ashes and the image of God, free choice requires a flexible response to challenges. A person can choose either to respond as a natural being or as a being with transcendent potential. Texts from rabbinic and medieval Jewish sources are used to demonstrate this contention.

582 Berkovits, Eliezer. Faith After the Holocaust. New York: Ktav Publishing House, 1973.

See the annotation at 256.

583 Fackenheim, Emil L. God's Presence in History: Jewish Affirmations and Philosophical Reflections. Harper Torchbooks. New York: Harper and Row, 1970.

See the annotation at 312.

584 Fackenheim, Emil L. "Human Freedom and Divine Power," in Quest for Past and Future: Essays in Jewish Theology, 338-343. Bloomington: Indiana University Press, 1968.

This early article by Fackenheim offers a profound view of the relationship between personal freedom and responsibility and an acceptance of God's power. It argues that while divine power is at the center of life, human responsibility is at the center of personhood. While the two ideas seem contradictory they in fact represent different logical systems. The system in which God's power is central is internally consistent; the system in which human responsibility is central is internally consistent.

585 Faur, Jose. "Reflections on Job and Situation Morality." Judaism 19 (1970): 219-225.

This probing article focusing on an analysis of the biblical book of Job suggests that the author's objective was to question the conventional morality of his time. In boundary situations such as he experienced rational ethics are shattered. The Holocaust represents such a shattering of normal ethics. There are times when a universal, rational ethics (like Kant's) is inappropriate. The critique of Job is needed in just those situations. While using a biblical tale as the basis for its reflection this is a Jewish confrontation with a modern, not merely biblical, problem.

586 Fox, Marvin. "Review Essay: Berkovits' Treatment of the Problem of Evil." Tradition 14 (1974): 116-124.

See the annotation at 269.

587 Grunblatt, Joseph. "Freedom of the Will: A Traditionalist's View." Tradition 10 (1969): 48-59.

This interesting, if not seminal or original article, reviews the Kantian demand for autonomous moral freedom in the light of Jewish sources from the Talmud through modern times. It suggests that the religious presupposition is that human beings are able to transcend their nature. The purpose of Jewish law is precisely that of training individuals to transcend themselves.

588 Katz, Steven S. Post-Holocaust Dialogues: Critical Studies in Modern Jewish Thought. New York: New York University Press, 1983.

See the annotation at 281.

589 Kushner, Harold. "Why Do the Righteous Suffer: Notes Toward a Theology of Tragedy." Judaism 28 (1979): 316-323.

This essay provides an early sketch of what was later to become a popular book and may be of interest because of this. Kushner suggests that emphasis should be given not to the evil but to free will, natural law, and the nature of a person's obligations to others. This is a rather typical and unexciting approach to the question of evil, but because the book became noteworthy the essay may be of interest.

590 Matt, Hershel J. "Man's Choice and God's Design." Judaism 21 (1972): 211-221.

See the annotation at 455.

591 Rubenstein, Richard. After Auschwitz. Indianapolis: The Bobbs-Merrill Company, 1968.

This early work in which Rubenstein describes his disillusionment with the values and claims of traditional religion argues that whatever the psychological or sociological relevance of Judaism once was it is no longer persuasive, particularly in the light of the radical evil of the Nazi Holocaust.

592 Rubenstein, Richard L. The Cunning of History: The Holocaust and the American Future. Harper Colophon Books. New York: Harper and Row Publishers, 1978.

This book offers one of the most profound and challenging interpretations of modern evil developed by a modern Jewish thinker. Rubenstein interprets modern history as a deterministic onslaught that undermines traditional values. The rationalization of human action and life has meant that the ideals which kept human greed and corruption in check are now rejected. The irony is that Jews who have been among the most modernized groups in contemporary life were the victims of modernity. The pessimistic sociological and psychological views he presents offer but limited possibility for human progress or hope.

593 Schachter, Zalman. "Patterns of Good and Evil." In Rediscovering Judaism: Reflections on a New Theology, edited by Arnold Jacob Wolf, 163-209. Chicago: Quadrangle Books, 1965.

The persuasive interpretation of evil offered here on the basis of Jewish sources contends that "free choice" is always the product of life situations and never easy since good and evil are not distinct entities but confused mixtures of right and wrong. The argument uses as a primary example the dilemma of the returnee to Judaism who seeks a resolution of crisis in Torah and contends that it does not solve problems but rather makes the dilemma more acute.

594 Schimmel, Solomon. "Free Will, Guilt, and Self-Control in Rabbinic Judaism and Contemporary Psychology." Judaism 26 (1977): 418-429.

In a brief but fascinating article Schimmel looks at the extraordinary psychological concerns of rabbinic literature and compares them to the major concerns of psychology. The two traditions share an emphasis on self-analysis, a desire to induce change, and a general theory of human nature. They diverge on the questions of whether to be normative or therapeutic and of whether to look at human nature as behaviorist or as exemplary of the image of God.

595 Schulweis, Harold M. Evil and the Morality of God. Jewish Perspectives 4. Cincinnati: Hebrew Union College Press, 1983.

This valuable theological essay surveys medieval ideas of God's perfection and the problem that poses given evil in the world. Schulweis contributes a sophisticated understanding of the idea of God, the question of progress, and the basis of morality to the entire discussion of freedom and ethics. Modern answers given by personalists, existentialists, and theologians are reviewed. In their place Schulweis suggests that the process be reversed. Rather than looking at God and deriving ethics, the question should be whether ethical ideals are godly. He argues for both the reality of the qualities of goodness, love, intelligence, and creativity and for their godliness.

596 Seeskin, Kenneth R. "The Reality of Radical Evil." Judaism 29 (1980): 450-453.

This is not a major article but demonstrates the continuing struggle of Jewish thinkers with the problem of evil. Seeskin admits that freedom of choice is a meager compensation for the suffering that radical evil creates. Instead of advocating an intellectual answer, however, he suggests that only an existential acceptance of one's own situation is possible.

598 Soloveitchik, Joseph B. "The Righteous Who Suffers Evil," in In Aloneness, In Togetherness: A Selection of Hebrew Writings [Hebrew], 331-400. Edited by Pinchas H. Peli. Jerusalem: Orot, 1976.

Soloveitchik considers evil and suffering part of the divine plan. When a righteous person suffers it is, according to this essay, a means by which a person is exalted and led to repentance. In the modern, post-Holocaust age, he suggests, there are six hopeful signs that reveal that out of evil good, even redemption, can come. This essay is a traditional view of the relationship between ethics and evil: evil is a reminder of the ethical task and suffering rededicates one to the task.

597 Sole, Moshe Zeev. "Faith in Free Will," in On the Essence of Judaism [Hebrew], 53-56. Jerusalem: Keriyat Sefer, 1969.

Sole notes that modern individuals feel the pressures of family and society impinging on freedom; he recalls the Kantian paradox that human beings act as if they are free but think as if all were determined. He looks at the problem from the perspective of modern Jewish thinkers like A.D.Gordon who considered free will the basic ethical presupposition. His major contention is that belief in free will is itself a psychological determinant that creates the possibility of freedom; he uses the midrashic explanation of the need for inner liberation after the Israelites were liberated from the external domination of the Egyptians to bolster his argument.

599 Spero, Shubert. "Freedom and Responsibility," in Morality, Halakha, and the Jewish Tradition, 236-273. The Library of Jewish Law and Ethics 9. New York: Ktav Publishing House, 1983.

This useful part of Spero's book (016) contends that no person is ever a fully completed, realized entity. People are always in the process of developing. Because of this process the elements making up both the self and the environment are constantly changing and are unpredictable. This unpredictability makes for freedom. Given freedom humans are not only developing, but they are in control of the course of their development. Responsibility entails shaping and directing how one develops.

600 Weinfeld, Abraham C. Basic Jewish Ethics and Freedom of the Will. New York: Bloch, 1968.

See the annotation at 018.

601 Worob, Avrohom. "The Problem of Evil," in Duties of the Mind: Essays on Jewish Philosophy, edited by Nova Worob, 43-44, Spring Valley: Shaare Emet, 1975.

This is a traditionalist address, homiletical rather than philosophic, suggesting that the response a Jew should make to evil is adherence to Torah. Through the practice of Torah the world will be redeemed, the messiah brought to earth, and evil eradicated. This is naive, hopeful, but also typical of many traditional Jewish thinkers. The essay should be compared with "The Free-Will Determinism Issue," pp. 44-46, which looks at a historical debate between the Pharisees and Sadducees and applies that debate to the modern controversy.

5
Jewish Ethics and Non-Jewish Ethical Theories

KANT, KIERKEGAARD, AND JEWISH ETHICS

602 Axinn, Sidney. "Kant on Judaism." Jewish Quarterly Review, n.s., 59 (1968): 9-23.

Axinn's article should be read as a commentary on Fackenheim's response to Kant's morality (see 313). Axinn claims that Kant's view of each person as part of a free willed kingdom of ends is analogous to the Jewish view of the chosen people: chosenness means freedom to choose and pursue a task. One need not reject Kant in the name of Judaism, Axinn contends. Kantian philosophy may not be sufficient for Jewish ethics, but it provides a basis upon which a Jewish ethics can be argued.

603 Bergman, Samuel Hugo. "The Sacrifice of Isaac and Contemporary Man," in The Quality of Faith: Essays on Judaism and Morality, 24-31. Trans. by Yehudah Hanegbi. Jerusalem: World Zionist Organization, 1970.

This well written and sophisticated analysis of the meaning of the binding of Isaac in Jewish tradition, Kierkegaard, and Kant rejects any theory of blind obedience as being dangerous and ethically misleading. From the standpoint of Kant human beings are given too much credit for autonomy; from the Kierkegaardian perspective too much trust is given to the divine will. Bergman claims that the best approach, and one he identifies with Judaism, is that of admitting human ignorance and acting out of limited knowledge and the desire to further the good of humanity. See 005; the essay is found on pp. 21-35 of the Hebrew version.

604 Brown, Michael. "Knight of Faith or Man of Doubt." Conservative Judaism 35 (1972): 17-23.

The debate over the morality of Abraham's willingness to sacrifice Isaac is continued in this essay. The rigors of theological investigation or agonized philosophical questions of autonomy are given slight attention. Despite its basically homiletical approach that looks at Abraham as an explorer of the unknown the essay is still an attractive discussion of the problem of sacrifice in religious ethics. Sacrifice emerges as the religious response to the dilemmas of human limitations combined with the human desire to fulfill the will of the deity. Taken as an address to religious individuals this essay is a fascinating exploration of religious obligation.

605 Ellenson, David. "Emil Fackenheim and the Revealed Morality of Judaism." Judaism 25 (1976): 402-413.

See the annotation at 311.

606 Fackenheim, Emil L. "Abraham and the Kantians: Moral Duties and Divine Commandments," in Encounters Between Judaism and Modern Philosophy: A Preface to Future Jewish Thought, 9-29. New York: Basic Books, 1973.

See the annotation at 313.

607 Fox, Marvin. "Kierkegaard and Rabbinic Judaism." In Faith and Reason: Essays in Judaism, edited by Robert Gordis and Ruth B. Waxman, 115-124. New York: Ktav Publishing House, 1973.

In an important study Fox confronts Kierkegaard's understanding of the binding of Isaac with talmudic and later rabbinic stories and insists on the radical difference between the two. Judaism does not emphasize the moral absurdity of the task but rather Abraham's rational understanding of the moral correctness of the divine demand.

608 Gordis, Robert. "The Faith of Abraham: A Note on Kierkegaard's 'Teleological Suspension of the Ethical'." Judaism 25 (1976): 414-419.

In a helpful sorting out of the major issues Gordis reflects on the continuing discussion of Kierkegaard's interpretation of the binding of Isaac. He argues that the rabbis found ethical dilemmas in the story, but that when the story is looked at in its biblical context it makes moral sense.

609 Green, Ronald M. "Abraham, Isaac and the Jewish Tradition: An Ethical Appraisal." Journal of Religious Ethics 10 (1982): 1-21.

See the annotation at 041.

610 Halevi, Jacob L. "Kierkegaard and the Midrash." In Faith and Reason: Essays in Judaism, edited by Robert Gordis and Ruth B. Waxman, 125- 140. New York: Ktav Publishing House, 1973.

This interesting, if not especially illuminating or important study of the binding of Isaac claims that midrash is exemplary because it embraces a variety of different approaches. The best use of this article is as a balance to Fox (605) whom Halevi criticizes for over simplifying a complex tradition.

611 Heschel, Abraham Joshua. A Passion for Truth. New York: Farrar, Straus and Giroux, 1973.

See the annotation at 241.

612 Jacobs, Louis. "The Problem of the Akeda in Jewish Thought." In Kierkegaard's "Fear and Trembling": Critical Appraisals, edited by Robert L. Perkins, 1-9. University: University of Alabama Press, 1981.

This essay, with an excellent bibliography, is the best introduction possible to the variety of approaches Jews take towards the story of Abraham's binding of his son Isaac. Jacobs surveys the various ways Jews have looked at the binding of Isaac. He notes that there are two major strands in confronting Kierkegaard: one, representing the rational tradition, stresses the Talmud, Maimonides, and the other approaches that seem antithetical to Kierkegaard; the second stresses midrash and existential response; from that standpoint Kierkegaard's view is an alternative option among many Jewish responses. Compare Jacob's discussion of this problem at annotation 055 and the response to it in 012.

613 Kasher, Naomi. "Leibowitz's view of Religion in Relationship to Kantian Ethics." In Sefer Yeshiyahu Leibowitz: A Collection of Essays on his Thought and in his Honor [Hebrew], edited by Asa Kasher and Jacob Levinger. Tel Aviv: Tel Aviv University Student Association, 1977.

See the annotation at 326.

614 Milch Robert J. "An Encounter with the 'Akeda'." Judaism 22 (1973): 397-399.

This homiletical essay suggests that the central concern in the story of Abraham's binding of Isaac is to delimit the scope of human knowledge. The binding story is taken as a reminder of how imperfect human ethics must always be. This straightforward view of the tale should be compared to more complex analyses in, for example 603, 607-610, 612.

615 Niewohner, Frederick. "Isaac Breuer und Kant." Neue Zeitschrifte fur Systematische Theologie und Religionsphilosophie 17 (1975): 142-150; 19 (1977): 172-185.

See the annotation at 332.

616 Samuelson, Norbert."Revealed Morality and Modern Thought." In Journal of the Central Conference of American Rabbis (1969): 18-30.

See the annotation at 320.

617 Seger, Ron. "Leibowitz and Kierkegaard." In Sefer Yeshiyahu Leibowitz: A Collection of Essays on his Thought and in his Honor [Hebrew], edited by Asa Kasher and Jacob Levinger, 42-46. Tel Aviv: Tel Aviv University Student Association, 1977.

Seger notes the shared concerns of Leibowitz and Kierkegaard and in this fine analysis of a modern Jewish thinker shows that the basic difference lies in the content attributed to faith. For Leibowitz that content is the halakhah, the traditional Jewish law while Kierkegaard develops a subjective supernaturalism. Seger argues that while Kierkegaard is unable to face the concrete world, Leibowitz enters the realm of concrete daily affairs.

618 Silman, Yohanan. "Kantian Motifs in the Thought of Leibowitz." In Sefer Yeshiyahu Leibowitz: A Collection of Essay on his Thought and in his Honor [Hebrew], edited by Asa Kasher and Jacob Levinger, 47-53. Tel Aviv: Tel Aviv University Student Association, 1977.

This valuable academic study shows how Leibowitz naturalizes Kantian ethics into Judaism as a response to Christian moral triumphalism. Silman contrasts the way Leibowitz uses Kant with the struggles of Hermann Cohen and Isaac Breuer to make Judaism and Kantian ethics fit together.

619 Spero, Shubert. "Morality and the Will of God," in Morality, Halakha, and the Jewish Tradition, 92-118. The Library of Jewish Law and Ethics 9. New York: Ktav Publishing House, 1983.

This good discussion of the relevance of divine morality for human life considers the binding of Isaac from the perspective of the discussion of Kierkegaard. Spero concludes that a divine morality incomprehensible to human beings cannot be the basis of imitation of God. As Spero shows elsewhere in his book the imitation of God is the central category of Jewish ethics (see the annotation at 016 and in particular the discussion pp.70-73). Therefore Kierkegaard's interpretation must ultimately be rejected.

620 Zac, Sylvain. "Kant et Le Probleme du Judaism." Les Nouveaux Cahiers 46 (1977): 32-49.

Zac who is well known for his studies of Spinoza, Mendelssohn, and other Enlightenment thinkers turns his attention to Kant's view of Judaism as theonomous religion. He rejects such a categorization and claims that Kant did not truly understand the autonomous nature of Judaism. Like other articles focused on Kant's thought this essay accepts his theories and seeks to fit Judaism into them. Both the Judaism and Kantianism involved reflect the thought of the Jewish neo-Kantian thinkers. It is an interesting if not seminal study.

PSYCHOLOGY AND JEWISH ETHICS

621 Abott, Samuel E. "New Approaches to Emotional Health and Moral Guidance." In Building Jewish Ethical Character, edited by Joseph Kaminetsky and Murray I. Friedman, 277-283. New York: The Fryer Foundation, 1975.

This informal analysis of Jewish teaching reveals traditional Jewish presuppositions about mental health. It notes the academic pressure on students in contemporary life and claims that the personal conflict involved brings stress and emotional problems. The proposed solution is to concentrate on emotional and mental health as well as upon academic subject matters through engagement in traditional Jewish studies.

622 Ackerman, Nathan W. "Ethical Issues in Psychotherapy." Conservative Judaism 23 (1969): 1-15.

Despite its appearance in an explicitly Jewish periodical this article has little specifically Jewish about it. Rather than reflect on Jewish concerns that must be raised in psychotherapy it dwells briefly on Freud's Judaism and then concentrates only on internal questions of psychotherapeutic ethics of patient/counselor relationships.

623 Amsel, Avrahom. "Judaism and Psychology." Tradition 11 (1970): 60-73.

In this short essay Amsel explains his views of the relationship between psychology and Judaism. He regards Freudian psychology to be the cause of many evils in contemporary society. While Freud recognized the danger of repressing healthy instincts, he neglected the need for balance. Amsel admits that human beings are guilty, but he suggests that not guilt but "teshuva," repentance, is the true focus of study. When a secularist reduces anxiety to false guilt he has "permitted his evil inclination to intervene and deceive him." Judaism is needed to reemphasize choice, fear of God and the creative use of human freedom. Amsel is not a naive opponent of all psychological investigation. He has a good background in psychology and knows the trends in that field. His diatribe, however, reflects the unease and restlessness with which many traditional Jews look at the therapeutic mentality. Compare 215.

624 Bulka, Reuven. "Hasidism and Logotherapy: An Encounter Through Anthology," in Mystics and Medics: A Comparison of Mystical and Psychotherapeutic Encounters, 104-118. New York: Human Sciences Press, 1979.

See the annotation at 236.

625 Bulka, Reuven. "Logotherapy and Judaism: Some Philosophical Comparisons." Tradition 12 (1972): 72-89.

This ambitious and informative essay hails Frankl as a Jewish exponent of psychology who undermines Freudian thought. The Jewishness of Frankl in opposition to Freud is said to consist of his emphasis on meaning and not pleasure, on freedom and not power, on social interrelationship rather than ego. While Bulka provides parallels to Frankl's ideas from the Talmud and rabbinic literature he fails to demonstrate any direct relationship between Frankl's thought and Frankl's Jewishness.

626 Bulka, Reuven. "Logotherapy as a Response to the Holocaust." Tradition 15 (1975): 89-96.

This serious essay joins theological and psychological concerns to argue that Viktor Frankl's psychological theory, an outgrowth of his experiences in the concentration camps, is also a theological contribution that represents an important strand of Jewish thinking. This is an interesting work by a committed Orthodox Jew who manages to see in a persuasive psychological system themes associated with traditional Judaism.

627 Fackenheim, Emil L. "Self Realization and the Search for God," in Quest for Past and Future: Essays in Jewish Theology, 27-51. Bloomington: Indiana University Press, 1968.

This early essay shows Fackenheim's awareness of psychology as a rival for religion. It notes that psychology has promised to help people express themselves and realize their full potential, but suggests that responsibility rather than self-expression is the path to Jewish ethics. The Jewish goal, it suggests, is not to realize the self but to become more closely like the divine. Compare Friedman (629).

628 Friedman, Maurice. "Psychology and Religion: The Limits of the Psyche as a Touchstone of Reality," in Touchstones of Reality: Existential Trust and the Community of Peace, 247-258. New York: E.P.Dutton and Company, 1974.

This important statement of the value of psychology in human development and its role in religious consciousness reviews the variety of approaches psychological theory has taken to religion, touching upon Freud, Jung, Fromm, and Huxley. It concludes by studying the Hebrew prophets and suggests that psychology only tells part of the story about human nature.

629 Friedman, Maurice. "Psychotherapy and the Human Image," in The Hidden Human Image: A Heartening Answer to the Dehumanizing Threats of Our Age, A Delta Book, 74-89. New York: Dell Publishing Company, 1974.

While the first part of this essay reproduces much in the previous entry, the last section reviews existentialist psychology, particularly that inspired by Martin Buber. The

I-Thou encounter becomes a test case for psychological awareness and sympathy in Friedman's thinking. A useful and sophisticated critique of psychology is also found in the essay "Aiming at the Self: The Paradox of Psychologism and Self-Realization," pp.274-285. This essay should be compared to that of Fackenheim in 627.

630 Friedman, Murray I. "Freudian Psychoanalysis in its relation to the Jewish Concept of Sin." In Building Jewish Ethical Character, edited by Joseph Kaminetsky and Murray I. Friedman, 300-312. New York: The Fryer Foundation, 1975.

This essay has a positive approach to the Freudian analysis of the human mind and draws parallels between it and Jewish literature, particularly the Zohar. Particular stress is given to the interpretation of of sin in Judaism as the struggle between the two inclinations takes on greater significance in the light of the Freudian understanding of the psyche. Sin is more clearly a matter of human choosing and the need for Torah conditioning is more clearly indicated when Freudian analysis is used as an explanatory hermeneutic.

631 Gersten, Leon (as told to Adina Miskoff). "The Mental Health needs of the Pious." Sh'ma 9 (1979): 52-55.

According to this report traditional Jews have a resistance to psychotherapy or mental health techniques. They have been trained to displace bad thoughts while therapy demands unmasking deep-rooted problems. Long term psychological analysis is therefore usually avoided. This is an interesting "field report" on the actual problems in bringing a meeting between Judaism and psychotherapy, not on a theoretical basis but on the practical basis of willing involvement in therapy.

632 Gottlieb, Mel. "Israel Salanter and Therapeutic Values." Tradition 15 (1975): 112-129.

See the annotation at 223.

633 Granatstein, Melvin. "The Dionysian Revolt and Halakhic Man." Tradition 11 (1970): 5-16.

This traditionalist diatribe against the excesses of psychology claims, citing Norman O. Brown and Herbert Marcuse, that some modern thinkers in the wake of the Freudian revolution have advocated greater appreciation of the body and its needs. While Judaism has a healthy affirmation of the body, it rejects the Dionysian style that posits a polarity in human experience.

634 Kagan, Jacob. "A Behavioral Analysis of Teaching Ethics." In Building Jewish Ethical Character, edited by Joseph Kaminetsky and Murray I. Friedman, 284-290; 296-299. New York: The Fryer Foundation, 1975.

This essay integrates traditional Jewish style and modern psychology and suggests that musar training exemplifies Skinnerian reenforcement techniques. This appreciation of behaviorism and use of its ideas is opposed by other Jewish thinkers (see especially 644). The struggle between traditionalists who utilize psychological theory and those who reject it is well illustrated by comparing the two positions on behaviorism. This debate is continued as Kagan responds to criticisms from Zalman Ury by suggesting that the mitzvot are all behaviorist and assume a contextual and situational determinism of human actions.

635 Katz, Robert L. "Martin Buber and Pyschotherapy." Hebrew Union College Annual 46 (1975): 413-431.

See the annotation at 280.

636 Rachlis, Arnold. "The Musar Movement and Psychotherapy." Judaism 23 (1974): 337-345.

See the annotation at 229.

637 Rubenstein, Richard L. Morality and Eros. New York: The McGraw-Hill Book Company, 1970.

See the annotation at 086.

638 Rubenstein, Richard L. The Religious Imagination: A Study in Psychoanalysis and Jewish Theology. New York: Bobbs-Merrill Company, 1968.

This fascinating and imaginative study uses Freudian techniques of analysis to move beyond Freud and note the psychological value of traditional images and practices and their ability to help Jews cope with the dilemmas of life in exile. It also concludes, however, that in the post-Auschwitz world it is impossible to naively accept those images and practices.

639 Sokol, Moshe. "The Psychology of Guilt and the Orthodox Jew." In Building Jewish Ethical Character, edited by Joseph Kaminetsky and Murray I. Friedman, 313-318. New York:The Fryer Foundation, 1975.

This essay celebrates guilt as an important element in the human psyche, valuable as an impetus to repentance despite the tendency in modern psychology to seek its eradication. This is a corrective essay that recognizes the limits to the psychotherapeutic process and thereby contributes not only to a Jewish view of psychology but to a wider psychological view of religious phenomenon. Although polemical in tone, the article's distinction between pathological and creative

640 Solomon, Andy. "Eros-Thanatos: A Modification of Freudian Instinct Theory in the Light of Torah Teachings." Tradition 14 (1973): 90-102.

This positive evaluation of the Freudian dichotomy between an instinct for life and an instinct for death claims that it is related to Judaism's view of the good instinct and the evil one. Judaism, however, is said to differ from Freud in refusing to absolutize this dichotomy and by teaching how it can be overcome and transformed.

641 Spero, Moshe Halevi. <u>Judaism and Psychology: Halakhic Perspectives</u>. New York: Ktav Publishing House, 1980.

This extraordinary collection of essays shows considerable psychological expertise and insight into traditional Judaism. All of the essays are worth examination from the standpoint of understanding how a traditional Jew struggles with meaning and morality in the modern world. The following essays are of particular interest: "Psychology as Halakha: Toward a Halakhic Metapsychology," 11-30, which is a programatic statement of how psychology and the <u>halakhah</u> are interrelated; "Sin as Neurosis-Neurosis as Sin: Further Implications of the Halakhic Metaphysic," 49-63, which sees Torah as a curative and therapeutic means of actualizing freedom; "A Reinterpretation of a Talmudic Instinct: Perspective on the Yezer Ha-Ra," 64-81, which claims that the sensual instincts have positive values that are recognized by Jewish tradition; "The Anxious Man of Repentance: Psychological, Religious, and Philosophical Implications," 82-98, which should be read in contrast to Sokol (639) as a positive view of anxiety and guilt.

642 Spero, Moshe Halevi. "Psychiatry, Psychotherapy and Halakha: A Torah Perspective on the Philosophy of Behavior Change." In <u>Jewish Bioethics</u>, edited by Fred Rosner and J.David Bleich, 221-241. New York: Sanhedrin Press, 1979.

Spero considers the <u>halakhic</u> precedent for behavior modification and concludes that Judaism recognizes that human beings can change and provides directives for that change. Spero does not reject psychology totally but rather understands its place as a tool in religious life. He neither exalts it as a full explanation of being human nor condemn it as a substitute for religion. Thus when correctly used psychoanalysis and therapy are appropriate means of attaining <u>halakhic</u> ends. Compare this view with the practical situation described in Gersten (631).

643 Spero, Moshe Halevi. "Thanatos, Id, and the Evil Impulse." <u>Tradition</u> 15 (1975): 97-111.

This is a response to Solomon (640) and should be read in the light of Spero (641). It argues that there is really no analogue between the Freudian death drive and the Yetzer ha-Rah, the evil instinct. Here Spero is less hospitable towards psychology than in the previous entry. This difference is traceable to a distinction between the practical uses of psychology which Spero accepts and its analysis of human nature which he rejects.

644 Ury, Zalman. "Beyond Behaviorism." In <u>Building Jewish Ethical Character</u>, edited by Joseph Kaminetsky and Murray I. Friedman, 291-215. New York: The Fryer Foundation, 1975.

This essay is a critique of a behaviorist interpretation of Jewish practice (see 634). Ury contends that the acceptance of modern psychological techniques threatens the concept of human freedom and responsibility. Human dignity and sanctity, he suggests, demands that the Jew advance beyond behaviorism. There is an interesting response to this criticism given by Jacob Kagan who demonstrates that the tradition has always used behavioral conditioning so that the use of such techniques is not a modern innovation or capitulation to contemporary society.

645 Wolf, Arnold Jacob. "Psychoanlysis and the Temperaments of Man." In <u>Rediscovering Judaism: Reflections On a New Theology</u>, edited by Arnold Jacob Wolf, 133-162. Chicago: Quadrangle Books, 1965.

This fascinating study of Freud and analysis of the Jewish view of the evil inclination from a Freudian perspective looks at Freud as a "psychological Jew" and shows parallels in his thought with Jewish writings on the evil inclination. It suggests that Freud is right and that for the immature immorality and idolatry are the same. Psychotherapy is interpreted in Judaic terms as "teshuva," a turning in which a person is modified and transformed.

JEWISH ETHICS AND MODERNITY

646 Blank, Irwin M. "Is There a Common Judeo-Christian Ethical Tradition?" <u>Journal of the Central Conference of American Rabbis</u> (1968): 75-84.

This essay criticizes the cliche of contrasting Judaism as a religion of law with Christianity as a religion of love. It also suggests that the period when Americans held one common ethic -- the Judeo-Christian Ethic has passed. A new period of interaction and exchange is predicted that will prove more productive than either polemical arguments or a common ethics. This essay is reprinted in Silver (126), 95-109.

647 Borowitz, Eugene B. <u>The Masks Jews Wear: The Self-Deceptions of American Jewry</u>. New York: Simon and Schuster, 1973.

This readable and challenging confrontation between Americanism and the Jewish spirit analyzes the dilemmas of contemporary philosophy and values. It contends that Jews have become disenchanted with civil religion and secular ethics. In the wake of that disenchantment they have sought to return to their roots and find in a religious morality that guidance and sense of purpose that they find lacking in contemporary life.

648 Fackenheim, Emil L. "Elijah and the Empiricists," in *Encounters Between Judaism and Modern Philosophy: A Preface to Future Jewish Thought*, 7-29. New York: Basic Books, Inc., 1973.

This is an important response to logical positivism and its reduction of religious claims to either psychological or emotive subjectivism or sheer nonsense. Fackenheim sees in history objective verification of Jewish claims and therefore an objective content in Jewish ethical statements.

649 Fackenheim, Emil L. "Judaism and the Idea of Progress," in *Quest for Past and Future: Essays in Jewish Theology*, 83-95. Bloomington: Indiana University Press, 1968.

This early essay challenges the conception that change is necessarily valuable and that evolution is progress. Fackenheim contends that the only basis for an optimistic view of human progress lies in the messianic hope and that moral progress takes place through adherence to the revealed law of Judaism.

650 Fackenheim, Emil L. ""Moses and the Hegelians: Jewish Existence in the Modern World," in *Encounters Between Judaism and Modern Philosophy: A Preface to Future Jewish Thought*, 79-169. New York: Basic Books, Inc., 1973.

This essay shows philosophical insight and Jewish sensitivity and is important reading on modern Jewish thought. The place of Jews in history and the morality of Jewish particularism is discussed with reference to medieval Jewish thought, nineteenth century Jewish responses to Hegel, and more recent Jewish reflection. Fackenheim claims that Torah is a force expressing free human self-activity. Jewish law is not only law but also grace and is a means of responding to the challenges of the present.

651 Goodman, Lenn Evan. "Equality and Human Rights: The Lockean and the Judaic Views." *Judaism* 25 (1976): 357-362.

Goodman, in a useful comparison of Jewish and philosophical approaches to human rights, contends that while Judaism emphasizes covenant and human task, Locke emphasizes human sinfulness and the need to restrict human power. There is, Goodman argues, a fundamental opposition between the naturalistic evaluation of human equality based on the depravity of human nature and the Jewish affirmation of equality based upon creation in the image of God.

652 Greenberg, Irving. "Jewish Values and the Changing American Ethic." *Tradition* 10 (1968): 42-74.

In a serious confrontation with contemporary American values Greenberg condemns the ethic of enjoyment, the "fun morality" with its emphasis on inner directed, individualistic concerns. He finds the American ethic to be self-indulgent and claims that a recapturing of the "ethics of Genesis" is needed in order to stress the interdependency of humanity and all creatures. Greenberg suggests that there are both positive and negative possibilities in a time of change; the Jew should try to make use of the positive opportunities which crisis presents. An expanded version of this essay is included in Bulka (102), 284-316.

653 Greenberg, Simon. "Some Affinities Between the Jewish and the American Historical Experience," in The Ethical in the Jewish and American Heritage, 219-232. Moreshet 4. New York: Jewish Theological Seminary and Ktav Publishing House, 1977.

This clear and ambitious study discusses separately the Jewish and American ethical systems and then turns to a comparison of the two. It suggests that in both cases the ideal has been a challenge never fully realized in practice. Defeat, in both cases, has been incorporated into the total value system, thus avoiding a triumphalism. In both their ideals and in their practical application Judaism and Americanism have many correspondences. These various similarities seem to Greenberg signs that the two systems are compatible.

654 Hel-Or, Yom Tov L. The Spiritual-Ethical Renaissance of the People of Israel. Trans. by Mendell Lewittes. Jerusalem: Or Yerushalayim, 1977.

See the annotation at 049.

655 Konvitz, Milton R. Judaism and the American Idea. New York: Schocken Books, Inc., 1980.

This collection of essays is unified by the theme of confronting and comparing Jewish and American ideals and values. Such subjects as equality, human dignity, constitutionality, and freedom of conscience are considered. Judaism and the democratic ideal as complementary values drawing from the same spiritual wells is the paradigm case that forms the model for all the essays included in the volume. See also 375, 507, 508, 571.

656 Lamm, Norman. "The Moral Revolution: A Jewish Evaluation." Tradition 10 (1969): 17-30.

Lamm confronts the new "situation" morality of American life and concludes that it contradicts basic Jewish values. The most important criticism he advances is that Judaism is realistic and acknowledges human imperfection whereas the new morality is based upon the assumption of human perfection. While the optimism informing this morality is congenial to Judaism the specific moral injunctions are judged inadequate. This essay is reprinted in Lamm (061), 247-269.

657 Pelkovitz, Ralph. <u>Danger and Opportunity</u>. New York: Shengold Publishers, 1976.

Pelkovitz is a leader in the Jewish Day School movement and most of the essays are centered on the relationship between the challenge of modernity and Jewish education. The moral element of Jewish learning in the midst of the modern world is emphasized as well as the growing influence of Yeshiva trained leaders. The essays are sermonic rather than academic in nature.

658 Plesur, Milton. <u>Jewish Life in Twentieth-Century America: Challenge and Accommodation</u>. Chicago: Nelson-Hall Company, 1982.

This investigation of Jewish history and ethical involvement begins at the opening of the twentieth century and continues to contemporary events. He finds the themes of social justice, search for tradition and ethnic consciousness, and Orthodox Jewish revivalism consistently arising. This is an interesting view of modern Jewish history with an ethical perspective pervading the work.

659 Posner, Zalman. "A Further Reflection on Tzniut." <u>Sh'ma</u> 12 (1982): 95-96.

In response to criticism to the following entry Posner claims that modesty in dress and action (<u>tzniut</u>, in Hebrew) is the best response to the challenge of today. The traditional Jew must answer the problematic morality of contemporary life by an increasing care and concern about even the seemingly trivial aspects of moral behavior. The essay is a good example of traditional Jewish restlessness with modern morality.

660 Posner, Zalman. "Modernity Must Make Room For Modesty." <u>Sh'ma</u> 9 (1978): 1-2.

Posner argues in a representative traditionalist attack on modern morality that modernity has emphasized immorality and lack of restraint. The Jew can counter this modern tendency by paying attention to details of modesty in dress and action. He advocates a return to traditional views about bodily exposure. Mere popularity or consensus that something is in style does not make it Jewishly correct, he argues. Clothes create an atmosphere that affects all of life. Modesty is, thus, for him the basis for any moral code of action.

661 Roth, Sol. "Two Concepts of Freedom." <u>Tradition</u> 13 (1972): 59-70.

In a restatement of traditional Judaism as an alternative to American values Roth contrasts the Jewish view of freedom with American views of liberty and finds them antithetical. The goal of a democracy, he argues, is for every individual to pursue the good life according to his own formula. Judaism, however, allows freedom as the basis for responsible decision making. While these two views are antithetical they are not contradictory. Roth suggests that the Jewish task in America is to use the freedom given by the government for the sake of the freedom emphasized in Judaism. In that way the two conceptions of freedom are complementary but not identical.

662 Schlesinger, G.N. "The Problem of Skepticism." Tradition 10 (1969): 86-92.

Schlesinger describes the situation in which the Musar Movement arose and concludes that it was the best response to the German Enlightenment. It countered skepticism not with argument and proof but with a demonstration that human emotions need religious training. He argues for such an approach today, an approach that he sees in the tradition of modern philosophy. Some traditionalists take issue with this approach of reconciling science and religion (see the discussion in 664).

663 Soloveitchik, Aaron. "Torah Tzniut Versus New Morality and Drugs." Tradition 13 (1973): 52-58.

This example of the hostility with which many Orthodox Jews view modern morality argues that the new morality is against all the principles of Judaism. Jewish teaching retains the a positive view of the impulses that are released in the new morality but sublimates them and channels them into a constructive and creative direction. Soloveitchik claims that there are important psychological insights in traditional Jewish modesty. The seven day refraining from sexual intercourse with one's wife, he suggests, makes marriage an ever new experience never totally routine. The use of drugs, he also argues, diminishes human dignity. Throughout he confronts the new morality with Jewish teachings and traditional Jewish values and behavioral prescriptions.

664 Spero, Shubert. "Is Religion a Separate Language Game?" Tradition 11 (1970): 51-59.

In opposition to positivist thought Spero claims that Judaism does make cognitive and empirical claims. He rejects either an emotive or prescriptive interpretation of religion and focuses on Jewish historical claims. The following entries offer alternative perspectives on the relationship between Jewish thought and non-Jewish philosophy.

665 Stepelevitch, Lawrence S. "Hegel and Judaism." Judaism 24 (1975): 215-224.

Stepelevitch in contrast to Fackenheim (649) rejects Hegel's system because of its misunderstanding of Judaism. This essay is useful to obtain a full sense of Hegel's place in contemporary Jewish thinking. It shows how Jewish thinkers struggle with contemporary philosophy and either reject or accept a philosopher based upon their own views of Judaism and Jewish ethics.

666 Weinberger, David and Geller, Ann. "A Philosophic Myth: Religion Vs Ethics." Sh'ma 10 (1980): 123-124.

This essay suggests that the putative conflict between autonomous, philosophical ethics and theonomous religious ethics is a myth. At their most profound both philosophy and religion combine and complement each other. This statement of the correlation of philosophy and religion would be rejected by many traditionalists but represents a major strand in contemporary Jewish ethical thinking.

Author Index

The index that follows contains only the primary authors or editors appearing in citations. References to the Introductory Survey are indicated by page number; references to the Bibliographical Survey are indicated by citation number.

Abott, Samuel E., 621
Ackerman, Nathan W., 622
Agus, Jacob Bernard, p.23; 001, 002, 003, 004, 019, 129, 130, 188,, 251, 252, 339, 340, 341, 424, 425, 476, 477, 483, 536, 581
Ahren, Yitzkak, 253
Altmann, Alexander, pp. 13, 14; 131, 163, 563
Amiel, Moshe Avigdor, 020, 342
Amsel, Avrahom, 215, 623
Appel, Gersion, 189, 343
Artz, Raphael, 344
Atlas, Samuel, 164, 478
Axinn, Sidney, 602
Baruk, Henri, 021, 022, 023
Bekritsky, Morris, 024
Belkin, Samuel, 426
Ben Horin, Schalom, 025
Berenbaum, Michael, 254
Bergman, Samuel Hugo, p. 9; 005, 026, 132, 479, 480, 603
Berkovits, Eliezer, 256, 345, 346, 421, 422, 427, 428, 481, 582
Berman, Lawrence V., 165
Berman, Saul, 133
Blanchard, Tzvi, 482
Blank, Irvin J., 646
Bleich, J. David, 124, 347,

Blidstein, Gerald J., 843, 537
Blomberg, Zeev, 166
Blue, Lionel, 027
Blumberg, Harry, 167
Bokser, Ben Zion, 201, 348
Borowitz, Eugene B., pp. 9; 028, 307, 308, 309, 349, 485, 647
Bourel Dominique, 257
Branson, Roy, 258, 486
Braude, Samuel G., 487
Breek, B., 029
Bulka, Reuven, pp. 9, 19; 102, 103, 236, 323, 351, 624, 625
Bulman, Nahman, 352
Butterworth, Charles E., 186
Breslauer, S. Daniel, 030, 202, 259, 350, 429
Brickner, Balfour, 538
Brog, Schmuel Elcohnen, 213
Brown, Michael, 604
Brusin, David, 310
Buber, Martin, pp. 9, 16, 564
Carmell, Aryeh, 104, 430,
Cohen, David, 488
Cohen, Hermann, p. 16; 260, 261
Cohen, Jack C., p. 9; 431
Cohen, Martin A., 489
Cohen, Seymour, 203

Cohon, Samuel S., 490
Damiel, Yitzhak, 031, 565
Dan, Joseph, 190, 191, 237
Daub, David, 539
Davidson, Herbert, 168
De Greef, J., 262
Deitrich, Wendel, 263
Djian, Jacques, 006
Domb, Cyril, 108, 430
Dorff, Elliot, 353
Dove, Y., 032, 540
Downing, Christine, 264
Dreier, Peter, 122
Dressler, Eliyahu, 033, 432, 541
Ebbinghaus, J., 265
Eckman, Lester Samuel, 216, 217
Edel, Abraham, 266
Efrati, Simhah, 034
Elkins, Dov Peretz, p. 9; 035, 354
Ellenson, David, 311, 604
Etkes, Emannuel, 218
Etkin, William, 433
Etzion, Isaac Raphael Halevi, 036, 169, 434
Faber, Salamon, 491
Fackenheim, Emil L., pp. 17, 21, 22; 267, 312, 313, 314, 355, 435, 492, 493, 584, 627, 648, 649, 650
Faierstein, Morris, 238
Faur, Jose 134, 585
Feldman, David M., p. 13; 007
Fenster, Myron, 494
Finkelstein, Louis, 135, 136
Fisch, Harold, 542
Fox, Marvin, p. 10; 008, 107, 170, 268, 269, 356, 357, 586
Frankel, Yonah, 137
Freudenstein, Eric G., 436
Friedman, Murray I., 037, 038, 110
Friedman, Maurice, 239, 270, 437, 495, 566, 628, 629
Galston, Miriam, 171, 358
Geller, Ann, 666
Gendler, Everett, 438
Gersten Leon, 631
Gewirtz, Leonard, 359
Gifter, Mordecai, 039, 543
Gilbert, Arthur, 496
Ginzberg, Louis, 219
Glicksberg, Abraham Abba, 040

Goldberg, Hillel, 108, 220, 221, 222
Goldenberg, Robert, 138
Goldman, Alex, 009
Goldman, Morris, 439
Goodman, Lenn Evan, 172, 651
Gordis, Robert, 109, 271, 361, 362, 363, 364, 440
Goren, Arthur, 272
Gottleib, Dale, 497
Gottleib, Mel, 223, 632
Granatstein, Melvin ,441, 633
Green, Ronald Michael, 041, 042, 043
Greenberg, Irving, 652
Greenberg, Moshe, 139, 498
Greenberg, Simon, 010, 044, 365, 441, 653
Greeves, Zeev, 240
Grunblatt, Joseph, 587
Guibal, Francis, 045, 273
Guttmann, Alexander, 315, 366
Hagi, Ben-Artzi, 192
Halevi, Jacob L., 610
Halivni, David Weiss, 140, 367
Harkavy, Solomon, 046
Harris, Monford, 324
Hartman, David, p. 15; 047, 173, 325, 368, 369
Harvey, Warren Zev, 048, 544, 567
Heilprin, Irving, 274
Hel-Or, Yom Tov L., 049, 654
Helfund, Jonathan, 443
Henning, Gunther, 275
Hershkovitz, S.A., 050
Herzog, Isaac, 051, 141, 142, 174, 370
Heschel, Abraham Joshua, p. 31; 052, 053, 241, 568
Himmelfarb, Milton, 545
Hirsch, Richard G., 499, 500
Hirsch, Samson Raphael, p. 23, 444
Hochbaum, Jerry, 501
Israel, Richard D., 502
Jacobs, Louis, 054, 055, 204, 371, 445, 546, 569, 612
Jonas, Hans, 276, 446
Jospe, Eva, 277
Jung, Leo, 056, 372, 503, 547
Kadushin, Max, pp. 8, 22; 057, 143, 373

Kagan, Jacob, 634
Kaminetsky, Joseph, 110
Kaplan, Asa, 447
Kaplan, Edward, 278
Kaplan, Mordecai, p.9 22; 058, 504
Kaplan, Simon, 279
Karff, Samuel E., 570
Kasher, Naomi, 326, 613
Katz, Dov, 224
Katz, Robert L., 280, 635
Katz, Steven, p. 30; 281, 588
Kegley, Charles W., 282
Kellner, Menahem Marc, p. 3, 35; 011, 111, 505
Kimmelman, Reuven, 144, 145, 506
Kirschenbaum, Aaron, 145
Klagsbrun, Francine, 112
Klausner, Joseph, 059, 548
Klein, Isaac, 374, 448, 449
Klein, Salomon J., 113
Kling, Simhah, 115,
Kluback, William, 283
Knoff, Josephine Z., 284
Konvitz, Milton R., 115, 375, 376, 507, 508, 571, 572, 655
Kook, Abraham Isaac, p.23; 060
Korn, Eugene B., 377
Kraut, Benny, 316
Kravetz, Julius, 147
Kuperstok, Nathan, 242
Kurzweil, Z'vi, 327
Kushner, Harold, 589
Lamm, Norman, 061, 062, 116, 225, 378, 450, 451, 573, 656
Landman, Leo, 148, 379, 509, 510, 511
Lawton, Philip W., Jr., 285
Lazaroff, Allan, 175, 193
Leibowitz, A.H., 226
Leibowitz, Yeshiyahu, p. 23-24; 063, 380, 381, 382
Leiman, Sid Z., 012
Leiser, Benton M., 383
Lelyveld, Arthur J., 064, 065
Levenson, Jon D., 512
Levi, Zeev, 066, 328
Levinas, Emmanuel, p. 16, 067, 068, 069, 070, 286, 287, 288, 452
Levine, Norman, 289
Levitz, Irving, 329
Levy, Bernard-Henri, 071
Levy, Leo, 453
Lichtenstein, Aaron, 149, 384, 385
Lightstone, Jack N., 150
Linzer, Norman, 575
Lipman, Eugene, 513
Loewe, Raphael, 118, 386
Lopian, Eliyahu, 072, 575
Lubarsky, Sandra D., 317, 454
Magnes, Judah L., 272
Mandelbaum, Bernard, 119, 151
Marcus, Ivan G., p. 14; 194, 195, 196, 197
Margolies, Morris, 330
Marmur, Dov, 073, 387, 514
Martinez-Miller, Orlando, 205
Marx, Tzvi, 388
Matt, Heskel J., 455, 590
McCollester, Charles, 290
Meltzer, Yehudah, 389
Meyer, Michael A., 318
Mihaly, Eugene, 390
Milch, Robert J., 614
Milishanski, Jacques K., 391
Mintz, Jerome, 243, 515, 517
Miskoff, Adina, 631
Moriel, Yehudah, 120
Motzkin, Aryeh Leo, 331
Nadler, Allan, 244
Nathan of Nemirov, 245
Neusner, Jacob, 121, 198, 206, 227, 392, 393
Newman, Eugene, 207
Niewohner, Frederick W., 176, 332, 615.
Novak, David, pp.10, 22; 074, 075, 291, 394, 395, 396, 456
Nulman, Louis, 076
Orbach, William, 457
Pachter, Mordecai, 208, 228
Pelkovitz, Ralph, 657
Perez, David Jose, 077
Petuchowski, Jakob J., 078 152, 397, 398, 549
Piekarz, Mendel, 209
Pines, Shelomo, 153, 550
Pines, Shelomo Zalman, 154
Plaut, W. Gunther, 399, 458
Plesur, Milton, 658
Plishkin, Zelig, p. 8; 013, 551
Polish, David F., 079, 516

Porter, Jack Nusan, 122, 253
Posner, Zalman, 659, 660
Priest, James E., 155, 518
Rabinkov, Zalman Baruch, 081, 519
Rabinovitch, Nahum L., 400, 401, 459, 460
Rachlis, Arnold, 229, 636
Rackman, Emanuel, 082, 402, 461, 552
Radkowsky, Alvin, 462
Rakefet-Rothkoff, Aaron, 520
Rawidowicz, Simon, 177
Reines, Chaim W. (See Reines, Chaim Zeev)
Reines, Chaim Zeev, 014, 083, 156, 157, 463, 553
Rittner, Steven, 015
Rosenberg, Shalom, 084, 333
Rosenblum, Noah H., 334
Rosenfeld, Leonora Cohen, 292
Rosenthal, Erwin J., 178, 403
Rosenthal, Gilbert S., 521
Rosner, Fred, 124
Ross, Jacob Joshua, 404, 464
Rotenberg, Mordecai, 246
Rotenstreich, Nathan, 293, 522
Roth, John K., 294
Roth, Sol, 085, 465, 523, 661
Rubenstein, Richard L., pp. 30, 32; 086, 591, 592, 637, 638
Samuelson, Norbert, 087, 179, 319, 320, 524, 554, 616
Sandmel, Samuel, 158
Schachter, Zalman, 593
Scherman, Nosson, 405
Schiller, Mordechai, 247
Schimmel, Solomon, 210, 594
Schlesinger, G.N., 662
Schneersohn, Menachem M., 466
Schochet, Immanuel J., 248
Schulweis, Harold M., 468, 595
Schwartz, Elkanah, 088, 230
Schwarzbach, Bertram E., 335, 406
Schwarzschild, Steven S., 089, 180, 295, 469, 525, 555
Schweid, Eliezer, 159, 181, 296, 297
Scult, Mel, p. 9, 321
Seeskin, Kenneth R., 596
Seger, Ron, 617
Shapiro, David S., 125, 160, 336 407, 470, 471, 556, 576, 577
Shatz, David, 526, 557
Sherwin, Byron, 211, 408, 558
Shilo, Schmuel, 527
Sidorsky, David, 409
Siegel, Seymour, 410, 411, 528
Silman, Yohanan, 618
Silver, Daniel Jeremy, 126, 529
Simon, Ernst, 412, 559
Singer, Sholom Alchanon, 199
Sobel, Ronald B., 127
Sokol, Moshe, 639
Sole, Moshe Zeev, 090, 298, 597
Solomon, Andy, 640
Soloveitchik, Aaron, 091, 413, 472, 663
Soloveitchik, Hayim, 200
Soloveitchik, Joseph Baer, pp. 16, 24; 092, 093, 337, 530, 531, 578, 579, 580, 598
Spero, Moshe Halevi, 641, 642, 643
Spero, Shubert, 016, 094, 414, 415, 473, 560, 599, 619, 664
Spiro, Solomon J., 416, 417
Stampter, Nathanial, 123
Stepelevitch, Lawrence S., 665
Stitskin, Leon D., 095, 182, 418
Sher, Isaac Aisik, 231
Strauss, Leo, 299
Swyhart, Barbara Ann, 322
Tishby, Isaiah, 128, 183, 212
Twersky, Isadore, 184, 419, 532
Ucko, Sinai, 300
Unterman, Allan, 017
Ury, Zalman F., 232-234, 644
Vajda, Georges, 185
Vogel, Manfred, 301, 474
Wallach, Sidney, 127
Waxman, Ruth B., 109
Weber, Stanley G., 096, 561
Wechsler, Harlan J., 475

Weinberg, Jacob S., 420
Weinberger, David, 666
Weinfeld, Abraham C., 018, 600
Weinstein, Deena, 097, 533
Weinstein, Michael A., 097, 533
Weiss, Abner, 098
Weiss, Raymond, 186
Wiesel, Elie, p. 17; 249, 534, 535
Wigder, Shabsie, 213
Wigoder, Geoffery, 187
Wineman, Aryeh, 250
Wolf, Arnold Jacob, 645
Worob, Avrohom, 161, 302, 338, 601
Wurzburger, Walter S., 421, 422, 423
Wyschogrod, Edith, 303, 304
Wyschogrod, Michael, 099, 100, 562
Yaffe, Martin D., 305
Yaged, Moshe, 162
Zac, Sylvain, 306, 620
Zacklad, Jean, 101, 214

Title Index

The references in this index are to the citation numbers of entries in which the title occurs either as the primary citation or as the anthology in which the primary title appears. Titles noted in the annotation are also included. Journal titles and published proceedings are not included.

Abraham Isaac Kook: The Lights of Penitence, the Moral Principles, Letters of Holiness, Essays, and Poems, 060
Abraham and the Kantians: Moral Duties and Divine Commandments, 606
Abraham, Isaac, and the Jewish Tradition: An Ethical Appraisal, 041, 609
After Auschwitz, 591
Ahavas Chesed, 039, 543
Aimer la Thora Plus Que Dieu, 286
Aiming at the Self: The Paradox of Psychologism and Self-Realization, 629
The Ambiguous Uses of Divine Personality, 467
And God Formed Man in His Own Likeness: A Jewish View On the Corporeality of Man, 025
Another Perspective on Jewish Ethics, 096, 561
An Anthology of the Words of the Sages, 106
Anthropocentricity and Theocentricity, 464
The Anxious Man of Repentance: Psychological, Religious, Philosophical Implications, 641
An Approach to Halakha, 374
The Artisan's Touch: Jewish Ethics and the Doctrine of Creation, 475
Asceticism in Sefer Hasidim, 192
The Attribute of Mercy, 432
Authentic Judaism and the Halakha, 346
The Authority Principle in Biblical Morality, 159
Authority in Jewish Law, 360
The Autonomous Jewish Self, 309
The Autonomy of Moral Objectivity, 409
Bachya's Asceticism Against its Rabbinic Background, 193
Basic Jewish Ethics and Freedom of the Will, 018, 600
A Basis for Morals: Ethics in a Technological Age, 271, 440
Beauty in the Bible and the Talmud, 156
The Beginning of Hassidism: Trends in Drush and Musar Literature, 209
A Behavioral Analysis of Teaching Ethics, 634

Belief and Behavior:
 Correspondences, 392
Between Man and His Fellow:
 Treatises on Human
 Relations in Judaism, 020,
 056, 080, 342, 519
Between Man and Man, 056,
 372, 503, 547
Beyond Behaviorism, 644
Beyond Survival: Reflections
 on the Future of Judaism,
 073, 387, 514
Beyond the Apologetics of
 Mission, 529
Beyond the Law: Ethics, 206
Biblical and Talmudic Ethics,
 154
The Body of Faith: Judaism
 as Corporeal Election, 099
The Book of the Light of Joy,
 034
The Book of Longsuffering,
 235
Bridging the Gap Between
 Ethical Theory and Practice,
 233
Buber's Concept of the
 Self, 302
Building Jewish Ethical
 Character, 024, 032, 037,
 038, 040, 076, 089, 091,
 110, 162, 226, 230, 233,
 234, 352, 413, 420, 472,
 448, 540, 543, 621, 630,
 634, 639, 644
The Bystander's Duty to
 Rescue in Jewish Law, 146
Can Democracy and Capitalism
 Be Jewish Values?: Mordecai
 Kaplan's Political
 Philosophy, 319, 524
Can There be a Judaism
 Without Revelation?, 435
Can Transgression Have an
 Agent?, 132, 479
Can a Religious Law Be
 Immoral?, 367
The Categorical Ethical
 Thrust of Halacha, 402
Causation and Choice in the
 Philosophy of Ibn Daud, 179
The Centrality of the Concept
 of Chesed, 082, 552
Challenge: Torah Views on
 Science and its Problems,
 104, 430, 433, 443, 453,
 459, 460, 462, 466

The Challenge of Eternity:
 Reflections on Our Times in
 the Light of the 'Mesilas
 Yeshorim', 213
Chochmas HaMusar, 226
Choices in Modern Jewish
 Thought: A Partisan Guide,
 307
Choose Life, 119
Christian and Jewish
 Ethics, 059, 548
The Chrysalis of Religion: A
 Guide to the Jewishness of
 Buber's I and Thou, 350,
 429
Civil Disobedience, 521
Civil Disobedience and the
 Jewish Tradition, 487
The Claim of Responsibility
 in Malamud's The Assistant,
 274
A Collection of Ethical
 Discourses, 231
Collective Responsibility,
 497
Commandment and Conscience
 in Talmudic Thought, 138
The Community, 530
Community Action for
 Orthodoxy: Priorities and
 Perspectives, 501
The Community of Otherness
 and the Covenant of Peace,
 495
Compassion: Remarks on
 Hermann Cohen, 300
The Concept of 'Chesed' in
 Judaism, 556
The Concept of 'Derech
 Eretz', 083
The Concept of 'Teshuva' in
 the Bible and Talmud, 152
The Concept of Responsibility
 in the Thought of Martin
 Buber, 301
Confrontation of Greek and
 Jewish Ethics: Philo's 'De
 Decalogo', 158
Confusion of Good and Evil,
 052
Conservative Judaism and
 Jewish Law, 360, 373, 410,
 411, 442
A Consuming Fire: Encounters
 with Elie Wiesel and the
 Holocaust, 294

Contemporary Jewish Ethics, 007, 011, 012,, 054, 111, 385, 546, 553, 564
Contemporary Problems in Ethics From a Jewish Perspective, 276
Contemporary Reform Jewish Thought, 398, 399
The Contemporary Relevance of the Philosophy of Maimonides, 164
The Covenant Concept: Particularistic, Pluralistic or Futuristic, 476
Covenantal Imperatives, 421
Creation, 445
Creation and Process: Halakhah and the Natural Order, 429
Creation and Value, 427
Crisis in Orthodoxy: The Ethical Paradox, 329
The Cunning of History: The Holocaust and the American Future, 592
Danger and Opportunity, 657
Deutschum und Judentum Bei Hermann Cohen, 265
Dialogue and Tradition: The Challenges of Contemporary Judeo-Christian Thought, 003, 339
Dialogue with Deviance: The Hasidic Ethic and the Theory of Social Contraction, 246
Different Paths, Common Thrust: The Shoaology of Berkovits and Frankl, 323
Difficile Liberte: Presences Du Judaisme, 067, 068
A Difficult Freedom, 285
The Dilemma of Liberal Judaism, 355
The Dimensions of Orthodox Judaism, 102, 243, 329, 397
Dina D'Malkhuta Delimited, 478
Dina DeMalkutha Dina: The Law of the Land is Law, 527
Dina d'Malkhuta Dina: Solely A Diaspora Concept, 510
The Dionysian Revolt and Halakhic Man, 633
The Discourse on Loving-kindness, 541

Dissenter in Zion: From the Writings of Judah L. Magnes, 272
A Distinctive Value Stance, 064
The Divine Helmsman: Studies on God's Control of Human Events, 179
Divine Law and Ethical Deed, 428
Do Noachides Have To Believe in Revelation, 469
Do Not Destroy, 444
The Doctrine of the Divine Spark in Man in Jewish Sources, 569
The Doctrine of the Image of God and Imitatio Dei, 576
Does Jewish Tradition Recognize an Ethic Independent of Halakha?, 385
Does Torah Mean Law?, 393
Duties of the Mind: Essays on Jewish Philosophy, 161, 338, 601
A Dynamic Halakha: Principles and Procedures of Jewish Law, 361
Ecology and the Jewish Tradition: A Postscript, 443
Ecology and the Jewish Tradition, 436
Ecology in Jewish Law and Theology, 450
Education of the Emotions in Jewish Devotional Literature, 210
Jewish Philosophers: In the Tradition of Personalism, 182
Elie Wiesel: The Job of Auschwitz, 270
Elijah and the Empiricists, 648
Emil Fackenheim and the Revealed Morality of Judaism, 311, 605
Emmanuel Levinas: The Problem of Ethical Metaphysics, 303
An Encounter with the Akeda, 614
Encounters Between Judaism and Modern Philosophy: A Preface to Future Jewish Thought, 267, 313, 606, 648, 650

Equality and Human Rights: The Lockean and the Judaic Views, 651
Eros-Thanatos: A Modification of Freudian Instinct Theory in the Light of Torah Teachings, 640
Essays and Investigations in Jewish Ethics and Law, 014, 083, 157, 463
Essays in Jewish Intellectual History, 163
Essays in Medieval Jewish and Islamic Philosophy, 168
Essays on the Occasion of the Seventieth Anniversary of the Dropsie University (1909-1979), 461, 571
Essence du Judaisme et Liberte de Conscience, 306
The Essence of the Halakha, 391
Eternal Life, 105
The Ethical Dimension in the Halakhah, 362
The Ethical Systems of Abraham Bar Hiyya, Joseph Ibn Zaddik, and Abraham Ibn Daud, 166
The Ethical in the Jewish and American Heritage, 010, 365, 653
Ethical Issues in Psychotherapy, 622
Ethical Standards in World Religions, I: Judaism, 017
The Ethical Values of Judaism, 090
Ethical Wills: A Modern Jewish Treasury, 123
The Ethical Writings of Maimonides, 186
Ethics and Halakha Once Again, 389
Ethics and Jewish Law, 377
Ethics and Law in Judaism, 365
Ethics and Majority, 481
Ethics and Religion, 036
Ethics and the Halakhah, 410
Ethics and Theodicy: Tensions in Emil Fackenheim's Thought, 317, 454
Ever Since Sinai: A Modern View of Torah, 078

Ethics as Transcendence and the Contemporary World: A Response to Emmanuel Levinas, 098
The Ethics of Anonymity Among the Pharisees, 135
The Ethics of Gilgul, 202
The Ethics of Jewish Self-Defense, 545
The Ethics of Preferring One's Own, 087, 554
The Ethics of the Pharisees, 136
Ethics, Religion and Judaism I, 010, 365
Ethics, Religion and Judaism II, 010
Ethique, Reflexion, et Histoire Chez Levinas, 262
Ethnic Activism: The Hasidic Example, 243, 516
La Etica Judia Y 'La Celestina' Como Alegoria, 205
Evil and the Morality of God, 595
Exigeant Judaism, 069
Exigences du Liberalism de Mendelssohn, 257
Expansion and Contraction in Jewish Ethics, 026
Extended Consciousness and Hasidic Thought, 242
Faith After the Holocaust, 255, 582
Faith and Doubt: Studies in Traditional Jewish Thought, 061, 225, 378, 450, 451, 656
Faith and Law, 339
Faith and Reason: Essays in Judaism, 059, 109, 431, 490, 548, 607, 610
Faith in Free Will, 597
Faith in Man and What is Above It, 031, 565
The Faith of Abraham: A Note on Kierkegaard's 'Teleological Suspension of the Ethical', 608
The Fear and Love of God, 040
The Fire of Sinai, 091, 472
For Its Own Sake and Not For Its Own Sake, 381

The Four Faces of God: Towards a Theology of Powerlessness, 457
Free Will and Predestination in Saadia, Bahya, and Maimonides, 163
Free Will, Guilt and Self-control in Rabbinic Judaism and Contemporary Psychology 594
The Free-will Determinism Issue, 601
Freedom and Determination, 581
Freedom and Responsibility, 599
Freedom of the Will: A Traditionalist's View, 587
Freudian Psychoanalysis in its Relation to the Jewish Concept of Sin, 630
From Mendelssohn to Rosenzweig: Jewish Philosophy in Modern Times, 293
From Reform Judaism to Ethical Culture: The Religious Evolution of Felix Adler, 316
From the Words of Shlomo, 046
Fundamental Assumptions for Discussions on Religion and Science, 447
A Further Note on 'The Law of the Kingdom is Law', 509
A Further Reflection on Tzniut, 659
God and the Ethical Impulse, 458
The God of Mordecai Kaplan, 310
God's Presence in History: Jewish Affirmations and Philosophical Reflections, 312
God, Man and History: A Jewish Interpretation, 345, 427, 428
God, Man, and Creation, 470
God, World, and Man, 471
The Good Society: Jewish Ethics in Action, 062, 116
Governmental and Judicial Ethics in the Bible and Rabbinic Literature, 155, 518

Greater Love Hath No Man...The Jewish View of Self-Sacrifice, 546
A Guide to the Repentant, 338
The Guilt Offering of the Defiled Nazirite, 148
Guilt and Responsibility in the Thought of Martin Buber, 264
The Halacha of Reform, 399
Halakah et Value Seculaires: La Philosophie Religieuse de Y. Leibowitz, 335, 406
Halakha and Aggadah: Jewish Law and Concretizing Jewish Value Concepts, 373
Halakha and History: Separate Realms, 371
Halakha and Other Systems of Ethics: Attitudes and Interactions, 081, 400
Halakha as Absolute, 347
Halakha as a Ground For Creating A Shared Spiritual Language, 368
Halakha as a Ground for Creating a Shared Spiritual Language: A Rejoinder, 416
Halakha is Absolute and Passe, 390
Halakha: Past, Present, Future: A Reply to the Responses, 363
Halakhic Man, 092, 578
Halakhic Man: Revealed and Concealed, 092
Hasidiana Americana: A Survey of American Literature on Hasidism, 238
Hasidic Conduct Literature as an Expression of Ethics, 240
Hasidism and Contemporary Man, 239
Hasidism and Logotherapy: An Encounter Through Anthology, 236, 624
The Heavens and The Earth: Reflections on Human Responsibility, 005
Hebrew Ethical Texts: Selected Texts With Introductions, Notes, and Commentaries 128, 183

Hebrew Ethical and
  Homiletical Literature: The
  Middle Ages and Early
  Modern Period, 190
Hegel and Judaism, 665
Hermann Cohen as a Biblical
  Exegete, 297
Hermann Cohen:The Challenge
  of A Religion of Reason,
  283
Hermann Cohen's Judaism: A
  Reevaluation, 277
The Hidden Human Image: A
  Heartening Answer To the
  Dehumanizing Threats of Our
  Age, 270, 437, 495, 629
The History of the Musar
  Movement: 1849-1945, 216
History, Religion, and
  Spiritual Democracy:
  Essays in Honor of Joseph
  L. Blau, 304
History, Rupture, and
  'Tikkun Olam': From
  Rosenzweig Beyond
  Heidegger, 493
Holiness: A Command to
  Imitatio Dei, 567
Homiletical and Ethical
  Literature of the Sages of
  Safed, 208
L'homme et La Creation Selon
  La Tradition Religieuse du
  Judaism, 474
Homo Imago Dei in Jewish and
  Christian Theology, 131,
  563
Human Dignity: From Creation
  to Constitution, A Phil-
  osophy of Human Rights From
  the Standpoint of Judaism,
  571
Human Freedom and Divine
  Power, 584
The Humanism of the
  Covenant, 480
Humanizing Jewish Life, 035,
  354
'I and Thou' and Jewish
  Ritual, 350
The Idea of Messianic
  Mankind in Hermann Cohen's
  Later Thought, 263
The Ideal Personality, 129
The Ideal Society, 130
The Ideological Foundations
  of the Halakha, 407

Ideology and Idealism, 070
Idolatry as a Modern
  Possibility, 267
The Image of Rabbi Joshua
  ben Levi in the Stories of
  The Babylonian Talmud, 137
Imitatio Dei, 564
Imperative and Conscience in
  Jewish Law: An Interview
  with Raphael Artz, 344
In Aloneness, In Togetherness
  A Selection of Hebrew
  Writings, 092, 337,
  531, 579, 598
In the Good Way: Commandments
  Between Man and Man
  According to the Sources of
  the Bible and the Oral Law,
  120
In the Light of The Torah,
  387
Individual Conscience and
  Group Consciousness in
  Israel and in the Diaspora,
  508
The Individual and the
  Commune: A Critique of
  Martin Buber's Social
  Philosophy, 258, 486
The Individual and the
  Community in Judaism,
  080, 519
The Infinite Dimension of
  Piety, 188
The Influence of Moses
  Hayyim Luzzatto on
  Hassidism, 212
The Innovations of Modern
  Orthodoxy, 359, 364
The Insecurity of Freedom,
  052, 568
Intellectual Honesty About
  Halacha, 405
The Interaction of Jewish
  Law and Morality, 353
Introduction, (to The
  Ethical Writings of
  Maimonides) 186
Introduction, (to The Good
  Society: Jewish Ethics in
  Action) 062
Introduction, (to
  Meditation of the Sad Soul
  by Abraham Bar Hiyya) 187
Introduction, (to Religion
  of Reason Out of the
  Sources of Judaism) 279

198 TITLE INDEX

Introduction, (to The Teachings of Hasidism) 237
Introduction, (to The Ways of the Righteous) 203
Introduction: Sources of Jewish Ethics, 037
Introduction to Jewish Ethics, 024
Introductory Essay, 299
Investigations in Questions of Faith, 169
Irrational Rational Man: Torah Psychology, 215
Is Religion a Separate Language Game?, 664
Is There a Common Judeo-Christian Ethical Tradition?, 646
Isaac Breuer und Kant: Ein Beitrag Zum Thema: Kant und Das Judentum, 332, 615
Israel Salanter, 219
Israel Salanter and Therapeutic Values, 223, 632
Israel Salanter: Selected Writings, 228
Israel Salanter: Text, Structure, Idea, The Ethics and Theology of an Early Psychologist of the Unconscious, 220
Issues in the Jewish-Christian Dialogue: Jewish Perspectives on Covenant, Mission, and Witness, 418, 489
The Jacob Dolnitsky Memorial Volume: Studies in Jewish Law, Philosophy, Literature and Language, 082, 421, 552
Jesus: Image of Man or Image of God, 566
The Jew and the State, 514
Jewish and Christian Elements in Philosophy: Their Share in Shaping the Modern Mind, 276
Jewish Bioethics, 124, 642
Jewish Ethics, 004, 054
Jewish Ethics 1970-1975: Retrospect and Prospect, 012
Jewish Ethics and the Virtue of Humility, 042
Jewish Ethics for the Twenty First Century, 015
Jewish Ethics: The Tension Between Particularism and Universalism, 097, 533
The Jewish Idea of Community 523, 567, 557
Jewish Life in Twentieth-Century America: Challenge and Accommodation, 658
The Jewish Mystical Tradition, 201
A Jewish Philosophy and Pattern of Life, 044
Jewish Philosophy: A Study in Personalism, 095
The Jewish Quest: Essays on Basic Concepts of Jewish Theology, 001, 004, 340, 425, 477
Jewish Radicalism: A Selected Anthology, 122
A Jewish Theology, 054, 445
Jewish Tradition and Political Action, 502
Jewish Values and the Changing American Ethic, 652
A Jewish View of World Community, 477
Jews and the State: Halakha is Our Guide, 483
Joy and Responsibility: Israel, Modernity, and the Renewal of Judaism, 047, 325, 364, 369
The Judaic Values of a Philosopher: Morris Raphael Cohen, 292
Judaism and the American Idea, 375, 507, 655
Judaism and the Democratic Ideal, 507
Judaism and Ethics, 126, 393, 458, 487, 496, 500, 513, 525, 529
Judaism and Human Rights, 079, 115, 426, 437, 444, 516, 572
Judaism and Humanistic Values, 066, 328
Judaism and the Idea of Progress, 649
Judaism and Psychology, 623
Judaism and Psychology: Halakhic Perspectives, 641
Judaism and the Secular State, 485

Judaism Confronts
  Contemporary Issues, 009
Judaism, Secularism, and
  Textual Criticism, 008
Judaism, The Jewish People,
  the State of Israel, 063,
  380, 381, 382
Judaism: Justice and Mercy
  of God, 043
Judaism: Law and Ethics, 051,
  141, 142, 174, 370
Judaism's Relation to
  Animals, 463
Judaismo E Universalismo, 077
Justice, Justice Shalt Thou
  Pursue: Papers Assembled on
  the Occasion of the Seventy
  Fifth Birthday of the
  Reverend Dr. Julius Mark,
  127, 135
The Kabbalistic World View,
  204
Kant et Le Probleme du
  Judaism, 620
Kant on Judaism, 602
Kantian Motifs in the
  Thought of Leibowitz, 619
Keddusha-Holiness, 372
Kibbud Ov: An Analysis, 162
Kierkegaard and Midrash,
  610
Kierkegaard and Rabbinic
  Judaism, 607
Kierkegaard's Fear and
  Trembling : Critical
  Appraisals, 612
Kindliness, 032, 540
Knight of Faith or Man of
  Doubt, 604
Law and Conscience: the
  Jewish View, 379, 511
  Law and Ethics in Modern
   Jewish Philosophy: The Case
   of Moses Mendelssohn, 268,
   356
  Law and Justice in Rabbinic
   Jurisprudence, 134
  Law and Love in Jewish
   Theology, 408, 558
  Law and Morality in Modern
   Society, 413
  Law and Morals, 376
  Law and Observance in Jewish
   Experience, 412
Law and Theology in Judaism,
  074, 394
Law and Theology in Judaism,
  2nd series, 075, 456
Law as the Basis of a Moral
  Society, 422
The Law in Rabbinic
  Judaism, 401
The Law of the Land in
  Halakhic Perspective, 520
The Law of the Red Heifer,
  141
The Legacy of Rabbi Israel
  Salanter, 234
Legends of Our Times, 535
Leibowitz and Kierkegaard,
  617
Leibowitz's View of Religion
  in Relationship to Kantian
  Ethics, 326, 613
A Letter on Science and
  Judaism, 466
Lev Eliyahu: A Collection of
  Talks, 072, 575
The Life and Teachings of
  Isaiah Horowitz, 207
Lifnim Mishurat Hadin, 133
The Light of Ethics, 117
Limitations on Self-
  Sacrifice in Jewish Law and
  Tradition, 539
The Limits of Self
  Sacrifice, 549
Liturgy and Ethics: Hermann
  Cohen and Franz Rosenzweig
  on the Day of Atonement, 305
Logotherapy and Judaism:
  Some Philosophical
  Comparisons, 625
Logotherapy as a Response to
  the Holocaust, 626
Love: The Beginning and the
  End of Torah, 048, 544
Love Your Neighbor: You and
  Your Fellow Man in the
  Light of Torah, 013, 551
Luzzatto's Ethico-Psycholog-
  ical Interpretation of
  Judaism: A Study in the
  Religious Philosophy of
  Samuel David Luzzatto, 334
Maimonides on the Fall of
  Man, 165
Maimonides' Shemonah Perakim
  and Al Farabi's Fusul al-
  Madani, 168
Maimonides' System of Ethics:
  Its Sources and Its Source,
  169

TITLE INDEX

Maimonides: Torah and Philosophic Quest, 173
Majesty and Humility, 093, 580
Major Themes in Modern Philosophies of Judaism, 250
Man as a Temporary Tenant, 426
Man's Choice and God's Design, 455, 590
Man's Dignity in God's World, 572
Man's Place in Nature, 439
Man's Power and Limits in a Technological Age, 570
Man's Smallness and Greatness, 051
Marital Relations, Birth Control, and Abortion in Jewish Law, 007
Martin Buber and Psychotherapy, 280, 635
Martin Buber and the American Jewish Counter Culture, 253
Martin Buber and the Drama of Otherness: The Dynamics of Love, Art and Faith, 278
Martin Buber's Ethics and the Problem of Norms, 282
Martin Buber and the No-Self Perspective, 304
The Masks Jews Wear: The Self-Deceptions of American Jewry, 647
The Meaning and Purpose of Jewish Survival, 496
The Meaning of Holiness in Judaism, 577
The Meaning of Jewish Law in Conservative Judaism: An Overview and Summary, 411
Medieval Jewish Mysticism: The Book of the Pious, 199
Meditation of the Sad Soul by Abraham Bar Hiyya, 187
The Mental Health Needs of the Pious, 631
The Mission of Israel After Auschwitz, 489
The Mission of Israel and Social Action, 513
Mitzvos as 'Springboards' for Ethical Behavior, 420
Modern Jewish Ethics: Theory and Practice, 089, 070, 081, 098, 107, 170, 385, 209, 542, 549, 559
Modernity Must Make Room For Modesty, 660
Modernizing Jewish Ethics, 259
The Moral Law as Halacha in Reform Judaism, 315, 366
The Moral Principles, 060
Moral Radicalism and 'Middlingness' in the Ethic of Maimonides, 180
The Moral Revolution: A Jewish Evaluation, 156
Morality and Eros, 086, 637
Morality and Halakhah, 414
Morality and the Law, 404
Morality and the Will of God, 619
Morality and Wisdom in the Bible, Ben Sirah, and the Rabbis, 157
Morality, Halakha, and the Jewish Tradition, 016, 094, 414, 415, 560, 599, 619
Moritz Lazarus: The Ethics of Judaism, 298
Moses and the Hegelians: Jewish existence in the Modern World, 650
Musar Anthology, 108, 221
Musar Avicha, 060
The Musar Movement, 232
The Musar Movement and Psychotherapy, 229, 636
The Musar Movement: History, Personalities, and Method, 224
Mystical Theology and Social Dissent: Judah Loewe of Prague, 211
Mysticism and Ethics, 198
Mystics and Medics: A Comparison of Mystical and Therapeutic Encounters, 103, 236, 242, 624
The Nature of Man in Judaism and Social Work, 574
The Neighbor Whom We Shall Love, 559
New Approaches to Emotional Health and Moral Guidance, 624

New Directions in Jewish Social Ethics: A Case for Traditional Conservatism, 528
New Directions in Jewish Social Ethics: More Concern, Less Doctrine, 494
A New Jewish Ethics, 030, 429
A New Jewish Theology in the Making, 307
The New Jews, 344, 438
A New Meaning for Mitzvah, 354
The non-Jew in Jewish Ethics, 537
Nonviolence in the Talmud, 144
A Note on the Function of 'The Law of the Kingdom is Law' in the Medieval Jewish Community, 484
Notes on the Concept of Imitatio Dei, 573
On Faith in Man and Its Meaning, 031, 565
On The Love of Torah and the Redemption of the Religious Spirit, 336, 531
On the Essence of Judaism, 090, 298, 597
On the Judaism of Nature, 438
On the Principle of Dina de-Malkhuta, 491
On the Rational Commandments in Saadia's Philosophy: A Reexamination, 170, 257
On the Supposed Anti-Asceticism or Anti-Naziritism of Simon the Just, 140
On the Theology of Jewish Survival, 525
One Generation After, 535
Order and Sequence in Maimonides Code, 174
Our Social Concerns Have a Jewish Ground, 482
The Particularism of Jewish Ethics, 100, 562
A Passion for Truth, 241, 611
Patterns of Good and Evil, 593
La Pensee Juive Aujourdui, 287
A Personal Code of Ethics, 076

Perspectives on Jews and Judaism: Essays in Honor of Wolfe Kelman, 367, 467
Pharisaism and Political Sovereignty, 517
Pharisaism in the Making: Selected Essays, 135
A Philosophic Myth: Religion Vs Ethics, 666
Philosophical Essays: From Ancient Creed to Technological Man, 276, 446
Philosophie des Forschritts: Hermann Cohens Rechtfertingung, 275
Philosophy as Duty, 177
Philosophy in the Talmud and the Midrash, 142
The Philosophy of Emmanuel Levinas, 290
The Philosophy of Lubavitch Activism, 248
A Philosophy of Mitzvot: The Religious-Ethical Concepts of Judaism Their Roots in Biblical Law and the Oral Tradition, 189
Piety and Politics: The Case of the Satmar Rebbe, 244
Piety and Society: The Jewish Pietists of Medieval Germany, 194
Plural Models and the Authority of Halakhah, 423
Plural Models within the Halakha, 357
Polarity in Jewish Ethics, 019, 536
The Politics and Ethics of Pietism in Judaism: The Hasidim of Medieval Germany, 196
Post-Holocaust Dialogues: Critical Studies in Modern Jewish Thought, 281, 588
The Position of Religious Ethics, 333
Potentialities and Limitations of Universalism in the Halakhah, 386
Pour Une Ethique De Dieu, 101, 214
The Power of Human Virtue and the Function of Suffering, 575
Poverty and the State in Biblical Thought, 512

Practical Commandments, 380
Precis De Morale Juive et de des Rapports Doctrinaux Avec Les Morales Chretienne et Marxiste, 006
The Presence of God in History: Jewish Affirmations and Philosophical Reflections, 312, 583
The Problem of the Akeda in Jewish Thought, 612
The Problem of Evil, 602
The Problem of Skepticism, 662
Problematics of Jewish Ethics, 318
La Probleme de La Philosophie Juive, 029
Problems and New Perspectives in the Study of Early Rabbinic Ethics, 150
Problems of Reform Halakha, 398
The Program of Kindness, 547
Psychiatry, Psychotherapy, and Halakha: A Torah Perspective on the Philosophy of Behavior Change, 642
Psychoanalysis and the Temperaments of Man, 645
Psychology and Religion: The Limits of the Psyche As A Touchstone of Reality, 628
Psychology as Halakha: Toward a Halakhic Metapsychology, 641
The Psychology of Guilt and the Orthodox Jew, 639
Psychotherapy and the Human Image, 629
The Purpose of the Law According to Maimonides, 171, 358
The Pursuit of Perfection, 230
The Quality of Faith: Essays on Judaism and Morality, 005 026, 132, 479, 480, 603
Quest for Past and Future: Essays in Jewish Theology, 313, 355, 435, 493, 584, 627, 649
The Question of Jewish Ethics Today, 089
The Question of Jewish Ethics Today II, 555
Rabbi Joseph K. Lookstein Memorial Volume, 573
Rabbi Nahman's Teachings, 245
The Rabbinic Ethics of Protest, 145, 506
The Rabbinic Mind, 143
Rabbinic Reflections on Defying Illegal Orders: Amasa, Abner, and Joab, 139, 498
A Rational Conception of Mitzvot, 343
The Reality of Radical Evil, 596
Reason and Hope: From the Jewish Writings of Hermann Cohen, 260
Reason, Emotion, and Habit in the Training of a Torah Personality, 352
The Recensions and Structure of Sefer Hasidim, 197
Reconstructionism: Hokhmah as an Ethical Principle, 322
Rediscovering Judaism: Reflections on a New Theology, 313, 593, 645
Reflections on Job and Situation Morality, 585
Reform Judaism: A Historical Perspective, Essays From the Yearbook of the Central Conference of American Rabbis, 164, 315
Reform Judaism Today III: How We Live, 028, 308, 349
Reform Through Tradition, 227
Reinterpretation of a Talmudic Instinct: Perspectives on the Yetzer Ha Ra, 641
Rejoinder to Tzvi Marx, 417
Rejoinder to a Rejoinder on 'Halakhah as a Ground for Creating a Shared Spiritual Language', 388
The Relationship Between Religion and Ethics in Jewish Thought, 055
The Relationship Between Science and Religion, 462
Religion and Law, 419

Religion and Morality: A Collection of Essays, 055
Religion in A Religious Age, 163, 419
The Religion of Ethical Nationhood: Judaism's Contribution to World Peace, 058, 504
Religion of Reason, Out of the Sources of Judaism, 261, 279, 299
The Religion of the Thinkers: Free Will and Predestination in Saadia, Bahya, and Maimonides, 163
Une Religione d'Adultes, 045, 273
Religious Ethics and Humanistic Ethics, 031
Religious Ethics on the Contemporary Scene, 004
The Religious Imagination: A Study in Psychoanalysis and Jewish Theology, 638
Religious Implications of Extraterrestrial Life, 451
The Religious Meaning of Contemporary Science, 433
Religious Reason: The Rational Basis of Religious Belief, 043
The Religious Responsibility for the Social Order, 493
Religious Virtuosi and the Religious Community: The Pietistic Mode in Judaism, 195
Rely on Tradition: It Transcends Itself, 383
Responsa and Halakhic Studies, 374, 448
A Response to Ernst Simon, 542
A Revealed Law: Torah MiSinai, The Divine Origin of Jewish Law, 442
Revealed Morality and Modern Thought, 320, 616
The Revealed Morality of Judaism: A Confrontation with Kant, 313
La Revelation, 452
La Revelation Dans La Tradition Juive, 452
Revelation as Quest: A Contribution to Ecumenical Thought, 424
Revered by All: The Life and Works of Rabbi Israel Meir Kagan, 217
Review Essay: Berkovits' Treatment of the Problem of Evil, 269, 586
The Right Way, 072
The Righteous Who Suffers Evil, 598
Risk and Uncertainty in Halakha, 369
The Role of the Individual in Jewish Law, 351
The Rule of Ethics, 050
The Rule of Law: Torah and Constitution, 375
Saadiah's Ethical Pluralism, 172
The Sacred Image of Man, 568
The Sacrifice of Isaac and Contemporary Man, 603
Sagesse et Religion, 185
Sagesse Humain et Morale Revle d'Apres Quelques Theologiens Juifs, 185
Samael, Lilith, and the Concept of Evil, 191
Samuel David Luzatto: Traditionalist and Scholar, 330
Samuel K. Mirsky Memorial Volume: Studies in Jewish Law, Philosophy, and Literature, 134, 336, 343, 421
Scholarship and Piety, 225, 378
Science and Religion, 465
Science and Scientism, 437
Science and Some Ethical Issues, 437
La Science du Juste: Le 'tsedek 'et Le Monotheism Hebreu, 023
Science in Torah Life, 453
Sefer Yeshiyahu Leibowitz: A Collection of Essays on His Thought and in His Honor, 066, 084, 326, 328, 333, 464, 613, 617, 618
Self Realization and the Search for God, 627
The Self and the Other, 560
The Self and the Other in Rabbinic Ethics, 553

Selfhood and Godhood in Jewish Thought and Modern Philosophy, 473
A Sense of Duty, 114
The Sense of Responsibility, 503
The Seven Laws of Noah, 149, 384
Shem U'Sheirit: An Anthology In Memory of Efraim Simhah Rozenfeld, 117
Should Government Legislate Halakhah?, 505
Silent Hate is Also a Sin, 538
Sin as Neurosis-Neurosis as Sin: Further Implications of the Halakhic Metaphysic, 641
Social Justice, Legal Justice, and Our Justice, 020, 342
Social Responsibility in an Age of Revolution, 136
Social Values in Judaism and Their Realization in the Reform Movement, 499
The Sociologist as Theologian: The Fundamental Assumptions of Mordecai Kaplan's Thought, 321
The Sociology of American Jews: A Critical Anthology 124
Soloveitchik's Response to Modernity: Reflection on 'The Lonely Man of Faith', 325
Solving Ethical Problems, 03
Some Affinities Between the Jewish and the American Historical Experience, 653
Some Aspects of the Jewish Attitude Toward the Welfare State, 532
Some Cautionary Remarks, 147
Some Current Trends in Ethical Theory, 266
Some Non-Halakhic Aspects of the Mishneh Torah, 184
Some Thoughts on Hasidism, 247
Somewhere-A Master: Further Hasidic Portraits and Legends, 249
Spinoza and Luzzatto: Philosophy and Religion, 331
The Spiritual-Ethical Renaissance of the People of Israel, 049, 654
The Standpoint of Religious Ethics, 084
Studies in the Shemoneh Perakim, 181
Systematic Aspects of Jewish Morality, 415
The Status and Value of the Individual in Spinoza, 297
Stoic and Talmudic Ethics: The Acceptable and the Adequate, 161
Strive For Truth: Michtavme Eliyahu, The Selected Writings of Eliyahu Eliezer Dressler, 033, 432, 541
The Structure of Jewish Ethics, 011
The Structure of Jewish Law, 007
The Struggle for Change, 348
Studies in Hebrew Law and Lore: Values and Evaluations, 391
Studies in History of Jewish Philosophy: The Transmission of Texts and Ideas, 153, 550
Studies in Jewish Law and Philosophy, 184, 532
Studies in Jewish Thought, 177
Studies in Jewish Thought 1, 125, 407, 556, 576, 577
Studies in Questions of Faith, 036
Studies in Rabbinic Judaism, 315, 366
Studies in Rationalism: Judaism and Universalism, 118, 178, 386, 403, 569
The Systems and Works of Rabbi Hayyim of Voloshin As a Response to the 'Mitnagdim' of Hasidism, 218
Take Judaism For Example, 195
The Teachings of Hasidism, 237

Technology and Responsibility: Reflections on the New Tasks of Ethics, 446
The Tenability of Herman Cohen's Construction of the Self, 295
The Testament of God, 071
Thanatos, Id, and the Evil Impulse, 643
Theocentricity in Jewish Law, 461
Theodicy and Belief, 441
A Theological Foundation for the Halakha, 340
Theological Modesty and the Idea of Divine Perfection, 468
The Theologico-Historical Thinking of Samuel David Luzzatto, 324
The Theology of Abraham Bibago: A Defense of the Divine Will, Knowledge and Providence in 15th Century Spanish-Jewish Philosophy, 175
Theories of Evil in Medieval Jewish Philosophy, 167
A Theory of Revelation, 456
Three Pathways from a Tradition-Centered to a Humanistic Ethic, 251
Three Themes in the Sefer Hasidim, 200
To Heaven With Scribes and Pharisees: The Lord of Hosts in Suburbia, the Jewish Path to God, 027
To Love the Torah More than God, 068, 288
To Mend the World: Foundations of Future Jewish Thought, 314, 492
Torah Tzniut Versus New Morality and Drugs, 663
Torah and Nomos in Medieval Jewish Philosophy, 178, 403
Torah and Science: Conflict or Complement, 459
Torah and the Spirit of Free Inquiry, 460
Torah into Prayer: 'Leqqutei Tifillot', 250
Touchstones of Reality: Existential Trust and the Community of Peace, 239, 627
Toward a Theology for Social Action, 500
Toward an Understanding of Israel Salanter, 222
Towards a Definition of Humility, 085
Towards a Theology of Ethics, 431
Tradition and Contemporary Experience: Essays on Jewish Thought and Life, 065, 412, 502
The Tragedy of Bourgeois Cosmopolitanism: On Martin Buber's Politics, 289
Transcending Denominational Labels, 395
Transient Isms and Abiding Values, 065
Tsedek, 021
Tsedek, Droit Hebraique et Science de l'Homme, 022
Two Concepts of Freedom, 661
Two Principles of Character Education in the Aggada, 151
Two Who Walk in the Desert, 153, 550
Understanding Jewish Theology: Classical Issues and Modern Perspectives, 121, 206, 392
Understanding Rabbinic Judaism: From Talmudic to Modern Times, 121, 198, 219, 227
The Unity of God as a Principle of Judaism and as the Basis of Jewish Morality 434
Universal Moral Law in Hermann Cohen, 291, 396
The Universal and the Particular in Judaism, 490
Universalism and Particularism, 522
Universalism in the Philosophy of Rabbi Joseph B. Soloveitchik, 327
Das Verhaltnis von Naturphilosophie und Ethik im More Nebuchim, 176
The Virtue of Obedience, 341
The Vision and the Way: an Interpretation of Jewish Ethics, 002, 129, 130, 188, 251, 252, 341, 581

The Vision and the Way in the Nineteenth Century, 252
The Vision of the Void: Theological Reflections on the Works of Elie Wiesel, 254
Voices of Wisdom: Jewish Ideals and Ethics for Everyday Living, 112
The Way of Torah and the Straight Path, 113
The Ways of Mentschlekhayt: A Study of Morality in Some Fiction of Bernard Malamud and Philip Roth, 284
The Ways of the Righteous, 203
What is Biblical Ethics to a Jew?, 382
Who is Man?, 052
Why do the Righteous Suffer: Notes Toward a Theology of Tragedy, 589
Wisdom and Knowledge of God in Biblical and Talmudic Thought, 160
Witnessing and Personal Religious Experience, 418
The Word of God, 449
The World Outlook of Rabbi Kook, 336
Worship and Ethics: A Study in Rabbinic Judaism, 057
The 'Yes' and the 'No' of Revelation, 425

Subject Index

This index includes subjects discussed in the Introductory Survey and in the Bibliographical Survey. References to the former are by page number; references to the latter are by entry number; the two are separated by a semi-colon. Where entries duplicate each other only the annotated entry is noted. Hebrew words are underlined.

Abner, 139
Aboab, Isaac, 205
Abortion, 007, 147
Abrabanel, Judah, 251
Abraham, p. 31; 041, 604, 608
Adam, p.24, 164
Adler, Felix, p. 21; 316
Agamemnon, p. 31
Aggadah, pp. 10, 11, 15 22, 25-26, 34-35; 017, 074, 075, 142, 151, 154
Agnon, Shmuel Yosef, 246
Agus, Bernard Jacob, p.23
Ahavas chesed See Lovingkindness
Ahad HaAm See Ginzberg, Asher
akeda See Isaac, binding of
Al Farabi, 168
Amalekites, p. 12; 139
Amasa, 139
America, 010, 271, 375, 507, 572, 653, 655, 657, 658, 661
American See America
Animals, 014, 463
Anonymity, 135
Anti-Semitism, p. 18
Anxiety, p. 32; 639, 641
Apologetics, 080
Aristotle, 169, 180, 186
Art, 178
Asceticism, p. 14; 140, 148, 192, 193, 197

Assimilation, 217
Atonement, 129
Authority, 159
Autonomy, pp. 30-31; 028, 084, 204, 266, 303, 309, 341, 354, 355, 409, 587, 666
Baeck, Leo, p.21; 307
Bar Hiyya, Abraham, 095, 166, 187
Beauty, 156
Ben Aaron, Elijah
Ben Levi, Joshua, 137
Berkovits, Eliezer, 181, 323
Bibago, Abraham, 175
Bible, pp. 11, 12, 14, 16, 27, 35; 010, 014, 015, 021, 023, 053, 129, 130, 131, 152, 154, 157. 160, 162, 270, 271, 296, 384
Biblical See Bible
Bioethics, 124, 429
Book of the Pious See Sefer HaHasidim
Breuer, Isaac, pp.16, 23, 618
Brown, Norman O., 633
Buber, Martin, p. 16; 044 095, 239, 252, 253, 256, 258, 278, 280, 281, 282, 289, 301, 302, 304, 324, 350, 421, 468, 513, 576, 629
Business, 013, 106
Capitalism, 319
Capital Punishment, 377

208 SUBJECT INDEX

Causation See Human being, freedom of
Celestina, La 205
Charity, 060, 129, 235
Children, 013, 163, 235
Choice, See Human being, freedom of
Chosen People See Particularism
Christianity, 006, 020, 022, 025, 041, 043, 052, 053, 059, 071, 131, 138, 190, 205, 237, 241, 246, 267, 276, 564, 566, 646, 647
Civil disobedience, 132, 139, 145, 379, 487, 521
Cohen, Hermann, p. 16; 029, 205, 252, 256, 260, 263, 265, 275, 277, 279, 283, 291, 293, 295, 296, 299, 300, 305, 307, 308, 318, 618
Cohen, Morris Raphael, 292
Community, pp. 20, 25, 28; 080, 239, 249, 477, 495, 523, 526, 530
Compassion, 054, 064, 116, 129, 261, 300, 324, 331
Conscience, 023, 132, 138, 139, 306, 344, 508, 655
Counter culture, 253
Covenant, 303, 421, 476, 480
Creation, pp. 18, 29-30; 025 061, 104, 124, 426, 427, 429, 436, 470, 474, 475, 477
Creation and design, pp. 29-30
Daniel, p. 11
Day of Atonement, 305
"De Decalogo," 158
Democracy, 115, 319, 322, 507
Derech eretz, 083, 106,
De Vitas, Elijah, 210
Dialogue, 030, 281, 285, 301, 302, 388
Dina d'malkhuta dina See Law of the kingdom.
Dresner, Samuel, 238
Dressler, Eliyahu, 215
Duty, 042, 114, 177, 280
Ebreo, Leon See Abravanel, Judah
Ecology, pp. 18, 29; 015, 429, 436, 443, 444, 470
Education, 035, 063, 110, 151, 210, 233, 382, 436, 657

Einhorn, David, p.21
Elijah, 648
Empiricism, p.31; 648
Enlightenment, the, pp.18-19; 216, 252, 257, 662
Equality, 651
Erikson, Erik, 295, 298
Eros, 640
Ethical Culture, 316
Ethics, American, 010
Ethics, Jewish, essence of, pp.34-35,
Ethics, Jewish, general, p.6; 010, 016, 017, 094, 105, 111
Ethics, Jewish, history of, pp. 4, 5, 13-14; 010, 014, 016, 018, 094, 111
Ethics, Jewish, modern, pp. 15-35; 004, 012, 015, 030, 086, 111, 122, 259
Ethics, Jewish, personal, p. 4; 013, 076, 110, 230, 231
Ethics, Jewish, principles of, pp.4, 6-9; 007, 008, 009, 010, 011, 016, 017, 019, 024, 026, 027, 034, 036, 037, 038, 039, 040, 055, 062, 064, 081, 088 090, 091, 094, 110, 111, 120, 133, 134, 135, 142, 143, 333, 362, 365, 367, 380, 381, 387, 389, 391, 392, 393, 414, 415, 460

Ethics, Jewish, social, pp.4, 21, 28-29; 020, 038, 111, 115, 116, 171, 258, 476, 477, 480, 482, 483, 488, 493, 494, 500, 502, 505, 528
Ethics, Jewish, sources of, pp. 9-15; 007, 010, 011, 016, 094, 110, 111
Ethics, varieties of Jewish, pp. 5, 34-35; 090, 111
Evil, p. 30; 167, 191, 269, 270, 281, 312, 314, 336, 589, 592, 593, 595, 601
Evil inclination, p. 32; 623, 630, 638, 640, 641, 643, 645
Evolution, 104, 124, 439
Exodus, 468
Fackenheim, Emil L., pp. 17, 21-22,; 311, 317, 320, 325

Faith, 031, 060, 072, 339
Family, 106, 116, 365
Feminism, 122, 191, 361, 365
Feuerbach, Ludwig, 066
Fichte, Johann, 077
Frankl, Viktor, 236, 323, 625, 626
Free will See Human being, freedom of,
Fromm, Erich, 628
Fusul Al Madani, 168
German Pietism See Hasidism, Ashkenazic
Gilgul, 202
Ginzberg, Asher, 059, 252
Gnosticism, 276
God, existence of, 068
God, fear of, 040, 060
God, general, 312, 313, 431, 441, 458, 467, 468, 473
God, imitation of, pp. 10, 26-29, 017, 042, 094, 095, 125, 136, 180, 182, 204, 310, 471, 473, 475, 564, 567, 573, 576, 577
God, knowledge of, 160, 175
God, power of, 079, 312, 457, 584, 595
God, unity of, p. 26; 017, 067, 260, 261, 275, 277, 434
Grace, 547
Guilt, p. 32; 264, 594, 623, 639
Hafetz Hayyim See Kagan, Israel Meir
Halacha See Halakhah.
Halakha See Halakhah.
Halakhah, pp. 6, 10, 11, 13, 15, 23, 25-26, 27, 33, 34, 35; 007, 016, 017, 062, 063, 066, 070, 074, 075, 081, 062, 094, 110, 143, 166, 173, 184, 315, 335, 340, 345, 346, 347, 348, 350, 353, 359-374, 380, 383, 385-391, 394-407, 410, 411, 412, 414, 416, 423, 429, 483, 577
HaNasi, Judah, p.12;
Hartman, David, p.15; 388, 416, 417
Hasid, pp. 11, 15, 20
Hasidism, Ashkenazic, p.11, 13-14; 191, 192, 194-200, 202
Hasidism, German See Hasidism, Ashkenazic

Hasidism, Polish, pp.20, 31; 052, 103, 202, 209, 218, 235-252, 304, 437, 495
Haskalah See Enlightenment
Hayyim, of Voloshin, 218
Hegel, Georg Wilhem Friedrich, See Philosophy, Hegelian
Heidegger, Martin, 492
Heifer, red, 141
Herberg, Will, 044, 267
Heschel, Abraham Joshua, p.31; 018, 044, 238, 256, 267, 325, 394, 574
Hesed See Lovingkindness.
High Holy Days, 119
Hillel, 477
Hirsch, Samson Raphael, 350
Hokmah See Wisdom
Holiness, 345, 372, 567, 576, 577
Holocaust, Nazi, pp. 17, 22; 072, 254, 255, 259, 267, 281, 286, 294, 312, 314, 323, 489, 534, 535, 591, 598, 626, 638
Horowitz, Isaiah, 207. 209
Human being, dignity of, p. 7, 24; 025, 051, 052, 072, 079, 080, 093, 115, 259, 260, 496, 569, 570, 571, 572, 574, 575, 645
Human being, freedom of, pp. 13, 29-31, 33-34; 018, 033, 061, 067, 106, 163, 179, 581, 584, 587, 589, 594, 596, 645, 655, 661
Human being, image of God, p. 27-28, 30; 025, 131, 461, 566, 568, 581, 594, 651
Human being, rights of, 079 115
Humanism, pp. 5, 7, 8, 9, 21; 005, 031, 063, 066, 286
Humility, pp. 7, 8, 23-24; 042, 051, 052, 060, 085
Husserel, Edmund, 295, 303
Huxley, Aldous, 628
Ibn Daud, Abraham, 166, 179
Ibn Gabirol, Solomon, 182, 185
Ibn Pakuda, Bachya, p.14; 163, 182, 185, 193, 202, 338
Ibn Zaddik, Joseph, 166, 185,
Id See Psychology, Freudian.
Ideology, 407
Idolatry, 267, 425

210 SUBJECT INDEX

Imitatio Dei See God, imitation of.
Isaac, binding of, pp. 12, 31; 377, 468, 603, 604, 607, 608, 610, 612, 614, 619
Israel, state of, pp.13, 28; 086, 107, 216, 259, 285, 287, 312, 337, 481, 508, 525, 531, 534, 535
Jacobs, Louis, 008
Jesus, See Christianity
Joab, 139
Job, 167, 585
Jonah, of Gerona, 209
Judaism, American, pp.8, 9, 21, 24-26; 009, 111, 243, 244, 247, 658
Judaism, Conservative, pp. 8-9, 21, 22-23, 24, 25; 009, 010, 011, 074, 075, 111, 360, 362, 394, 410, 411
Judaism, essence of, pp. 6, 7, 21, 34-35.
Judaism, European, pp.9, 21; 021, 022, 029
Judaism, liberal, pp. 5, 7, 9, 16-18, 21; 027, 099, 266, 318, 355
Judaism, Orthodox, pp. 7,8, 15-21, 23-24; 008, 009, 011, 017, 063, 099, 102, 111, 329, 359, 364, 368, 501, 658
Judaism, rabbinic, pp.4, 12-15, 35; 078, 121, 127, 129, 130, 134, 135, 136, 138, 139, 142, 143, 144, 145, 147, 150
Judaism, Reconstructionist, pp.21, 22; 009, 307, 310, 319, 321, 322
Judaism, Reform, pp. 16-17, 21- 22, 24; 009, 011, 028, 054, 064, 065, 111, 126, 227, 272, 307, 308, 309, 316, 324, 335, 363, 398, 423, 499
Judaism, traditional, pp. 3-5, 7, 8, 15-18, 20-25, 30,31
Judeo-Christian Tradition, 646
Jung, Carl Gustav, 628
Justice, p.31; 020, 132, 134, 155, 290
Kabbalah See Mysticism.
Kadushin, Max, p. 22; 044, 393

Kagan, Israel Meir, 217
Kaplan, Mordecai, p. 22; 018, 307, 310, 319, 321, 322, 513
Karo, Joseph, p. 12;
Kierkegaard, Soren, pp. 30-31, 35; 041, 241, 468, 607, 608, 610, 612, 617, 619
Kindness See Lovingkindness 313, 315, 344, 345, 346, 353, 354, 355, 360, 375 380, 385-394, 401, 408, 411, 412, 413, 419, 421, 422, 428, 461
Kook, Abraham Isaac, p.23; 049, 336, 572
Kotzk, Menahem Mendel of, p. 31; 241
Language, pp. 16-18, 31;
Law, Jewish, pp.4, 6-7, 10, 12-13, 23-28, 33; 007, 020, 062, 070, 071, 078, 094, 099, 107, 129, 138, 155, 166, 170, 171, 173, 206, 268
Law, Noahide, pp. 27-28; 066, 149, 271, 291, 386, 469
Law, of the kingdom, pp.13, 28-29; 478, 484, 487, 491, 509, 520, 527
Lazarus, Moritz, 084, 252, 291, 293, 298, 318
Leibowitz, Yeshiyahu, pp. 23-24; 066, 084, 325, 326, 335, 368, 389, 464, 617, 618
Lequtei Tifillot, 252
Levinas, Emmanuel, p.16; 045, 068, 098, 262, 285, 288, 290, 303
Lichtenstein, Aaron, 012
Lifnim Mi Shurat HaDin, 133, 134, 385
Lilith, 191
Literature, p. 17;
Locke, John, 651
Loewe, Judah, of Prague, 211
Logos, 393
Logotherapy, p.19; 103, 236, 625, 628
Love, of God, 040, 068, 173, 177, 541
Love ,of neighbor, 013, 033, 048, 064, 107, 116, 146, 537, 538, 541, 542, 559
Lovingkindness, pp.7, 11, 26; 032, 033, 039, 048, 082, 105, 330, 541, 547, 556
Lurianic Kabbalah, p.11; 302

SUBJECT INDEX   211

Luzzatto, Moses Hayyim, 188, 206, 212, 213
Luzzatto, Samuel David, p.23; 054, 252, 293, 324, 330, 331
Magnes, Judah L., 272
Maimonides, Moses, pp. 12, 14, 15; 022, 054, 095, 128, 163, 164, 165, 168, 169, 171, 172, 173, 174, 176, 177, 180, 181, 182, 184, 186, 197, 297, 338, 469, 477, 612
Malamud, Bernard, p. 17, 274, 284
Marcuse, Herbert, 633
Marrano, 535
Marxism, 006, 018, 275, 289.
Maybaum, Ignaz, 281
Mendelssohn, Moses, pp. 16-18, 30; 066, 164, 251, 257, 268, 306, 469
Mentschlekhayt, 284
Mercy, 033, 043, 432
Mitzvoth See Mitzvah
Messianism, 130, 136, 137, 260, 261, 263, 275, 277, 492, 493, 496, 513, 514, 601
Micah, 310
Midrash, pp. 12, 13, 17, 22, 31; 021, 312, 314, 326, 612
Mishnah, p. 12; 181
Mishneh Torah, p.12; 184
Mission, 489, 513, 529
Mitnagdim, 218
Mitzvah, pp. 10, 23, 26; 319, 339, 354, 380, 381, 420
Modernity, pp. 3-6, 14-25, 30-33; 005, 045, 047, 049, 056, 070, 071, 072, 086, 216, 247, 271, 277, 325
Modesty, p. 33; 659, 660, 663
Monotheism See God, unity of
Morality, pp. 6, 15, 18, 20, 32, 35-36; 005, 010, 026, 027, 028, 034, 035, 057, 061, 086, 105, 110, 111, 112, 315, 376, 377, 404, 409, 413, 414, 415, 422, 652, 656, 659, 660, 663
Moses, 650
M'silas Yeshorim, 213
Musar, pp. 10, 19-20, 35; 033, 034, 046, 072, 105, 106, 108, 113, 117

Musar Movement, pp. 10, 19-20; 017, 050, 054, 108, 215-294, 662
Mysticism, pp. 3, 4, 8, 11, 14-15, 23, 35; 007, 060, 101, 103, 106, 143, 191, 198-200, 201-214, 237, 242, 302, 314, 457, 569, 573
Nahman, of Bratzlav, 235, 240, 245, 246, 250
Nationalism, pp. 5,18;058, 122
Nature, 156, 438, 439
Nazirite, 140, 148
Nietzsche, Friedrich Wilhelm, 304
Norms, 282, 301
Nomos, 178, 393
Nonviolence, 144
Obedience See Autonomy
Ozick, Cynthia, 574
Particularism, pp. 5, 16, 18, 22, 26-28; 026, 028, 077, 080, 087, 090, 096, 097, 099, 100, 319, 380, 381, 476, 490, 522, 526
Passover, 106
Peace See War
Personality, 129, 352
Pharisees, 078, 135, 136, 517, 601
Phenomenology, 067, 070, 098,
Philo, of Alexandria, 158, 477
Philosophy, Analytic, 043, 648, 664
Philosophy, Existential, p.32; 092, 369
Philosophy, Greek, p. 3; 153, 158, 160, 161, 169, 330, 331, 376, 377, 393, 446, 452, 564, 577
Philosophy, Hegelian, 650, 665
Philosophy, Jewish, pp. 3, 4, 13-19, 30-31;
Philosophy, Kantian, pp. 16, 23, 24, 30-31, 35; 029, 041, 042, 077, 092, 100, 164, 266, 281, 283, 291, 293, 298, 303, 309, 311, 313, 320, 326, 332, 402, 421, 585, 587, 602, 603, 618, 620
Philosophy, medieval Jewish, pp. 3-4, 12-15; 006, 017, 095, 127, 128, 163-187

SUBJECT INDEX

Philosophy, modern, pp. 13, 15-17; 017, 029, 031, 095, 100
Philosophy, non-Jewish, pp. 13, 31-32; 017
Pietism, p.14; 088, 188-200,
Politeness, p. 7
Politics, 171, 243, 244, 312, 322, 481, 485, 501, 502, 507, 517, 528
Poverty, 512, 532
Pragmatism, p. 31;
Prayer, 250
Predestination See Human being, freedom of
Priest, 003, 004
Progress, p.31; 645
Prophet, 003, 004, 260, 261, 628
Psychology, behaviorism, pp. 31-33; 634, 644
Psychology, existential, p. 32;
Psychology, Freudian, p. 32; 215, 622, 623, 625, 628, 638, 639, 640, 641, 643, 645
Psychology, general, pp. 19-20, 31-33; 072, 086, 103, 334, 591, 594, 597, 621, 628, 629, 631, 633, 642
Psychology, musar, 215, 220, 229, 280, 633
Redemption, 477, 480, 492, 503, 531, 601
Reincarnation See Gilgul.
Repentance, 072, 152, 338, 574, 623, 639, 641, 645
Responsa, pp. 12-13;
Responsibility, 038, 152, 264, 282, 301, 493, 497, 584, 599
Revelation, pp. 18, 27-18; 037, 061, 075, 158, 185, 189, 345, 424, 425, 435, 442, 449, 452, 456, 477
Ritual, 028, 034, 075, 078 231, 303, 305, 579
Rokeah, Eliezer, 194-197
Rosenzweig, Franz, 067, 252, 256, 301, 314, 350, 421, 492
Roth, Philip, 284
Rubenstein, Richard, pp. 30, 32; 254, 281, 294,
Saadiah Gaon, p. 13; 022, 095, 170, 172, 186

Sabbath, 106, 365, 429, 450, 576
Sadducees, 601
Safed, 208
Sage, 003, 004
Salanter, Israel, p.19; 219, 220, 222, 223, 224, 227, 228, 233, 234, 338
Salvation, 319
Samael, 191
Sartre, Jean Paul, 295
Satmar, Rebbe of, 244
Saul, p.12
Scholem, Gershom, 202
Schwarzschild, Steven, 019
Science, 102, 124, 271, 359, 433, 437, 447, 448, 450, 453, 459, 462, 465, 466
Secularism, p. 3; 008, 072
Sefer Hasidim, 191, 192, 194-200
Sefer Hinnuk, 189,
Self, the, 295, 302, 304, 473, 629
Self-realization, 627, 629
Self-sacrifice, p. 27; 031, 146, 153, 539, 546, 549, 553, 560
Sexuality, 007, 013, 015
Shemoneh Perakim, 181
Shnei Luchot Ha Berit, 207
Shulhan Arukh, 184, 338, 532
Simon, the Just, 140, 148
Sin, p. 32; 072, 132, 638, 641
Skepticism, 662
Social justice, 020, 258
Society, 116, 130
Sociology, 086, 321
Soloveitchik, Joseph B., pp. 16, 24; 325, 327, 368, 394, 574
Spinoza, Baruch, 004, 067, 251, 257, 297, 314, 324, 469
Strawson, P. F., 295
Stoicism, 153, 158, 160, 161, 162
Subconscious, p.33
Suffering, 072, 097, 575, 589, 596
Talmud, p. 12; 003, 014, 031, 039, 078, 176
Technology, 271, 276, 446, 450
Teshuva, See Repentance.

Theodicy, 317, 595, 596, 598, 601
Tikkun, p. 11; 314, 425, 492
Tikkunei HaZohar, 101
Torah, p. 7; 178, 225, 235, 319, 393, 442
Transgression See Sin
Tribalism, 086
Trust, 106
Tsedek, 021-023
Universalism, pp. 15, 26, 27; 026, 028, 029, 063, 066, 077, 079, 080, 087, 089, 099, 100, 176, 265, 327, 336, 381, 386, 476, 490, 522, 545, 555
Upright Path, the See M'silas Yeshorim
Value-concepts, pp. 8-9; 057, 064, 065
Virtue, 013, 231
War, 015, 116, 130, 144, 147, 155, 444, 520
Welfare state, 532
Wiesel, Elie, p. 17; 238, 254, 270, 294, 494
Wills, ethical, 123
Wisdom, 157, 160, 322
Yetzer Ha-Ra See Evil inclination
Zaddik, 237
Zen, 304
Zionism, 004, 058, 071, 216, 258, 260, 359

About the Compiler

S. Daniel Breslauer is Associate Professor of Religious Studies at the University of Kansas, Lawrence. He contributed to *A Dictionary of the Jewish-Christian Dialogue*, edited by Leon Klenicki and Geoffrey Wigoder.